☆☆☆☆ THE ☆☆☆☆
AMERICAN
EXPERIENCE
·IN·
EDUCATION

★★★★ THE ★★★★
AMERICAN
EXPERIENCE
IN
EDUCATION

EDITED BY JOHN BARNARD & DAVID BURNER

NEW VIEWPOINTS | A DIVISION OF FRANKLIN WATTS, INC. | NEW YORK, 1975

Library of Congress Cataloging in Publication Data

Barnard, John, 1932–   comp.
    The American experience in education.

    Includes bibliographical references.
    CONTENTS: Cremin, L. A. Education in the house-
holds and schools of colonial America.—Kett, J. F. Grow-
ing up in rural New England, 1800–1840.—Rapson, R. L.
The American child as seen by British travelers,
1845–1935. [etc.]
    1. Education—United States—History.   I. Burner,
David, 1937–   joint comp.   II. Title.
LA205.B36   370′.973   74-13455
ISBN 0-531-05361-X
ISBN 0-531-05569-8 (pbk.)

CONTENTS

CONTRIBUTORS

Lawrence A. Cremin is President of Teachers College, Columbia University.

Joseph F. Kett is a professor in the Department of History at the University of Virginia.

Richard L. Rapson is in the history department at the University of Hawaii.

Ruth M. Elson is a member of the faculty of Finch College.

William R. Taylor is Professor of History at the State University of New York, Stony Brook.

Howard K. Beale was formerly a professor of history at the University of Wisconsin.

Robert F. Berkhofer, Jr., is Professor of History at the University of Michigan.

Barbara M. Cross was a member of the faculties of Bryn Mawr College and Barnard College.

Clifford E. Clark, Jr., teaches at Carleton College.

David B. Tyack is a member of the history and education faculties at Stanford University.

Robert D. Cross is Professor of History at the University of Virginia.

Merle Curti formerly taught history at the University of Wisconsin.

Oscar Handlin is Charles Warren Professor of American History at Harvard University.

Clarence J. Karier is Professor of the History of Education at the University of Illinois, Champaign-Urbana.

David Potter was formerly Coe Professor of American History at Stanford University.

ACKNOWLEDGMENTS

Chapter 1
From pp. 123–137, 192–195, *American Education: The Colonial Experience, 1607–1783* by Lawrence A. Cremin. Copyright © 1970 by Lawrence A. Cremin. By permission of Harper & Row, Publishers.

Chapter 2
Joseph F. Kett, "Growing Up in Rural New England, 1800–1840," pp. 1–14 in Tamara K. Hareven, ed., *Anonymous Americans: Explorations in Nineteenth-Century Social History*, © 1971. Reprinted by permission of Prentice-Hall, Inc., Englewood Cliffs, N.J.

Chapter 3
Richard Rapson, "The American Child As Seen by British Travelers, 1845–1935," *American Quarterly*, 17, 1965, pp. 520–34. Copyright 1965, Trustees of the University of Pennsylvania.

Chapter 4
From pp. 1–2, 8–11, 65–71, 87–89, 92–94, 96–98, 212–217, 337–342, Ruth M. Elson: *Guardians of Tradition*. Copyright © 1964 by permission of the University of Nebraska Press.

Chapter 5
William R. Taylor, "Toward a Definition of Orthodoxy," *Harvard Educational Review*, 36, 1966, pp. 412–426. Copyright © 1966 by President and Fellows of Harvard College.

Chapter 6
Reprinted by permission of Charles Scribner's Sons from *A History of Freedom of Teaching in American Schools* by Howard K. Beale, pp. 112–115, 116–132. Copyright 1941 Howard K. Beale; renewal copyright © 1969 Georgia Robinson Beale.

Chapter 7
Robert F. Berkhofer, Jr., "Model Zions for the American Indian," *American Quarterly*, 15, 1963, pp. 176–90. Copyright 1963, Trustees of the University of Pennsylvania.

Chapter 8
Reprinted by permission of the publisher from Barbara M. Cross (ed.), *The Educated Woman in America: Selected Writings of Catherine Beecher, Maraget Fuller, and M. Carey Thomas*. (New York: Teachers College Press, 1965, copyright by Teachers College, Columbia University), 1–48.

Chapter 9
Clark, Jr., Clifford E., "The Changing Nature of Protestantism in Mid-nineteenth Century America: Henry Ward Beecher's *Seven Lectures to Young Men*," *Journal of American History*, 57, 1971, pp. 832–846.

Chapter 10
David Tyack, "Bureaucracy and the Common School," *American Quarterly*, 19, 1967, pp. 475–98. Copyright 1967, Trustees of the University of Pennsylvania.

Chapter 11
Robert D. Cross, "Origins of the Catholic Parochial Schools in America," from *American Benedictine Review* 16, 1965, pp. 194–209. Reprinted by permission.

Chapter 12
Excerpt from pp. 288–309 of *The Social Ideas of American Educators* by Merle Curti is used with the permission of Charles Scribner's Sons. Copyright 1935 Charles Scribner's Sons.

Chapter 13
(Entire book) *John Dewey's Challenge to Education* by Oscar Handlin. Copyright © 1959 by Harper & Row, Publishers, Inc. By permission of the publishers.

Chapter 14
Clarence J. Karier, "Testing for Order and Control in the Corporate Liberal State," *Educational Theory*, 22, 1972, pp. 158–170 and 175–176 as noted.

Chapter 15
From David Potter, *People of Plenty*, 1963, pp. 192–200. Reprinted courtesy University of Chicago Press.

PREFACE

This anthology includes some of the more recent and provocative writings on the history of American education. In the case of this subject, as in any field of knowledge, both the results of new research and the reinterpretations of events and trends first appear in scholarly periodicals and monographs. There they remain relatively inaccessible to students who are becoming acquainted with the subject for the first time. The best of these writings deserve as large an audience as possible and, for the convenience of students and instructors in courses about the history of American education, they should be available in a single volume.

The authors of these essays are jointly the authors of this book. Less burdensome than authorship yet still with its own difficulties, the task of the editors was to select from the many writings deserving consideration only those few that could be included in this volume. In making our selection we have followed four guidelines. First, we wanted to move beyond the educational experiences of white, middle-class boys and youths to include essays on the education of American Indians, blacks, and women. Although our leading educational traditions and standards reflect the needs and expectations of white youths, there have been so many variations and exceptions in practice that an exclusive emphasis on the dominant tradition would seriously distort our history.

Second, we chose to follow the lead of many thoughtful writers on this subject by recognizing that much of education—the shaping, that is, of the form and content of the mind—occurs outside of schools. This point of view derives from the assumption, amply borne out in everyday observation, that all of the human relationships that involve the young, whatever their institutional settings, are potentially educational. Historically, the most important of these institutions has been the family, but religious, economic, and governmental institutions, the prevailing popular culture, and the total impress of the structure of a society have all had educational effects. Historians have only just begun the systematic study of the educational impact of the social and cultural environment; nevertheless, the results of some of their investigations into children's education and the conditions of their lives outside the schoolroom are included in this volume.

Third, we believe that education is above all an experience of children and the young. The history of education becomes a part of the history of ideas, politics, economics, and social reform, but its impact on the young should be one of the historian's principal concerns. Wherever possible, then, we included writings that at least supply a foundation in fact and concept for inferences about personal and group educational outcomes. In many cases, however, the reader must draw these out for himself.

Fourth, we have tried to avoid a selection of articles that express only one interpretive viewpoint. Like other fields of study, the growth and vitality of educational history depends upon the interplay of different perspectives. Recently, historians have placed emphasis on social and economic class differences in education, and the educational apparatus has been closely tied in idea and operation to class order and control; however, racial, ethnic, religious, and sexual differentials have also existed and must be taken into consideration.

In closing, we should point out that we have deliberately omitted writings on the history of higher education. Since the colleges and universities, throughout much of the American past, have faced quite a different set of conditions and problems than the schools, we feared it would be impossible to do justice to the subject in the space at our disposal.

INTRODUCTION

Most social institutions have a single function. Political institutions distribute power according to accepted concepts of order and justice, economic institutions channel and regulate the energies that go into meeting and enriching material wants, and the family facilitates the orderly succession of the generations. But the function of education is more difficult to define. Characteristically, educational activities fall into two separate and even somewhat conflicting categories. From the earliest and simplest to the most recent and complex, all societies have relied on education to encourage acceptance of a set of beliefs and values, using it as a method of conveying its faith, creed, and way of life to the young through formal instruction as well as through custom, ritual, and a variety of other devices. On the other hand, education has also been responsible for stimulating the development of mental capacity, dexterity, and creativity. Ironically, the expansion and awakening of the mind's power and energy have often led to a critical skepticism toward the very beliefs and practices that society hopes to perpetuate. With some measure of tension always present between its elements, education has consisted of a continuing process of acceptance and challenge. A realistic study of the historical development of education may begin by assuming this dual character and impact. From the historian's point of view, education is not solely a device for social control or an instrument for enlarging the scope of human freedom, but a shifting point of equilibrium between the two.

Events in American history have shaped and accentuated this innate tension; educational purposes and activities have traveled the full range between seeking consensus and initiating choice and change.

The migration of peoples to America from other countries and the internal movements of a restless people from East to West, from South to North, and from country to city and town emphasized the need for cultural and social norms shared by all amidst the variety and novelty. A common core of values eased movement into and out of different regions, occupations, and social strata, acting as a social lubricant. At the same time, this disruptive freedom of movement, with freedom of thought and of expression, threatened to undermine accepted ways and values and to fragment shared experiences.

Examples of the mixed effects of movement on social consensus and personal choice abound in American history; an especially relevant instance lies in the historical relationship between schooling and the schooled. The schools, in their official capacity, have been designed primarily to transmit and reinforce accepted social and cultural values, heavily emphasizing the need for consensus. Simultaneously, there has been a tendency to grant the young, with some important exceptions, a separate and generally exalted place in society and, therefore, to enhance the area of choice. Age groups early emerged in American experience as important social categories, perhaps owing initially to the belief that people could indeed change and improve their condition, a belief tangibly expressed in the decision to migrate itself. Whether the immigrant's principal purpose was to seek a refuge for religious worship, or to find work, acquire property, and get rich, or to escape conscription in Europe, there was no point in undergoing the risk, travail, and disruption of resettlement unless he believed that life would improve significantly.

The significance of age divisions flowed from the fact of movement. Older people, those whose lives were largely behind them, whose important personal decisions had already been made, were underrepresented among migrants. Of course, some of the more influential and prominent migrants were older, but the appeal of migration was mainly to those who still had most of life before them. Young adults and boys and girls made up the bulk of immigrants from abroad. The requisite qualities of good health, energy, strength, and ambition weighted the composition of the immigrant flow in their favor. Although adults expected to benefit from migration, the encounter with the new reality often suggested that the benefits would be less than anticipated. When difficult problems of adjustment resisted solution, the sustaining hope tended to center on the coming generation. The old immigrant, both historically and as depicted in fiction, was often a tragic figure, unable to meet the demands of his new, chosen environment. In Willa Cather's *My Ántonia*, the father of the immigrant family, a cultivated and kindly but bewildered and ineffectual man, was driven to suicide when he realized how seriously he burdened the younger members of the family in their struggle to survive the first winter on the Nebraska prairie.

The main justification for undertaking the hazardous voyage to the new world for the Plymouth pilgrims was the benefit that might be expected for their children and later generations. Similarly, in the Massachusetts Bay Colony, Samuel Willard, an eminent divine and vice-president of Harvard College, recalled in a sermon of 1682 the purpose that had moved the founders of the colony over fifty years before. "The main errand which brought your fathers into this wilderness," he said, "was not only that they might themselves enjoy, but that they might settle for their children, and leave them in full possession of the free, pure, and uncorrupted liberties of the Covenant of Grace." The characteristic expectations of migration tended to set in motion a cycle of hope and anguish revolving around coming generations. When the immigrant thought about the meaning of his decision and experience, his mind swiftly turned to posterity.

The hopes and fears of immigrant parents were intensified by cultural isolation and abrupt change. Later migrants, speaking an alien language, settled in a relatively unrewarding occupation, and shut off from native American culture in many ways, found the transition to a new life more difficult than did their children. The plasticity of the young, their susceptibility to the education of the streets, the shops, and popular culture, as well as that of the schools, meant that the child often taught the parent the novel ways of Americans. Ease of travel within America also acted to exalt the young; long distances emphasized their separateness and their individual significance. The sons and daughters of parents living in areas of economic decline, such as the upland New England towns and farms of the early nineteenth century, often struck out for the fertile lands of the West or the factories of eastern cities to find better opportunities. The old were left behind.

The characteristic religious orientation of Americans also catered to the young. Evangelical Protestantism, the dominant faith, regardless of denomination, held that while it was always possible for an aged sinner to be redeemed, the moment of insight upon which salvation depended, the personal decision that settled one's destiny for eternity and produced a transforming spiritual fulfillment, typically occurred during youth. In sum, American experiences reinforced an inclination to think of young people as set apart from others and to invest that period of life with substantial personal and social significance.

In contrast to the elevation of youth's status, the schools carried a heavy burden of social indoctrination. This purpose is evident in schools everywhere, but there may have been differences of degree and style in the American approach. Social conformity dictated the patterns in such patently germane parts of schooling as the curriculum, textbooks, and methods of instruction. It was further reflected in the process of recruiting teachers, their social status and material rewards, the control of schools by local elites, and the commitment to a public policy of uniform, compulsory schooling for all children. The reliance on the schools for social indoctrination and control testifies to the ineffectiveness of other institutions that might have served to secure order and consent. In other countries there were alternative means of guaranteeing consensus and continuity—occupational and other kinds of economic controls, closed social classes, a state church, an extensive administrative system, and the presence of centrally controlled police and military forces among the civilian population. But in America social order issued from voluntarily extended choice and consent to an unusual degree, and the school served as the most convenient and acceptable instrument for guiding choice and securing consent. So great was the dependence on schools as a social stabilizer that one historian has suggested that the characteristic nineteenth-century American concept of a proper social order consisted of anarchy plus a schoolmaster.

Since a just and orderly society rested on the foundation of schooling, correct formal instruction was an essential element in social calculations. In view of this assumption, the interest in schooling of statesmen and thinkers like Franklin and Jefferson is readily understandable. If American society was to function correctly and predictably, the schools had to meet their responsibilities. Yet this reliance on instruction placed the schools in a difficult, even paradoxical, situation. They were indispensable in establishing order; they were also an important means of individual fulfillment and of liberation from ignorance, superstition, and prejudice. There has often been disagreement and confusion about their ultimate purpose and impact.

In practice, the status of youth and the pressure of school indoctrination have often been in balance, each acting as a countervailing force to circumscribe and temper the other. The homage paid to the young encouraged self-reliance and created opportunities for autonomy, self-expression, and initiative. Yet the temptation for youth to form its conception of itself solely on the basis of its status was checked by the pressures the schools exerted to guide choice toward approved ends and secure assent to the existing order. One result was a kind of social precocity, an almost instant adulthood. Another was an intellectual simplicity that was induced in part by the sanctioned mechanisms and even content of instruction. Not that the schools were entirely immune from the claims of autonomous youth; they could be exploited, or subverted, to serve its purposes. The remarkable scope and significance of extracurricular and other peer group activities within and around American schools reflected the determination of the young to make every situation they entered an instrument of their wishes and needs. The young were free to form associations and determine their course within a broad framework of individualism, the moral law, and republicanism.

For many young Americans, there was a tolerable equilibrium between the status they enjoyed and the demands of social control. For some others, such as blacks and Indians and, in a different way, all women, this balance never existed. These outsiders were, so to speak, denied the status of youth, with its many prerogatives and opportunities. Blacks and Indians did not trace their American origins to a voluntary migration, that crucial act of self-election for oneself and one's posterity to membership in the American community. Nor could women, owing to their traditional role in European societies, ordinarily initiate the process of joining. These elements in the population had little freedom of movement or access to other ways of life and, in consequence, they were not partners in the tacit agreement to share the benefits, prestige, and security of being Americans. Historically, their educational experiences, both in and out of school, became a lopsided exercise in social control, with an exposure to alien roles and concepts established by and for others. Although some of the conditions and decisions that originally produced this pattern have either disappeared or retreated to the corners of the mind, their heritage continues to shape the educational experience of many young Americans.

EDUCATION IN THE HOUSEHOLDS AND SCHOOLS OF COLONIAL AMERICA
Lawrence A. Cremin

The history of education has usually been concerned with the schoolhouse and schoolroom activities. Historians have studied the legal, social, and economic organization of schools, the changes in courses of study and methods of instruction, the recruitment and training of teachers, and the several philosophies of education that have stimulated and justified different approaches to educational problems. While no one now denies the significance of the schoolroom, many historians are trying to come to terms with the clear fact that the outlooks and lives of the young take shape within a broad institutional and historical setting in which the school is only one of many elements. This has directed attention to the educational influences of the family, church, workshop, factory, and playground—in fact, to all of society's institutions that deal with the young. In this excerpt from his masterful work *American Education: The Colonial Experience, 1607–1783,* Lawrence A. Cremin discusses the primacy of the household in the education of children in the American colonies. Cremin's study should be consulted for all aspects of education in the colonial period.

The place of children in English society and policy is the subject of Ivy Pinchbeck and Margaret Hewitt, *Children in English Society, Volume One: From Tudor Times to the Eighteenth Century* (London: Routledge & Kegan Paul, 1969). Studies of colonial American domestic and school relationships include Bernard Bailyn, *Education in the Forming of American Society* (Chapel Hill: University of North Carolina Press, 1960); Edmund Morgan, *The Puritan Family*, rev. ed. (New York: Harper Torchbooks, 1966); John Demos, *A Little Commonwealth: Family Life in Plymouth Colony* (New York: Oxford University Press, 1970); and Philip J. Grevan, Jr., *Four Generations: Population, Land, and Family in Colonial Andover, Massachusetts* (Ithaca, N.Y.: Cornell University Press, 1970). The history of schooling may be followed in Samuel E. Morison, *The Intellectual Life of Colonial New England* (Ithaca, N.Y.: Cornell University Press, Great Seal Books, 1960); Robert Middlekauff, *Ancients and Axioms: Secondary Education in Eighteenth-Century New England* (New Haven: Yale University Press, 1963); and the documents in Edgar W. Knight, ed., *A Documentary History of Education in the South Before 1860*, 5 vols. (Chapel Hill: University of North Carolina Press, 1949–1953).

Dutchmen, Frenchmen, Swedes, Finns, and Walloons notwithstanding, it was predominantly Englishmen who peopled the colonies. But it was not a truly representative cross-section of England that came, and this is important to bear in mind in studying the transplanting of institutions. However active the nobility and elite gentry may have been in sponsoring and financing the colonizing enterprises, few members of these classes actually immigrated, and some who did stayed only temporarily as representatives of the Crown. The lesser gentry, the merchants, and the professionals were somewhat better represented and, indeed, exercised an influence out of proportion to their numbers during the initial decades of settlement. By far the greatest number of migrants were "middling people"—yeomen, husbandmen, artisans, and tradesmen—who acquired their own farms and shops either immediately or after a brief period of indentured servitude. Finally, there were the unskilled laborers, many of whom did not even come voluntarily; virtually all such laborers arrived in some sort of indentured status, though it is important to note that this class never constituted a majority of the indentured servants.

Colonial society, then, was generally representative of contemporary

English society, though it had a comparative preponderance of middling people and a comparative paucity of the well-born and the absolutely unskilled. Not unexpectedly, colonial communities comprised a broad range of contemporary familial styles, again with a comparative preponderance of nuclear families characteristic of middling Englishmen and a comparative paucity of both large upper-class households and vagrant unattached laborers. To be sure, the colonists brought with them English ideas of degree, priority, and prestige; and, when they had the wherewithal, many strove to imitate the gentry, in family style as in everything else. Hence, the early acceptance in the colonies of two paradigms, one formed by the accepted norm of the nuclear household, the other formed by the prestigious ideal of the extended household. And hence, too, the coexistence there of nuclear families that spawned additional nuclear families, of extended families that remained extended over several generations, of nuclear families that in a generation or two acquired sufficient land and maintained sufficient stability to become extended, as younger sons and daughters married but remained in the vicinity of the patriarchal household, and of extended families that in a few generations became nuclear, as younger sons and daughters struck out on their own.

Whatever the variation in the size and character of these families, it is clear that their educational responsibilities were both augmented and intensified by the New World situation. The colonists were heir to Renaissance traditions stressing the centrality of the household as the primary agency of human association and education; and they were instructed—indeed harangued—by Puritan tracts and sermons proclaiming the correctness and significance of those traditions. Moreover, at the very time that the need for education seemed most urgent, given the threat of barbarism implicit in the wilderness, they found themselves with far less access than their metropolitan contemporaries to churches, schools, colleges, and other institutions that might share the task. In short, they were Renaissance Englishmen of Puritan loyalties—or at least propensities—who were frightened; and the result was an increased familial responsibility for education, both imposed from without and assumed from within.

The imposition from without came in the form of statutes legally compelling households to do what in England they had long been accustomed to doing. An oft-cited example is the Massachusetts law of

3

1642 empowering the selectmen of each town "to take account from time to time of all parents and masters, and of their children, concerning their calling and employment of their children, especially of their ability to read and understand the principles of religion and the capital laws of this country," and authorizing them, with the consent of any court or magistrate, to "put forth apprentices the children of such as they shall [find] not to be able and fit to employ and bring them up." The statute was more than an affirmation of the value of education per se; it came as part of a vigorous legislative effort to increase the political and economic self-sufficiency of the colony. And, significantly, the responsibility for encouraging and overseeing familial education, which had been held by the clergy under the various Royal Injunctions of the Tudor era, was now vested in the selectmen.

Connecticut passed similar legislation in 1650, requiring that children and servants be taught to read English, that they be instructed in the capital laws, that they be catechized weekly, and that they be brought up in husbandry or some trade profitable to themselves and to the commonwealth. New Haven followed suit in 1655, New York in 1665 (the Duke's Laws, after all, were "collected out of the several laws now in force in His Majesty's American colonies and plantations"), and Plymouth in 1671. And, in 1683, an ordinance of the new colony of Pennsylvania provided that all parents and guardians of children "shall cause such to be instructed in reading and writing, so that they may be able to read the Scriptures and to write by the time they attain to twelve years of age; and that then they be taught some useful trade or skill, that the poor may work to live, and the rich, if they become poor, may not want; of which every county court shall take care." Virginia dealt with the matter less directly but no less firmly, by requiring parents and masters to send their children and servants to weekly religious instruction at local churches, by ordering churchwardens to present "such masters and mistresses as shall be delinquents in the catechizing the youth and ignorant persons," and by imposing a substantial fine on parents and masters for failure to comply.

With respect to apprenticeship, there were numerous laws authorizing the putting out of children whose parents were not "able and fit to employ and bring them up," as well as various statutes providing for the public purchase of tools and raw materials for apprentices to use in their work. In addition, there was occasional legislation seeking to force unmarried persons into service within households, or at least into residence within households, and defining minimum standards for the maintenance of households. But the Statute of Artificers itself was never duplicated in the colonies, and the Poor Law of 1601 was explicitly incorporated only in Virginia.

These laws relating to household education are best viewed as essentially normative but only partially descriptive, and we shall never know precisely the extent to which they were actually honored or obeyed. From time to time, one or another of the Massachusetts towns would crack down on parents and masters whose dependents remained ignorant and illiterate, and in 1668 the general court, sensing widespread social discontent, felt obliged to reenact the law of 1642 and remind the selectmen of their responsibilities under it. On the other hand, there is no evidence that any Virginia parent was ever fined five hundred pounds of tobacco for failing to send his children to religious instruction, as ordered in the law of 1646. Throughout the colonies, the most common relevant judicial actions were those dealing with apprenticeship contracts or with the oversight of orphans or other public dependents.

In any case, there is every indication that the colonial household was even more important as an agency of education than its metropolitan counterpart. As in England, it was the fundamental unit of social organization, serving simultaneously as a center of human association, a producer of food and manufactured articles, and a focus of religious life. Colonial houses were for the most part small and almost always crowded; and though they provided the family itself with a measure of privacy, they afforded little privacy to the individuals within the family. In their most elemental form, they simply combined sleeping space with living space. The sleeping space comprised one or more bedchambers, in which parents, children, lodgers, servants, and occasional visitors mingled—two, three, or four to a room and often two, three, or four to a bed. The living space was the kitchen, an all-purpose area revolving around a hearth, which might at any time be the scene of eating, working, or playing, cooking, baking, or brewing, knitting, spinning, or weaving, the dipping of candles, the saying of prayers, or the reading of books.

As in England, too, the diurnal business of getting a living was in most households an extension of the activities of the kitchen. On farms,

5

the master of the family and his sons, perhaps with the assistance of a servant or two, worked the fields of rye, wheat, hay, corn, and tobacco, frequently using scythes, hoes, sickles, and shovels that had been fashioned within the home. More often than not, the women managed the several enclosures that constituted the home lot—barnyard, cattleyard, pigpen, garden, and orchard. But there was no sharp division of labor; and, in times of sickness or need, everyone did everything, not only during the busy periods of planting and harvesting, but in the late autumn and early winter, when there was equipment to be repaired, manure to be spread, grain to be threshed, and corn to be husked.

Similarly, shopkeepers and artisans used either part of the home itself or additional houses or sheds on the "homelot" area to pursue their trades. Indeed, farms and shops were often combined, in New England, where a town tradesman might own and cultivate strips of outlying acreage (or have them cultivated by sons, servants, or tenants), as well as in Virginia, where the combination of farm and shop was frequently dictated by the sparseness of settlement. Thus, for example, the extensive and diversified activities at Denbigh, the estate of Captain Samuel Mathews on the north side of the James between Deep Creek and Warwick River: "He hath a fine house, and all things answerable to it, he sows yearly store of hemp and flax, and causes it to be spun; he keeps weavers and has a tan house, causes leather to be dressed, has eight shoemakers employed in their trade, has forty Negro servants, brings them up to trades in his house: he yearly sows abundance of wheat, barley, etc. The wheat he selleth at four shillings the bushel; kills store of beavers, and sells them to victual the ships when they come thither; has abundance of kine, a brave dairy, swine great store, and poultry."

Whatever the extent of specialization—and it must have been greater in Captain Mathews's household than in most—the opportunities for varied learning amid such surroundings were legion. One saw and heard and took part as soon as one was able; indeed, given the lack of privacy and the burden of necessity, there was literally no escape from learning. The labor of each child was required as early as possible, and, in the nature of things, the everyday activities of the household provided a continuous general apprenticeship in the diverse arts of living.

But, beyond this, the household was also the scene of a good deal of sustained and systematic instruction. In the first place, there was reading, which was as commonly learned at home as anywhere, both in En-

6

gland and in the colonies. "My younger days were attended with the follies and vanities incident to youth," John Cotton's grandson Josiah (1680–1756) noted in his diary; "howsoever I quickly learned to read, without going to any school I remember." The experience was characteristic in an age when it was assumed that a youngster ready to undertake formal classwork would have a certain rudimentary ability to read in the vernacular. Once again, the evidence is fragmentary, but there is every indication that individual reading, responsive reading, and communal reading were daily activities in many colonial households, and that reading was often taught on an each-one-teach-one basis by parents or other elders, or by siblings or peers. For youngsters growing up in homes in which no one was equipped to teach reading, there was frequently a neighboring household where they might acquire the skill. And, indeed, when an occasional New England goodwife decided to teach reading on a regular basis in her kitchen and charge a modest fee, she thereby became a "dame school"; or, when an occasional Virginia family decided to have a servant (or tutor) undertake the task for its own and perhaps some neighbors' children, the servant became a "petty school." Such enterprises were schools, to be sure, but they were also household activities, and the easy shading of one into the other is a significant educational fact of the seventeenth century.

In the teaching of reading, a family might use a textbook like Edmund Coote's *The English Schoole-Maister* (1596); or a simple hornbook or ABC, which presented the alphabet, a few syllables combining a consonant with a vowel, and a prayer or grace, usually the Lord's Prayer or the Apostles' Creed; or perhaps some combination of hornbook or ABC and primer or catechism, a primer being an elementary book of religious material usually including the Lord's Prayer, the Apostles' Creed, and the Decalogue, a catechism being a series of questions and answers setting forth the fundamentals of religious belief. *The English Schoole-Maister* was the most formal: it was addressed "unto the unskillful, which desire to make use of it for their own private benefit: and unto such men and women of trades (as tailors, weavers, shopkeepers, seamsters, and such other) as have undertaken the charge of teaching others"; and it went systematically from letters, syllables, and words, to sentences, paragraphs, and colloquies. The hornbook, ABC, primer, and catechism, on the other hand, were the most characteristic: they were addressed to the same untutored audience as *The English*

7

Schoole-Maister, but they were explicitly tied to the oral tradition of the liturgy, the characteristic thing about them being that they taught the art of reading using passages with which the learner was probably familiar. This was equally true of the Bible itself, which was frequently used as a reading text. Doubtless many a colonial youngster learned to read by mastering the letters and syllables phonetically and then hearing Scriptural passages again and again, with the reader pointing to each word until the relationship between the printed and oral passages became manifest.

Reading was taught for many reasons, not the least so that the Bible might be personally known and interpreted. Yet there was always the inherent Protestant problem of ensuring that the Scriptures would be interpreted and applied properly; and here, too, families were assiduous in their instruction, relying heavily upon the catechetical mode. Initially, of course, English catechisms were used, the most popular of which was probably William Perkins's *The Foundation of Christian Religion, Gathered into Six Principles* (c. 1590). After 1641, however, when the Massachusetts general court "desired that the elders would make a catechism for the instruction of youth in the grounds of religion," there was a steady procession of native catechisms. Hugh Peter and Edward Norris each prepared one for the use of the Salem congregation; James Noyes produced one for Newbury, Ezekiel Rogers for Rowley, John Norton for Ipswich, and Thomas Shepard for Cambridge. John Cotton, characteristically, wrote two catechisms for the members of Boston's First Church, one of which was *Milke for Babes* (c. 1646), later to appear in so many editions of *The New-England Primer*. The Westminster Assembly's Shorter Catechism became available in 1647 and was widely used in the New World, but the proliferation of American catechisms continued unabated. By 1679, Increase Mather felt obliged to observe: "These last ages have abounded in labors of this kind; one speaketh of no less than five hundred catechisms extant: which of these is most eligible, I shall leave unto others to determine. I suppose there is no particular catechism, of which it may be said, it is the best for every family, or for every congregation."

There was also a good deal of systematic study of the more popular devotional works that were acknowledged as authoritative guides to the Christian life. The *Book of Martyrs*, *The Practise of Pietie*, *The Whole Duty of Man*, *The Poor Man's Family Book*, and *The Pilgrim's Progress* have already been discussed.* To these must be added at least one native product of unrivaled popularity, Michael Wigglesworth's *The Day of Doom* (1662). Cast in contemporary ballad form, 224 stanzas in length, Wigglesworth's poem portrayed Judgment Day in lurid and sulphurous detail: the awesome wrath of God, the fruitless pleas of sinners, and the terrible torments of hell. Many a child learned the ballad early and in its entirety, and remembered it for the rest of his days. And this, of course, is the crucial point about all this material: it was read and reread, often in groups and almost always aloud; much of it was memorized and thus passed into the oral tradition, where it influenced many who could not themselves read; and, ultimately, it provided a world view and system of values that families held in common and that communities could therefore assume as a basis of law and expectation.

For many colonial families, piety simply incorporated civility, and since *The Practise of Pietie, The Whole Duty of Man,* and *The Poor Man's Family Book* dealt in detail with the cardinal virtues and their application in human affairs, there seemed no need to go beyond these manuals in the teaching of conduct. For other families, *The Compleat Gentleman, The English Gentleman,* and *The Gentleman's Calling* served as texts for the nurture of proper deportment and demeanor. Interestingly, one looks in vain for evidence of traditional books of manners, such as Hugh Rhodes's *The Boke of Nurture* (1545), or Francis Seager's *The Schoole of Vertue* (1557), or William Fiston's *The Schoole of Good Manners* (1609), or Richard West's *The School of Vertue* (1619), though the colonists made considerable use of a volume called *The Academy of Complements* (1639), which promised readers "the best expressions of choice complemental language" for every occasion, from a lovers' tryst to a long journey requiring small talk.

Books, of course, were but the visible core of a general household education in values and conduct that was as pointed as it was persistent. The goal was cultivation of piety and civility, and the pedagogy, insofar as it can be gleaned from contemporary biographies and autobiographies, was essentially Hebraic, assuming an overall context of patriarchal surveillance, using the methods of encouragement, emulation, and punishment, and relying heavily on casuistry. "He wanted not the cares of his father to bestow a good education on him," Cotton Mather

---

* These well known works by English authors were discussed by Cremin in an earlier portion of his work that is not reprinted here.

9

wrote of his late brother, Nathaniel, "which God blessed for the restraining him from the lewd and wild courses by which too many children are betimes resigned up to the possession of the Devil, and for the furnishing him with such accomplishments as give an 'ornament of grace unto the head of youth.' He did live where he might learn, and under the continual prayers and pains of some that looked after him, he became an instance of unusual industry and no common piety; so that when he died, which was October 17th, 1688, he was become in less than twenty years, 'an old man without gray hairs upon him.' " Now Increase Mather was no ordinary father, and Nathaniel Mather was no ordinary son, but the prayerful and painful education Nathaniel received in his home during the 1670s was exemplary for the age.

Within the context of patriarchal surveillance, fathers, mothers, tutors, and other parent surrogates in the household used a variety of ancient devices for training up the child in the way he should go. At one level, it was assumed, as the Pilgrim preacher John Robinson once put it, that "there is in all children, though not alike, a stubbornness, and stoutness of mind arising from natural pride, which must, in the first place, be broken and beaten down; that so the foundation of their education being laid in humility and tractableness, other virtues may, in their time, be built thereon." In order to beat down "stubbornness and stoutness of mind," parents frequently resorted to castigation and chastisement. At another level, however, they sought to encourage proper behavior by apt example and casuistical reasoning, using shame and fear in place of chastisement and, wherever possible, the promise of salvation in place of all three. Pedagogically as well as politically, the family was truly "an original to states and churches"; indeed, certain essential tactics of the three institutions for the exercise of authority and the enforcement of conformity were virtually interchangeable.

Beyond the nurture of piety and civility, the family undertook the training of children "in some honest lawful calling, labor or employment." In a subsistence economy, this meant at the very least that boys would be instructed by their fathers in the multifarious arts required for the management of household, farm, and shop, while girls would be similarly instructed by their mothers. For those who wished to follow some calling not pursued in their own homes, it meant apprenticeship in another household, where the new mystery or art would by systematically taught by a parent surrogate. For the few who wished to practice one of the more learned professions, a period of formal schooling might be substituted for the apprenticeship, though even here it was assumed that the masters of the school stood *in loco parentis,* and the curriculum either incorporated or was supplemented by an apprenticeship component. The essential pedagogical feature of all such apprenticeship instruction was the combination of direct example and immediate participation. While an occasional household could boast a copy of one or another of the contemporary works on farming, there is no indication that printed manuals played a significant part in training for husbandry or the crafts. Possibly the only assistance beyond the day-by-day demonstration, explanation, and appraisal of parent or master came via an oral tradition that was partly proverbial and partly derived from such popular books as Thomas Tusser's *Five Hundred Pointes of Good Husbandrie* (1557, 1580). Thus the colonial apprentice to agriculture may have chanted a rhyme such as the following while weeding newly planted shrub cuttings after a spring rain:

Banks newly quicksetted, some weeding do crave,
  the kindlier nourishment thereby to have.
Then after a shower to weeding a snatch,
  more easily weed with the root to dispatch.

And his sister may have mused over one of the standard commonplaces of contemporary housewifery:

Good flax and good hemp for to have of her own,
  in May a good housewife will see it be sown.
And afterward trim it, to serve at a need,
  the fimble to spin and the carl for her seed.

In the matter of formal apprenticeship, though English custom generally prevailed, a number of departures from contemporary English practice grew directly out of the conditions of colonial life. For one thing, there was a persistent shortage of labor in the colonies, and it is probable that youngsters entered into apprenticeship arrangements earlier than they did in England, that the period during which they served was shorter than the customary seven years, and that traditional entry fees and property restrictions were either relaxed or abandoned entirely. And, for another, the guilds of merchants and craftsmen, which, along with networks of informers, played an important role in enforcing the Statute of Artificers, never became as numerous or as powerful in the

11

colonies. Consequently access to the trades was comparatively easy in America, and training requirements comparatively lenient—a fact of political as well as economic significance, given the inextricable ties between economic self-sufficiency, the opportunity to start a household, and freemanship.

A final dimension of household education involved the direct transmission of learning itself. Here the key was almost always the family library, used either for formal instruction by parent or tutor or for systematic self-instruction. Such instruction was certainly given in the household of William Brewster in Plymouth, of Increase Mather in Boston, of Gysberg van Imborch in New Amsterdam, and of John Carter in Lancaster County, Virginia, who provided in his will of 1669 that his son Robert "during his minority have a man or youth servant bought for him that hath been brought up in the Latin school and that he constantly tend upon him not only to teach him his books either in English or Latin according to his capacity (for my will is that he shall learn both Latin and English and to write) but also to preserve him from harm and from doing evil." And, given the utilitarian character of many colonial libraries, with their volumes on law, medicine, husbandry, and military tactics shelved beside the standard works of divinity and belles lettres, it is not surprising that they were regarded as centers of information and culture, and that borrowing and lending among friends and acquaintances were both frequent and spirited.

The family, then, was the principal unit of social organization in the colonies and the most important agency of popular education; and it assumed an educational significance that went considerably beyond that of its English counterpart. Whereas England had by the 1640s and 1650s placed churches within the reach of virtually every household, schools within the reach of most, and universities within the reach of at least the more ambitious and able, the colonies were only beginning their efforts in those directions. Hence, while metropolitan families could take for granted the ready availability of other institutions to assist in the educational task, colonial families could not. As a result, the colonial household simply took unto itself, by force of circumstance, educational responsibilities that the English family commonly shared with other agencies. And this, of course, was but one manifestation of a more general tendency of institutions to "double up," so to speak, under the wilderness conditions of the initial decades, that is, to assume responsibilities not traditionally carried, or carried in some bygone age but subsequently discarded. The phenomenon was nowhere more apparent than in the widespread practice of requiring masters to teach their apprentices reading, writing, and the principles of religion, in addition to the mysteries of a particular trade or trades. In sum, families did more and taught more, in the process nurturing a versatility in the young that was highly significant for the development of colonial society.

Yet, given this generalization, at least two caveats must be entered. First, there were critical educational differences between the dispersed farmsteads of the Chesapeake colonies and the tightly knit agricultural villages of New England. In the former, isolation was a salient feature of existence, and, though the well-to-do managed to get from one place to another rather easily and frequently, the yeomen seem to have had little contact with the outside world. Hence, geography alone would have necessitated a greater educational self-sufficiency on the part of southern households. By contrast, the village communities of the several townships of New England afforded ample opportunity for social intercourse among the members of different families and for joint sponsorship of readily accessible churches and schools. There it was ideology rather than geography that established the primacy of the household; for the Puritans considered the family the basic unit of church and commonwealth and, ultimately, the nursery of sainthood. True, geographical necessity and ideological propensity often converged both in New England and on the Chesapeake, but it is important to distinguish them if one is to understand the subtle differences in the educational patterns of the two regions.

Second, however much the educational responsibilities of the European colonial family increased under wilderness conditions—and obviously not all families rose equally to the task—it is important to bear in mind at least two ancillary developments: the sharp disruption of family life and education among the native Indians, who withdrew from the tribal context and sought to live according to European ways, and the even sharper disruption of family life and education among those African blacks who were brought forcibly to America as servants or slaves and placed within colonial households. Deprived of their tribal affiliations, the latter played ill-defined roles in the seventeenth century, with some achieving freedom and attempting to live like the European colonists, with others trying to maintain versions of Christian family life within white households, and with still others forced to form matrifocal families unprecedented in Anglo-Saxon or Christian law. We know next to nothing about the education provided in such families: they were often the instruments of white households and white missionaries, and they doubtless transmitted to their young a poignant version of African tribal lore, modified and confused by the effort to adapt it to New World circumstances.

Finally, as the basic unit of social organization, the family was the principal agency through which the colonists worked out responses to the new conditions in which they found themselves, consolidated what they learned, and transmitted that learning to subsequent generations. This is best seen, perhaps, in agriculture, where the production of maize and tobacco was early learned from the Indians and where certain traditional practices associated with the intensive cultivation of valuable but relatively exhausted English soil quickly gave way to quite different practices devised for the extensive cultivation of cheap and relatively virgin American soil. It is seen too in the social and economic arrangements worked out by the New England merchants who, in the face of early Puritan attempts to develop a strictly regulated economy based on agriculture, local fur-trading, and native industry, devised an elaborate commercial network between Boston, London, and the West Indies, which enabled them to challenge and eventually defeat the original restrictive efforts.

The knowledge, skills, and values associated with these innovations were not to be gained from books and manuals or learned in schools and colleges; they were developed, codified into lore, and transmitted orally by families. The enterprise, of course, was far from new for the seventeenth-century English-speaking household, which, given the social and geographical mobility of the Tudor and Stuart eras, had been serving as a mediator of change for several generations. But in the colonies it was crucial. At a time when church, school, college, and press were slowly adapting a fairly explicit and well-defined tradition to colonial needs, the family, for all its commitment to disciplining, civilizing, and spiritualizing children, managed within a single generation to work out and regularize new attitudes and behaviour and to transmit these orally to the young. In effect, the colonial family became the critical agency for institutionalizing change—for nurturing the versatility, the flexibility, and the pragmatism so vital to the successful transplantation and modification of metropolitan institutions. . . .

In transplanting schooling during the seventeenth century, the colonists inevitably transplanted something of the revolution in contemporary English education. True, that revolution took on a different flavor in a wilderness three thousand miles from the principal sources of culture, but it remained a revolution nonetheless. The idea that schooling ought to be generally available for the advancement of piety, civility, and learning was accepted throughout the colonies: in New England, that acceptance was manifested by the actual existence of a substantial number of schools; in Virginia and Maryland, where scattered settlement rendered this less feasible, that acceptance was manifested by a continuing concern that more schools be brought into being—e.g., Nathaniel Bacon's insistent questioning of Governor Berkeley as to "what arts, sciences, schools of learning, or manufactories, have been promoted [by those] in authority."

Wherever it took root, schooling was viewed as a device for promoting uniformity, and in that sense the educational revolution was institutionalized in the colonies and put to the purposes of the controlling elements of society; indeed, that institutionalization may well explain why there was no suspicious retreat from schooling in the latter half of the century, comparable to that in Restoration England. Yet, whatever the purposes of those in control, schooling did advance literacy, and it did help immerse a significant number of Americans in the classical tradition. And, like all other institutions of education, schools inevitably liberated at the same time that they socialized, and many a colonial youngster was doubtless freed from the social and intellectual constraints of a particular household, church, or neighborhood by attending a nearby school, which opened doors to new ideas, new occupations, and new life-styles.

Granted this, the transplanted revolution encountered a series of novel problems in the colonies. For one thing, there was the initial blurring of lines between institutions, which makes it exceedingly difficult to assess the number and concentration of formally established schools. What the sources clearly indicate is that schooling went on anywhere and everywhere, not only in schoolrooms, but in kitchens, manses, churches, meetinghouses, sheds erected in fields, and shops erected in towns; that pupils were taught by anyone and everyone, not

15

only by schoolmasters, but by parents, tutors, clergymen, lay readers, precentors, physicians, lawyers, artisans, and shopkeepers; and that most teaching proceeded on an individual basis, so that whatever lines there were in the metropolis between petty schooling and grammar schooling were virtually absent in the colonies: the content and sequence of learning remained fairly well defined, and each student progressed from textbook to textbook at his own pace.

The counterpoint to all this variation, however, was the fact that education became increasingly a matter of "public concernment" in the colonies. The companies, the legislatures, the county and village courts, and the towns were early involved in education, but, as in England, their involvement took quite different forms. Geraldine Murphy * provides ample documentation of the diversity in her excellent study of seventeenth-century Massachusetts: the various ways in which the towns initially concerned themselves with schooling; the gradual—and often reluctant—settlement on town-sponsored schooling; the shift from control by the town meeting to control by the selectmen to control by special committees of selectmen; and, finally, the role of the general court in gently guiding these developments. Her study reveals, too, the concomitant variety in sources of support: the initial efforts to raise adequate funds via subscription, rents, tuition, and grants of land, and the gradual—and, again, often reluctant—settlement on town rates, once it became clear that the abundance of land rendered more traditional modes of endowment unsatisfactory. And her study indicates, finally, the multiplicity of meanings of "free school": in Roxbury, the term "free" meant free to the children of subscribers, in Salem free to all poor children, in Ipswich free to a limited number of children, and in Dedham free to all children; as the years passed, the last meaning came to prevail fairly generally throughout the colony.

While these particular lines of development are less clear outside New England, "public concernment" with education was everywhere evident: in the Virginia assembly's abortive effort of 1661 to erect a college and a free school for "the advancement of learning, promoting piety and provision of an able and successive ministry"; in the similarly fruitless effort of the Maryland assembly in 1671; and in the general tendency to place the responsibility for certifying and licensing teachers in

* *Massachusetts Bay Colony: The Role of Government in Education*, unpublished doctoral thesis, Radcliffe College, 1960.

the hands of lay rather than ecclesiastical officials—the selectmen in New England and the resident governors in New York and Virginia.

Finally, there was the insistent problem of clientele. By the seventeenth century, access to English schools had been substantially increased, and this increase continued in the colonies, where school attendance was a function more often of propinquity than of social status, at least for white children. The accessibility of schooling to Indians and Negroes, on the other hand, was much more problematical. In Virginia, there as an abrupt retreat from neighborliness toward the Indians after the hostilities of 1622. "The way of conquering them is mich more easy than of civilizing them by fair means," stated a formal report to the Virginia Company, "for they are a rude, barbarous, and naked people, scattered in small companies, which are helps to victory, but hindrances to civility: Besides that, a conquest may be of many and at once; but civility is in particular, and, slow, the effect of long time, and great industry." In New England, although the Puritans remained as ambivalent about the Indian's educability as they were about his salvation, Indian schooling was vigorously promoted, especially in the years before King Philip's War: there is evidence that, as early as 1650, Indian children were attending the common schools of Massachusetts side by side with whites, and, indeed, the Harvard charter of that year mentioned "the education of the English and Indian youth of this country." In 1653, the Society for Propagation of the Gospel in New England asked the Commissioners of the United Colonies to erect an Indian College at Harvard, and shortly thereafter a program was started in which selected Indian youngsters undertook preparatory studies with Elijah Corlet at the Cambridge Grammar School and with Daniel Weld at Roxbury. Finally, owing largely to the efforts of John Eliot and Daniel Gookin, there were schools for both youngsters and adults in the several praying towns of Massachusetts. No other region did as well as New England, though attempts to school the Indians doubtless accompanied missionary endeavors in all the colonies. As far as the blacks are concerned, it appears that only a handful attended school along with the whites, and there is no evidence at all of the establishment of any all-black schools. Apart from the suggestions of John Eliot and Morgan Godwyn, little was proposed and little was accomplished, beyond such "schooling" as might have come on the fringes of household or church instruction for whites.

★ 2 ★

GROWING UP IN RURAL NEW ENGLAND, 1800–1840
Joseph F. Kett

Whatever their particular concern, historians always confront the question of continuity or change. Does the past consist of unbroken trends that last throughout the superficial changes of successive eras, or are there watersheds of abrupt change that clearly distinguish one historical period from another? What combination of continuity and change is found at a particular time and place? Joseph F. Kett contends that growing up in early nineteenth-century New England was very different from growing up today. In premodern American society, there were neither uniform conceptions of normal boyhood nor common conditions of life for boys of different regions and classes.

A work on the history of French children and youth is Philippe Aries, *Centuries of Childhood: A Social History of Family Life*, trans. Robert Baldick (New York: Vintage Books, 1965). Writings on American attitudes toward children and youth include Oscar and Mary F. Handlin, *Facing Life: Youth and the Family in American History* (Boston: Little, Brown and Company, 1971), and Bernard Wishy, *The Child and the Republic: The Dawn of Modern American Child Nurture* (Philadelphia: University of Pennsylvania Press, 1968).

A concern with the adolescent has been a distinctive feature of twentieth-century social thought. Psychologists and others have written books on the teen years as frequently as nineteenth-century theologians turned out concordances of the Bible. Whole journals have been devoted to the psychological and social significance of adolescence. Professional writers on youth have enjoyed successful careers, while youth culture has become so pervasive that it is often dominant over adult culture. All of this presupposes the existence of typical adolescents, so that one can generalize from the experience of a sample group to that of untested groups. We assume that street-corner society in Brooklyn is like street-corner society in Cicero, that the Grosse Pointe teen-ager shares common experiences with the Mamaroneck teen-ager. Few early adolescents work; the great majority attend school of a special type, the high school. There they are segregated by age with peers, exposed to similar subjects, and expected to engage in carefully regulated and age-graded pursuits, whether cheerleading or sports, proms or debating.

Nothing remotely resembling this pattern existed in early nineteenth-century America. The experience of growing up differed, often profoundly, from one youth to the next. There was no set age for leaving school, leaving home, or starting to work. Variations among regions were at least as deep-seated as those among classes or individuals. The dominance of regional variation arose from two sources: the differing character of work demands and opportunities in settled and in frontier areas, and the immense discrepancy among the kinds of schooling available in the Northeast, the South, and the West. These variations often had an intensely personal application. The boy who started to grow up in New England might find himself at the age of ten in Ohio and at fifteen in Michigan. His attachment to his family would be the only constant factor as he was ruthlessly ushered from one setting to the next.

The pattern of random experience, however, could extend just as readily to the family itself. Families were constantly being disrupted by the death of one or both parents, not simply because of higher mortality from disease, but also because of the length of time which usually elapsed between the birth of the first and the last child. A man who fathered his first child at twenty-five might not father his last until he was forty or even forty-five. It was a statistical probability that the father would be dead before the youngest child reached maturity. The frequency of being orphaned in the early nineteenth century had a personal as well as a demographic significance, for it meant that the plans laid by youth were subject to drastic shattering by chance.

All of these factors make it difficult to reconstruct the experience of growing up in the early nineteenth century. Even if we confine our attention to New England between 1800 and 1840 and exclude from consideration sons of the very rich and the very poor, we only assuage the problem. The most typical experience of any child in the early nineteenth century was coming into contact with death before he reached the age of five. Although writers in the period did not produce a significant body of literature on the teen years, they did often talk of childhood and youth, indicating that they were conscious of some model experiences, and thereby tempting the historian to explore the nature of growing up.

FEMININE CONTROL IN THE EARLY YEARS

Very early in the nineteenth century a consensus emerged in published literature to the effect that the first five or six years of childhood were primarily the mother's responsibility. These were the years of "infancy," not in its modern connotation of reference to suckling babes, but used more broadly to indicate the years of maternal control of the child. The same literature which affirmed the preeminent role of the mother insisted on two corollaries: the need to pay attention to little children, and the superiority of moral suasion over corporal punishment in discipline.

In all likelihood, the simple conditions of farm life did more to reinforce than to frustrate the accomplishment of the prescribed regimen. Although mothers were busy managing large families and cooking meals for husbands and field hands, they could expect and command assistance from older daughters for these tasks. During the winter, moreover, the workload for all parties eased and more time could be found for children. In the summer, especially in the busy hours before noon (the time of the principal meal), children under eight were usually sent to district schools, which functioned virtually as nurseries in the planting, haying, and harvesting seasons. Summer schools, which usually served three- to eight-year-olds, were taught by women, and never acquired the unsavory reputation for disorder which marked the winter schools. The absence of older boys in summer sessions meant that discipline for younger children could be mild, an extension of approved family discipline.

20

The first of many jarring discontinuities involved in the experience of growing up usually came not in "infancy" but between the ages of six or eight to twelve, and was an outgrowth of new experiences in school, work, and, often, religion. After the age of eight or nine, boys customarily attended only winter schools, being kept at home to work on the farm in summer. The transition to winter school was, in a fundamental way, abrupt.

District schools in the winter bore little resemblance in either composition or discipline to summer sessions. Prior to the 1840s, the former were usually taught by men of all ages and temperaments. Some were college students, some academy students, and others were local farmers who had advanced to the rule of three, if little beyond. Differences among the pupils were even greater. Most winter schools included "large boys" of sixteen and seventeen, and many had young men of eighteen or twenty. The majority of pupils, however, were between eight and fifteen. Sometimes efforts were made to seat the smaller children separately, but they would still be in the same room with older boys, since no effective grading system existed outside of large cities before 1840.

Available evidence suggests that disorderly conditions were the norm in winter schools. Even progressive educators and reformers attached primary importance to the establishment of order. School was occasionally broken up by the "carrying out" of the schoolmaster. Although such complete dismantling was rare, chaos, or a measure of order purchased by brutal discipline, was common. Discipline itself consisted in a combination of corporal punishment and humiliation, especially the latter. There was nothing in theory to exempt younger boys from this regimen, but in practice schoolmasters had to focus on the teen-agers, who, by all accounts, made the most trouble. This preoccupation gave a random quality to the kind of discipline experienced by the younger boys. But such discipline could be as unsettling as systematic chastisement. Autobiographers frequently commented on the shame they felt when they were first singled out for correction, for severe discipline occasionally administered was likely to produce a more profound sense of shame and guilt than the daily drubbing to which the older boys became inured.

21

If the years of seven and eight were significant as the time when most boys started to attend winter schools, these years had importance in other respects as well. At about the age of seven a boy was expected to begin work on the farm. How much he would do was dependent on a host of factors including his size, the number and age of his male siblings, the health of his father, and the size of the farm. Whatever the variables, however, direction in his daily routine now came both at school and work from older boys or men.

The third experience which occurred with some regularity between the ages of eight and twelve was the commencement of religious anxiety. Religious instruction began earlier, just after infancy, but most autobiographers traced the start of personal religion to the period between eight and twelve. At times, especially among girls, religious conversion took place this early, but the expectation, at least up to the 1840s, was that conversion would come later. At eight or nine children were expected to evince no more than "early piety" and to become subjects of "hopeful conversion." Early piety usually involved lying awake most of the night in anxiety about salvation, a morbid fear of death, and a tendency to meet together with peers, sometimes in district schools, in prayer meetings. This is the syndrome which emerges in autobiographies of evangelicals, and considerable evidence points to its spread among those who never went on to become ministers. Some of it was undoubtedly due to the intense desire of most boys between eight and twelve for peer group acceptance. Contemporary skeptics put forward a version of this argument, attributing early piety to mere "sympathetic enthusiasm," but there was also an aspect of solitary introspection to it not explicable in terms of any current developmental model.

Although peer group pressure is not an altogether satisfactory explanation for the prevalence of morbid piety among children in early nineteenth-century New England, other leads are available. The kind of regimen of guilt and shame to which most schoolchildren were exposed could produce feelings of inadequacy which led to juvenile religious anxiety. Early nineteenth-century New England Calvinism, moreover, took a paradoxical approach to childhood. Children were told that they were damned unless converted, that they had to repent, but that they could not do so without divine aid. Finally, they were told that such assistance was not likely to come before the age of seventeen or eighteen.

The approved practice in much of New England before 1840 was to usher children into religious anxiety but not to let them out. To take an apt if anachronistic analogy, children from eight to seventeen or eighteen were put into a kind of moral pressure cooker.

CHILDREN OF THE WEALTHY

There were, naturally, differences among classes in the experience of growing up. Children of moderately wealthy or well-educated parents were less likely to be exposed to the district school's winter session. Instead, they were sent to private schools or academies where classes were smaller, the curriculum much more difficult, and discipline more regular. The regimen of moderately wealthy children was not softer but more consistent, for all academies stressed punctuality, and, at least within a given term, regular attendance. After 1840 the school reform movement had the effect of bringing practices in public schools more in line with those of private schools, but the gap in the previous period between the discipline of boys who, for whatever reason, never went beyond district schooling and those who were exposed to private schools and academies was substantial. In a general way, this represented a class difference.

The years from eight to twelve comprised a unit in the lives of most boys, marked primarily by the commencement of work and winter schooling and often by the start of religious anxiety. Neither idleness nor leaving home was an ingredient of this unit. An artisan's son was likely to work in the shop, close to his father or an older brother. A farmer's boy would follow the plough and perform odd jobs around home. Both would be sent to district schools in the winter. There were exceptions, coming, oddly enough, at opposite ends of the social ladder. Children of poor people were often sent away to work, because they could not easily be incorporated into the family routine. When the father did not own his own shop or farm, it was difficult for him to find a suitable place for his son close to home, even though such a father would need all the money a son could earn. Similarly, children of ministers or of wealthy parents were often sent away to school at extremely early ages. Wealthy mill owners and manufacturers, who were not, as a rule, great believers in prolonged schooling, often put their sons into the family factory at eight or nine, making them child laborers. Length of dependency did not correlate neatly with rising social class. In fact,

23

there seems to have been an inverse correlation. Children of wealthy parents were thrust out into the world at an earlier age than sons of middle-class farmers. Thus one encounters sixteen-year-old sons of merchants traveling to St. Petersburg as supercargo and being taken in as partners of the firm at nineteen. In the course of the nineteenth century a reaction to this did take place, and by 1900 the sons of the rich usually enjoyed a more protected and sheltered upbringing than did the sons of the middle classes. But this reaction had little effect before 1840.

DEPENDENCY AND DISCONTINUITIES

It is difficult to say exactly when the period of total dependency ended, simply because youthful experiences in the early republic were not determined in any precise way by numerical age. Still, sometime after the age of twelve and before the age of fifteen or sixteen, middle-class boys passed into a new stage of semidependency. Sons of artisans and small manufacturers were likely to be apprenticed, sometimes to their fathers, sometimes to relatives, sometimes outside the family altogether. Those who were not apprentices in theory were usually apprentices in fact, having entered machine shops or mills to learn the routine. The pattern does not seem to have involved continual employment at the same position until twenty-one, but rather a moving about from job to job or apprenticeship to apprenticeship. Thus, while tradition sanctioned a lengthy apprenticeship to occupy the remaining years of minority, social conditions facilitated short-term apprenticeships with frequent removals.

Sons of farmers experienced a different pattern. They were likely after the age of twelve or fourteen to be withdrawn from winter schooling and encouraged to seek employment or possibly advanced schooling away from home during the winter. Late spring, summer, and early fall would find them back on the farm again, thus completing the cycle of home leaving and homecoming. Although there was an element of regularity in the summer employment of farm boys, their winter occupations had little consistency. Some clerked in country stores, others went to academies, others found employment in such winter work as lumbering. Although many stopped attending winter school between twelve and fourteen, there was nothing to stop them from resuming attendance at sixteen or seventeen.

Whether one is discussing sons of artisans or small manufacturers or sons of farmers, there were certain discontinuities which beset the life experiences of teen-agers in early nineteenth-century New England regardless of occupation or parentage. The first of these was between school and work. In the twentieth century work normally follows a period of schooling, but in the early nineteenth century the relationship was less definite. Many apprentices had the right to a month or two of annual schooling stipulated in their contracts with masters, and farm boys often managed to snatch a few months of schooling in the winter. Two aspects of the school experience of teen-agers might be noted. First, prior to the middle of the century, there seems to have been little understanding that teen-agers might need a type of discipline different from that given to younger children. If there was any difference of emphasis in pedagogical thought, it was that older boys were more unruly and hence greater effort had to be made to break their wills. Second, in virtually all types of school (including colleges), few efforts were made before 1840 to segregate pupils by age. Pupils of fifteen or sixteen, both in academies and common schools, were likely to be grouped with much younger children in classes and exposed to a more severe version of the same type of discipline experienced by the eight- or nine-year-olds. Quite obviously, the adult roles which teen-agers often played in one part of the year were followed by demands for childish submission during the rest of the year.

The major educational innovation of the late eighteenth and early nineteenth century, the New England academy, dramatically accentuated these tendencies. Although the academy offered a valuable opportunity for intermediate education between the district school and the college, academy students were subject to many of the same anomalies as district school pupils. One encountered in academies, as in winter district schools, students of eight or nine to twenty or twenty-five years of age, with the concentration falling in the ten- to twenty-year-old category. Teen-agers were constantly matched first against children and then against mature men. We sometimes indulge in a stereotype of nineteenth-century boyhood which postulates that boys were then exposed much more than now to the company of adults. The stereotype has an element of truth, but older men were also periodically classified with children. Like the experience of work, the academy experience presented boys with alternating demands, now for childish submission, now for adult responsibility.

The fact that many boys had already worked for a number of years before attending academies accentuated the anomaly. This accounted for the unusual age distribution of academy students: for some, attendance at the academy was the first departure from home, for others, it represented a respite from job demands. Moreover, for nearly everyone, attendance at academies did not exclude the performance of useful work during part of the year. Attendance usually fell off in the winter as students went out to teach or labor, and again in the summer, when any strong male, boy or adult, could command high wages on the farm. The academy was a form of seasonal education to complement the seasonal labor pattern of an economically active but preindustrial society. Academy pupils thus experienced the same odd shifting from dependent to independent to dependent status which characterized the lives of boys who never attended school beyond the age of twelve.

The critical constituent of the teen years was, therefore, an endless shifting of situations—home to work, work to school—in a society in which discipline was determined not so much by numerical age as by situation. Flogging was much less common in academies and colleges than in common schools, yet pupils in the latter were often older than students in either of the former. Similar factors dominated the experience of work. Because of rapid economic change in New England in the early nineteenth century, boys often had to give up one type of employment to learn a new trade; one could be nearly self-sufficient at fourteen and an apprentice at sixteen. This was especially true of farm boys, who often did not enter apprenticeships until their late teens after years of semi-independent manual labor in winters, but it was also at least partly true of sons of artisans. Although the institution of apprenticeship no longer existed in its Elizabethan form, it still involved a master-dependent relationship, with the latter receiving low wages for the duration. The pattern of discontinuity was not only horizontal, between work and school, but vertical, between types of work and types of schooling.

A second tension in the lives of teen-agers was between their desire for ultimate independence and the fact of their semidependence. Because of the new economic opportunities created by the beginnings of industrialization and by territorial expansion, many teen-agers were largely self-supporting. Even those who sought higher education in the academies could probably earn enough in the winter and summer months to pay the meager tuition demands. There were even instances of boys becoming factory overseers at sixteen or seventeen. But traditional assumptions about maturity persisted, assumptions which thus ran counter to the new economic forces. Although the latter made possible an earlier independence than ever before, the former still provided that a boy became a man at the age of twenty-one. Before that age he was conceived of as a piece of property under obligation to work for his father. Even where there were more sons than could possibly be settled on family land, as was often the case in New England, fathers could usually use their sons' labor in the late spring, summer, and early fall. There was no easy or consistent resolution of this problem. A few boys simply left home at fifteen or sixteen, never to return; a few stayed on the farm until twenty-five or later. For most, however, the critical period came between seventeen and twenty-one. By the age of seventeen, many youths had acquired enough capital to launch themselves in the world and saw that there was no future for them on the farm. If a father resisted his son's demands for independence, the likeliest solution was for the son to make a cash payment to the father in lieu of his services, thus in effect ending the contractual relationship.

A final, and central, ingredient of the teen years in the early nineteenth century was religious crisis, which was often followed by conversion. Evangelical clergymen involved in the Second Great Awakening in the early 1800s noted time and again the frequency of religious conversion among "youth" or the "young people." There had been some foreshadowing of this in the Great Awakening of the eighteenth century, although young converts at that time were more likely to be in their late twenties than in their teens. In the early nineteenth century, by contrast, a pattern of teen-age conversion began to emerge. It is impossible to compute the average or median age of conversion, and it would be pointless, since some individuals experienced a religious crisis in their teens without going through conversion, and others experienced conversion without a religious crisis. A huge number of published autobiographical conversion narratives of the nineteenth century, however, point to the predominance of conversions between the ages of fifteen and twenty-one.

Conversion narratives emphasized three themes. Two were traditional—the idleness and sinfulness of the convert's past life and the appeal of conversion as a decisive break with the past. But a third theme was relatively novel in the early nineteenth century: the importance of a sudden, quick transformation. Although seventeenth-century Puritans had emphasized a gradual conversion experience, the distinctive feature of early nineteenth-century thought, encapsulated in the doctrine of regeneration or rebirth, was that one could experience the turning point in an instant.

Given this rhetoric of the Second Awakening, it is possible to locate at least one factor in the experience of middle-class New England boys which would dispose them to evangelical conversion. Enough has been said to indicate that the need to make choices was, perhaps as never before, incumbent on every youth. The beginnings of industrialization, the spread of commercialization, increasing pressure on the available land, and proliferation of educational opportunities for teen-agers gave the experience of maturation novel dimensions. But the religious dimension of choice was no less important. In seventeenth-century Massachusetts the principal sects had been Congregationalism and Anglicanism. Dissenters such as Baptists and Quakers could be isolated in places such as Rhode Island. From 1750 on, however, the number of dissenters increased, and arguments and even fistfights among dissenters and between dissenters and the orthodox became more common. By 1820 even small villages in New England were likely to have, besides the "standing order," a number of free-will Baptists, Methodists, and Universalists.

The extravagant claims of each sect only further necessitated the importance of making a choice. In his autobiography, Joseph Smith, who had grown up in Vermont but moved to western New York State—the so-called burnt-over district which was to be the scene of extraordinary religious commotion in the years 1820–1845—drew a revealing portrait of small-town religious excitement:

> Indeed, the whole district of country seemed affected by it, and great multitudes united themselves to the different religious parties, which created no small stir among the people, some crying, "Lo, here!" and others, "Lo, there!" Some were contending for the Methodist faith,

some for the Presbyterian, and some for the Baptist. . . . During this time of great excitement my mind was called up to serious reflection and great uneasiness. . . . In process of time my mind became somewhat partial to the Methodist sect and I felt some desire to be united with them; but so great were the confusion and strife among the different denominations that it was impossible for a person young as I was and so unacquainted with men and things, to come to any certain conclusion who was right and who was wrong. . . . In the midst of this war of words and tumult of opinions, I often said to myself, what is to be done? Who of all these parties are right; or are they all wrong together? If any one of them be right, which is it, and how shall I know it?

Smith, only fifteen at the time, resolved his crisis with the discovery of the Book of Mormon and the launching of a new religion. While his resolution was atypical, the kind of anxiety he expressed at confrontation with religious choice found expression elsewhere.

In one sense religious choice was part of the larger pattern of choice; in another sense it held forth to the convert the lure of finality. Although many lapsed after making a religious identification, in theory religious choice was absolute. Therein lay part of its appeal to the young, for it was the choice to end all choices in a society in which young people were subjected to an apparently endless sequence of role changes.

THE TURBULENCE OF ADOLESCENCE

In the twentieth century a variety of factors have conspired to make the teen years difficult. The evidence indicates that they were also turbulent in early nineteenth-century New England, but for different reasons. The significance of adolescence today lies in its following a protected and sanitized period of childhood and in the forced economic inactivity of teen-agers. Neither of these conditions was present in the early nineteenth century. Although attitudes toward childhood were changing in the direction of sentimentality, social conditions scarcely permitted sealing off the cares of adulthood from the life of the child. One might illustrate this by taking so simple yet pervasive a concern as death. People generally did not die in hospitals in early nineteenth-century New England, but in homes, right in front of the family. Although intense religious anxiety often marked the teen years, religious concern, the so-called early piety, was expected to begin before the age of twelve. In the experience of work, a farm boy of nine or ten toiled in the field alongside his older brother of fourteen. Many aspects of adolescent life were thus simply extensions of patterns launched in late childhood.

Although adolescence as we know it did not exist in 1820, boys did experience an intermediate period between childhood and adulthood. An opposing view is sometimes presented. The period of dependency, it is asserted, was very short in the early nineteenth century. Boys left home and became men at fifteen, if not earlier, and thus scarcely experienced a period of youth. It is true that the period of total dependency was brief, but the intermediate stage of semidependency was often lengthy. However, even the period of semidependency was getting shorter after 1750. Research on the seventeenth century has indicated that boys commonly stayed around the homestead until their middle twenties. Between about 1750 and 1820, pressure on the land and availability of attractive alternatives to following the plough were operating to end the period of semidependency in the late teens. But the very fact that the period of semidependency was shortening made it even more turbulent. As long as young people were not expected to make important decisions until they reached twenty-one, semidependency had more chronological than psychological content; it was long but not critical. One could have dependency without youth, without a time of erratic indecision. In this sense, youth hardly existed in the seventeenth century, even though the period of semidependency was long. It did exist by the early nineteenth century, largely because of the contraction of the outer limits of semidependency.

What effect did the kind of experience described have on the attitudes of those who went through it? It would be ridiculous to suppose that it had any uniform effect; personalities differed as much in the nineteenth century as they do in the twentieth. But Americans born between 1800 and 1840, especially those born in New England, were more prone than any previous generation to assign importance to boyhood and youth. Two themes in their romanticization of boyhood did have a traceable connection to the actual experience of growing up: the idea that such a boyhood was free, and that it encouraged initiative or individualism. It was free, not because parents or teachers were indulgent, but because the social institutions which came to bear on youth had a loose and indefinite character. An economically active but largely preindustrial society allowed boys, and adults, a footloose life. The cycle of the seasons rather than the time clock or an office manager regulated the routine of work. Home authority could be severe, when one was home, but a great deal of time was spent outside the home. Discontinuity of experience, frustrating in one respect, was liberating in another, since it meant that no single regimen had to be submitted to for long.

Finally, the experience of growing up in New England between 1800 and 1840 did encourage initiative. There were abundant opportunities but no fixed experiences which automatically led the young to success. One had to respond to and make the best of a complicated situation. What writers in the late nineteenth century had to say about the early initiative nurtured by a rural boyhood certainly had its fanciful elements. Whole segments of society—Negroes, women, paupers, and immigrants—were excluded from even the opportunity of making a choice, and the mere presence of choice did not ensure that those who could choose would make the right choices. Moreover, an ability to make choices was a precondition, even if not a guarantee, of success in life.

★ 3 ★

THE AMERICAN CHILD AS SEEN BY BRITISH
TRAVELERS, 1845–1935
Richard L. Rapson

The only sure way to detect and analyze the causes of
change, some historians claim, is through comparative
study. When two broadly similar societies or cultures are
compared, the variables that determine the differences between them may be identified. Foreign travelers have been
an important source of comparative data and opinion, although their observations must be evaluated in the light of
their biases. British travelers to this country provide a particularly useful approach to the study of American education
because their culture and traditions were close enough to
American conditions to make an intelligent study of them
possible, yet sufficiently different to throw our native peculiarities into relief. In the essay below Richard Rapson studies some of the variations between the two countries in their
ways of child rearing.

While British travelers to American shores disagreed with one another
on many topics between the years 1845 and 1935, they spoke with practically one voice upon two subjects: American schools and American
children. On the whole they thought the public school system admirable; with near unanimity they found the children detestable.

This adds up to a paradox, for if the innovation of free public education was, as most of these visitors contended, the best thing about
America, surely some decent effect upon the schools' young charges
should have been faintly discernible. Yet the British were not at all

charmed by the youngsters, and the foreign observers had very few kind things to say in behalf of American children.

The paradox as stated must leave one unsatisfied. In any nation one should expect the child to stamp his impress upon the climate of the entire society; the detestable child should become the detestable adult. But especially in a nation which the British characterized by the term "youthful"—the epithet more often used in a complimentary rather than a deprecatory fashion—one would with reason expect to find some association between the word and the actual young people of the country.

There was no question as to what quality in the children did most to nettle the Englishmen. As David Macrae said in 1867, "American children are undoubtedly precocious." In the same year, Greville Chester explained a little this theme, which appeared with more monotonous regularity than did any other in these books. "Many of the children in this country," he said, "appear to be painfully precocious—small stuck-up caricatures of men and women, with but little of the fresh ingenuousness and playfulness of childhood."

Again in that same uneventful year of 1867, the Robertsons embellished this developing portrait thus:

> *Their infant lips utter smart sayings, and baby oaths are too often encouraged . . . even by their own parents, whose counsel and restraint they quickly learn wholly to despise. It is not uncommon to see children of ten calling for liquor at the bar, or puffing a cigar in the streets. In the cars we met a youth of respectable and gentlemanly exterior who thought no shame to say that he learned to smoke at eight, got first "tight" at twelve, and by fourteen had run the whole course of debauchery.*

Every year American youth was similarly berated for its precocity. "Precocity" politely expressed the British feeling that American children were pert, impertinent, disrespectful, arrogant brats. But "precocious" meant more than that; it implied that American children weren't children at all. Three British mothers made this point. Therese Yelverton exclaimed that "in the course of my travels I never discovered that there were any American *children*. Diminutive men and women in process of growing into big ones, I have met with; but the child in the full sense attached to that word in England—a child with rosy cheeks and bright joyous laugh, its docile obedience and simplicity, its healthful play and its disciplined work, is a being almost unknown in America."

Daniel Boorstin in the introduction to a new edition of *A Lady's Life in the Rocky Mountains* wrote of how Isabella Bird "saw a society where, in a sense, everyone was young, yet where the most painful sight was 'the extinction of childhood. I have never seen any children, only debased imitations of men and women.' " And Lady Emmeline Stuart-Wortley, before the Civil War, commented: "Little America is unhappily, generally, only grown-up America, seen through a telescope turned the wrong way. The one point, perhaps, in which I must concur with other writers on the United States, is there being no real child-like children here."

Eyre Crowe tells how he and his traveling companion, William Makepeace Thackeray, came across a youngster reading a newspaper, "already devouring the toughest leaders, and mastering the news of the world whilst whiffing his cigar, and not without making shies at a huge expectorator close at hand." The picture of the cigar-smoking cherub flashed recurrently in these accounts.

The visitors did not have to search far for an explanation—at least, a superficial explanation—for this disconcerting childhood behavior. Although a few of them remarked at the leniency of the common schools and regretted the lack of corporal punishment handed out there, many more felt that the only doses of discipline ever received by the child were administered, even if in small quantities, in the schoolrooms. No, it was unquestionably in the home that the child was indulged, and indulgence gave him his swagger.

His parents either could not or else chose not to discipline their offspring. To be sure, the school system was not blameless. Many, like Fraser, regarded the school "as an extension of the family," which, by its very effectiveness made matters more difficult for mother and father.

. . . *It must be allowed that schools are robbing parents of the power to control their families. The school has drawn to itself so much of the love and veneration of the young that in the homes missing its spell they grow unruly. Parents are not experts in the management of children, nor have they the moral weight of an institution to back them up, hence they fail to keep up the smooth ascendancy of the school.*

34

P. A. Vaile blamed the American mother: "She is refusing to perform her part of the contract. First she 'went back' on raising her children now she does not want to have any children at all." Mrs. Humphreys raged at "the conspicuous absence of maternal instinct as a feature of American marriages."

Many others accused fathers, but usually with greater sympathy. After all, the father simply worked too hard all day to have much time, interest, or energy to devote to his little ones. "The husband had his occupations, friends, and amusements."

No matter which parent had to bear the burden of guilt, many an Englishman simply felt that home life in the United States just wasn't homelike; it lacked atmosphere, comfort, love, play, and warmth. It never became the cozy, friendly hearth which imparted to a family a sense of kinship, identity, or oneness. Long after young couples had forsaken the custom of dwelling in boarding houses or hotels and exposing their tiny ones to the dregs of society—a custom deplored by every Englishman—long after this, W. L. George, along with most others, refused to admit that Americans still had any idea as to what constituted a "real" home.

> *The hard child [he said] suggests the hard home, which is characteristic of America. I visited many houses in the United States, and except among the definitely rich, I found them rather uncomfortable. They felt bare, untenanted; they were too neat, too new . . . one missed the comfortable accumulation of broken screens, old fire irons, and seven-year-old volumes of the* Illustrated London News, *which make up the dusty, frowsy feeling of home. The American house is not a place where one lives, but a place where one merely sleeps, eats, sits, works.*

George may have been a bit unfair to expect to find "seven-year-old volumes of the *Illustrated London News*" lying about, but he had a right to notice the lack of age; it takes years for a family to implant its brand on a structure of brick and mortar. Perhaps, as many visitors rightly pointed out, Americans were too much on the go, too mobile for them ever to fulfill George's requirements for home-ness. This nonetheless did not excuse the parents from their failure to bring up their children appropriately. Joseph Hatton, in 1881, begged the mothers and fathers to take their responsibilities as parents more seriously than they were and to realize, as any sensible person must, that their overindulgence of the child was "excessive and injurious."

Little Fritz, a pretty little American boy who sat as the subject for one of Philip Burne-Jones' paintings, told his grandmother, in the artist's presence, "I'll kick your head!" After being chided and asked to apologize, there was "dead silence on the part of Fritz." Finally, after some more pleading, Fritz relented and uttered "a few perfunctory and scarcely audible sounds, which were generously construed by the family as expressive of contrition and penitence; and Fritz started again with a clear record, for a brief period. His mother had absolutely no influence on him whatever, and she admitted as much."

Other American parents admitted as much also; they were fully aware of their inability to control their little ones, but they just didn't know what to do about it. L. P. Jacks, in 1933, let an American mother speak her heart about her utter helplessness and frustration in a way that was rather revealing and even poignant:

> We mothers are rapidly losing all influence over our children, and I don't know how we can recover it. We have little or no control over them, whether boys or girls. The schools and the colleges take them out of our hands. They give them everything for nothing, and that is what the children expect when they come home. Their standards and their ideals are formed in the school atmosphere, and more by their companions than their teachers. They become more and more intractable to home influence and there is nothing for it but to let them go their own way.

But the majority of the Britons did not accept either the influence of the schools or the social fact of mobility as sufficient explanations for the precocious child; they would have had little justification for disliking the child with the fervor they did and deploring the parents' follies so strongly if these impersonal forces accounted adequately for the situation.

They felt, rather, that causes ran deeper, in more insidious channels. Not only did the parents spoil their children, but they *wanted* to spoil them. Not only did the mothers and fathers put up with more than they should have, but they were actually proud of their babies. The Britons were especially distressed when they decided that parents felt, as a rule,

36

not the least bit guilty over their own efforts or over the way their boys and girls were turning out. The travelers came not to the conclusion that American parents were unable to discipline their sons and daughters, but that they deliberately chose to "let them go their own way." This either infuriated the by now bewildered visitor, or else made him desperate to figure out just how this insanity could possibly reign.

William Howard Russell could not accept the excuse that the schools pre-empted parental power since "there is nothing in the American [school] system to prevent the teaching of religious and moral duties by parents at home; but it would seem as if very little of that kind of instruction was given by the busy fathers and anxious mothers of the Republic. . . ."

Horace Vachell, as did many others, told a child story that turned into a mother story. It seems that one day the author was in the parlor of a ship filled with ailing people, including the author's own mother, who was suffering with a bad headache. Into this sickly assemblage trooped our hero—a small American boy who decided to soothe the aches of all by playing on the bagpipes! "The wildest pibroch ever played in Highland glen was sweet melody compared to the strains produced by this urchin." He naturally continued to play, louder than ever, despite the daggered glances hurled at him from all around the parlor; he stopped only when he tired. Then, instead of permitting sweet peace, "he flung down the pipes, walked to the piano, opened it, sat down, and began to hammer the keys with his feet."

At this turn of events, our long-suffering author had had enough. " 'You play very nicely with your feet,' I ventured to say, as I lifted him from the stool, 'but some of these ladies are suffering with headache, and your music distresses them. Run away, like a good boy, and don't come back again.' "

But Vachell's story did not end here because, in the final analysis, this is more of a mother tale than a child story. "The mother was furious. Had I been Herod the Great, red-handed after the slaughter of the Innocents, she could not have looked more indignant or reproachful. I was interfering with the sacred rights of the American child to do what he pleased, where he pleased, and when he pleased."

Vachell's first conclusion inevitably was that American children were unspeakable monsters, utterly lacking in "sense of duty, reverence, humility, obedience." His second conclusion was, however, more inter-esting and more important, namely, that parents actually "encourage the egoism latent in all children, till each becomes an autocrat."

Once this appalling discovery had been verified, it occurred to the more curious of the Britons to raise the appropriate question: how could the American parents be proud of these diminutive devils?

Sir Edwin Arnold presented a question of this sort, in more general form, to one whom he regarded as an expert on this strange *genus Americanus*: Walt Whitman. " 'But have you reverence enough among your people?' I asked. 'Do the American children respect and obey their parents sufficiently, and are the common people grateful enough to the best men, their statesmen, leaders, teachers, poets, and "betters" gener-ally?' "

To this most fundamental of all inquiries Whitman responded, " 'Al-lons, comrade!, your old world has been soaked and saturated in rever-entiality. We are laying here in America the basements and foundation rooms of a new era. And we are doing it, on the whole, pretty well and substantially. By-and-by, when that job is through, *we will look after the steeples and pinnacles.*' "

Whitman and Arnold included childhood precocity within the larger framework of a new people refusing to pay homage to their betters, refusing to revere their "superiors." Such reverence constitutes one of the necessary ingredients of an aristocratically-oriented society. Lack of that reverence suggests an egalitarian society, and these two distin-guished men of letters were implying that the precocious child was symptomatic not merely of weak, stupid, willful parents, but rather of the pervasiveness in American society of the principle of equality. In fact no generalization about America was made more forcefully or repeatedly by the commentators en masse than that the thrust of the American belief in equality (understood as opportunity to rise more than as classlessness) was ubiquitous; it extended into every corner of the daily institutional fabric of American life—into the schools wherein all children had the right to a free education, into politics where all had the right to vote, into the enhanced place of women in American society, into the fluid class structure, into the churches wherein voluntary re-ligion was the rule, and, perhaps most astonishing of all, apparently even into the homes where little boys and little girls were granted un-heard-of liberties.

Captain Marryat, as early as 1839, related a well-known example illustrating this last point:

Imagine a child of three years old in England behaving thus:—
"Johnny, my dear, come here," says his mamma.
"I won't," cries Johnny.
"You must, my love, you are all wet, and you'll catch cold."
"I won't," replies Johnny.
"Come, my sweet, and I've something for you."
"I won't."
"Oh! Mr. ——, do, pray make Johnny come in."
"Come in, Johnny," says the father.
"I won't."
"I tell you, come in directly, sir—do you hear?"
"I won't," replies the urchin, taking to his heels.
"A sturdy republican, sir," says his father to me, smiling at the boy's resolute disobedience.

In 1845 Francis Wyse generalized upon incidents like these, placing them in a broad social context. "There is seldom any very great restraint," he noted, "imposed upon the youth of America whose precocious intellect, brought forth and exercised at an early, and somewhat premature age, and otherwise encouraged under the republican institutions of the country, has generally made them impatient of parental authority."

Parental authority did not sensibly differ from any other exercise of power: royal, military, governmental, or private. Americans had established their independence in rebellion against authority; they had rejected all artificially imposed forms of superiority; and they had proclaimed the equality of man. Surely these principles should extend to the family. Indeed, Jacks talked aptly of the way in which children had applied (with considerable parental approval) the Declaration of Independence to themselves. And James Fullarton Muirhead, who composed one of the most informative chapters on this topic, formulated the grand generalization thus: "The theory of the equality of man is rampant in the nursery." He referred to the infants as "young republicans," "democratic sucklings," "budding citizens of a free republic."

Here then was another application of the theory of equality—one which even the friendly Muirhead could not get himself to smile upon.

It "hardly tends," he patiently tried to explain, "to make the American child an attractive object to the stranger from without. On the contrary, it is very apt to make said stranger long strenuously to spank these budding citizens of a free republic, and to send them to bed *instanter*."

One must, of course, sympathize with the British traveler as he suffered through each encounter with these young specimens of the New World. But their hate affair is as much beside the point as their love affair with the schools. Both child-rearing at home and the nationwide system of compulsory public education were faithful to the omnipresent force of equality, and the paradox which began this chapter turns out to be no paradox at all. The commentators liked what they saw in the classrooms because authority was being exercised. It was being exercised by teachers who wielded it in the interests of learning and morality. When the visitors confronted the child outside the schools and in the context of home and family they were appalled by what they believed to be the universal and inexcusable betrayal of authority by the parents.

This reversal in the roles of authority *vis-à-vis* children disoriented the observers to such an extent that many of them never realized that, just a few chapters before their excoriation of the American child, they had been blessing his development in the schoolrooms. Although the traveler frequently sensed that the "success" of the teachers and the indulgent "failures " of the parents were related to each other, and that both stemmed from the same peculiar general assumptions in which American society was rooted, not one of them ever managed to pose squarely the problem of how and whether dual authority *could* be exerted on the child, of just how parent and teacher *should* combine their efforts in child-rearing, given the public school system and the widespread assumption that the child was an equal partner in the family "team."

The origins of this dilemma may be traced back to colonial days when, under the pressure of new conditions, the familiar family pattern brought over from the Old World suffered major transformations affecting both child-rearing practices and the role of education.

The traditional family was the wide kinship group with the source of power vested in the father and extending outward to include not only wife and children, but cousins, other relatives, and servants as well. The father was the chief educator, transferring the traditions of his culture and vocational training itself to his sons. But authority and traditionalism were, as revealed in an excellent study by Bernard Bailyn, inadequate for conditions in the New World, where problems were new, land abundant, labor scarce, and old solutions to old problems irrelevant. In these circumstances "the young—less bound by prescriptive memories, more adaptable, more vigorous—stood often at advantage. Learning faster, they came to see the world more familiarly, to concede more readily to unexpected necessities, to sense more accurately the phasing of a new life. They and not their parents became the effective guides to a new world, and they thereby gained a strange, anomalous authority difficult to accommodate within the ancient structure of family life."

While the details need not concern us here, the traditional family and educative pattern could not survive these challenges.

By the middle of the eighteenth century the classic lineaments of the American family as modern sociologists describe them—the "isolation of the conjugal unit," the "maximum of dispersion of the lines of descent," partible inheritances, and multilineal growth—had appeared. The consequences can hardly be exaggerated. Fundamental aspects of social life were affected. In the reduced, nuclear family, thrown back upon itself, traditional gradations in status tended to fall to the level of necessity. Relationships tended more toward achievement than ascription. The status of women rose; marriage, even in the eyes of the law, tended to become a contract between equals. Above all, the development of the child was affected.

One of the effects on the child cited by Bailyn concerned the passage of the child into society as "the once elaborate interpenetration of family and community dissolved." A result was that "the individual acquired an insulation of consciousness," a "heightened . . . sense of separateness" from society, and particularly from the state, which no longer could "command his automatic involvement." Perhaps this is what the British meant by precocity.

A second result came as the Puritans transferred the primary educative responsibilities from "the maimed . . . family to formal instructional institutions, and in so doing not only endowed schools with a new importance but expanded their purpose beyond pragmatic vocationalism toward vaguer but more basic cultural goals." Perhaps this explains why the British abused American parents.

41

The commentators who believed that parents must exercise authority over children were not pleased by what they saw in American families. In order to muster any kind words it was necessary to revise traditional conceptions of the family and accept a measure of equality in the home, accept the notion that the various family members could be close friends.

Dicey was one who was able to take this step. He concluded one of his volumes in 1863 in praise of "the great charm which surrounds all family relations in the North. Compared with Europe, domestic scandals are unknown; and between parents and their grown-up children, there exists a degree of familiarity and intimacy which one seldom witnesses in this country."

There were other companions besides the parents and grown-up children. Growing boys and their fathers were companions, wrote Zincke in 1868. "In America the father never loses sight of his child, who thus grows up as his companion, and is soon treated as a companion, and as in some sort an equal." Zincke went on to relate a pleasant incident he observed on a train between a fourteen-year-old boy and his father:

They had long been talking on a footing of equality. . . . At last, to while away the time, they began to sing together. First they accompanied each other. Then they took alternate lines; at last alternate words. In this of course they tripped frequently, each laughing at the other for his mistakes. There was no attempt at keeping up the dignity of a parent, as might have been considered necessary and proper with us. There was no reserve. They were in a certain sense already on an equal footing of persons of the same age.

Mothers and daughters were companions, Low maintained. "Daughters are much with their mothers, and they become their companions younger than they do in Europe. At an age when the French girl, for instance, is still demurely attending her convent, or the English girl is in the hands of her governess, her more emancipated sister across the Atlantic is calling with her mother on her friends, or assisting her in the drawing-room on her reception days."

Sons and daughters received equal treatment, claimed Saunders. Whereas "in an English family, as a rule, the greatest consideration is shown to the boys," in America, if anything, "the wishes of the girls would be first listened to, and their education provided for." The boy, after all, "is as eager to start life on his own account as is a greyhound to rush after the hare." "In the matter of early independence both sexes are equal."

Even husbands and wives were companions. While the wife "will not consent to being submerged by her children, she gives much of her time to them, and is still able to find time to be with her husband. The average American husband makes a confidante and a companion of his wife. . . ."

The patriarchies and matriarchies of the past had been replaced by a family team composed of equals. The British perceived this family revolution as being directly parallel to the fundamental cultural difference between the New World which blurred distinctions and the Old which honored and preserved them. As Muirhead put it: "The reason—or at any rate one reason—of the normal attitude of the American parent towards his child is not far to seek. It is almost undoubtedly one of the direct consequences of the circumambient spirit of democracy. The American is so accustomed to recognize the essential equality of others that he sometimes carries a good thing to excess. . . . The present child may be described as one of the experiments of democracy."

Americans enthroned their children not merely out of blind obedience to some social ethos which compelled them to do in the home something consonant with what the nation proclaimed to the world as its faith. Americans, as Zincke's story of the singing father and son so nicely shows, were often quite fond of their children, and rather than being harried or intimidated, they were not infrequently joyful parents. In fact, the Americans, according to the British, believed in their young ones in much the same way that they believed in their future. Let the youths' natural spirit triumph and they would not only participate in a grand future, but they would be the chief forgers of that future; the child was the future. Children could be heard as well as seen because they represented hope in "the land of youth." "Nowhere," said Muirhead, "is the child so constantly in evidence; nowhere are his wishes so carefully consulted; nowhere is he allowed to make his mark so strongly on society in general." Richard DeBary chimed in that "America is wholly convinced . . . that the young child can take it all in. The child is given kingship and becomes the king."

Those few Englishmen who thought well of American children praised precisely the same qualities which the detractors abominated.

Arnold Bennett, for example, came across one "captivating creature whose society I enjoyed at frequent intervals throughout my stay in America. . . . [She] was a mirror in which I saw the whole American race of children—their independence, their self-confidence, their adorable charm, and their neat sauciness." The reformer George Holyoake liked "the American habit of training their children to independence" more than he did England's "unwise domestic paternalism, which encourages a costly dependence."

John Strathesk did not employ the term "precocious" in a deprecating manner when he decided that "the girls and boys of America are very frank, even precocious." And Sir Philip Gibbs expanded upon this theme. "The children of America," he said, "have the qualities of their nation, simplicity, common sense, and self-reliance. They are not so bashful as English boys and girls, and they are free from the little constraints of nursery etiquette which make so many English children afraid to open their mouths. They are also free entirely from that juvenile snobbishness which is still cultivated in English society, where boys and girls of well-to-do parents are taught to look down with contempt upon children of the poorer classes."

It may be noticed that the adjectives used to depict the child are similar, whether used in delight or disgust: saucy, self-reliant, wild, spontaneous, immodest, independent, demanding, irreverent. It may furthermore be observed that they bear resemblance to adjectives which some Englishmen thought applicable to the young nation as a whole. Some visitors also found the terms suitable for characterizing American adults as well.

The blurring of lines between young and old in the New World furnished an invitation to some British writers to caricature both American parents and children. But to Margaret Mead this leveling tendency forms an explicable part of a peculiarly national approach to child-rearing which she has called "third-generation American." The American child, contends this anthropologist, is expected to traverse a course very different from his father's, and "with this orientation towards a different future for the child comes also the expectation that the child will pass beyond his parents and leave their standards behind him." Thus "it comes about that American parents lack the sure hand on the rudder which parents in other societies display." Or, approaching the matter from a different perspective than either the historian Bailyn or Miss

Mead, Erik Erikson supports their findings when he writes that "the psychoanalysis of the children of immigrants clearly reveals to what extent they, as the first real Americans in their family, become their parents' cultural parents."

As Erikson and many other psychologists have stressed, the high prestige accorded youth, understandable though it may be considering the abundant resources, the scarcity of labor, the virgin conditions, and the rapid pace of change in the egalitarian New World, is not without cost to Americans. The child himself has to pay a price for his exalted place; the compulsion to achieve, to succeed, can be taxing and perhaps ultimately futile. Unlike his Old World counterpart who begins life with a position of ascribed status which he knows is his own, the American child can never let up.

The society, too, has to pay a price for its cult of youth. It is paid not only in the primitive music, the puerile television, and the domestic tyranny to which the adult world is exposed at the command of teenagers, and to which the adults meekly succumb. It is paid also in the sacrifice of wisdom, of standards, of permanence, of serenity under the frantic injunction to constantly "think young." The quiet contemplation of the past and the present is sacrificed when all must worship at the altar of the future.

The most repeated consensus at which the travelers arrived concerning the "American character" was that that character resembled, at heart, the character of a child. If there were no childlike children, if there were only miniature adults in "the land of youth," then the reverse was equally true—there were few adultlike adults; there were only adults trying to be young. "There are no old in America at all," said George Steevens in 1900. By this he meant two things. First, that adult virtues are uncultivated in the New World; the American "retains all his life a want of discipline, an incapacity for ordered and corporate effort."

Steevens's second meaning centered on the fate of those who were actually aged. "They are shouldered unmercifully out of existence," he claimed. "I found in New York a correspondence on the open question whether the old have any right to respect. Many of the public thought, quite seriously, they had no right even to existence."

The dearest price of all is paid neither by the children nor by the society but by the adults who have to be "boys" at the office, who as parents must "live for their children," who as mature women must forever look and act like eighteen-year-olds, who as elderly must join the other aged in some zippy retirement community quarantined from the rest of mankind.

The cult of youth has perhaps permitted a more spontaneous family life to develop, and it has, no doubt, lent to our national life a special vigor and freshness. But in exalting childhood and early youth to the consummatory positions in life, it follows that maturity and old age should become anticlimactic. Indeed, in America, as one ages, one declines, and the reward of lower movie admission fees for "senior citizens" furnishes rather ineffectual solace. One can only guess at the extent to which the American fixation on the earlier stages of the life cycle is related to our tendency to deny the reality of old age and to put from our minds all thoughts of death. And it is not possible to do more here than to raise the question which then becomes inescapable: what kinds of spiritual reserves might this habit of mind take from the individual as he passes through life?

Thirty years after his 1869 visit to America, the Reverend Mr. Macrae returned and noted that the "independence and precocious intellect of the American children" had not diminished; but he was "less struck with these features this time." The reason he was less struck was precisely the same that made Harold Spender think better of the American children in 1920, twenty years after *his* first visit. "Our English child in the interval," said Spender, substituting his native land for Macrae's Scotland, "has become a little more American." By the early years of the twentieth century, America's startling departure in raising children and in inflating the status of the youngsters in the family hierarchy was, like various other American innovations, becoming more general in the Old World also.

46

★ 4 ★

I
AMERICAN SCHOOL BOOKS IN
THE NINETEENTH CENTURY
Ruth M. Elson

Teachers have long relied on school books for instruction.
Their importance was especially great in the nineteenth
century, since simple recitation from texts was then the
usual school exercise. The textbooks were repositories of
conventional wisdom and common belief and aspiration.
This selection from Ruth Elson's careful and thorough
study of nineteenth-century school books recounts the place
of texts in instruction and examines some of their teachings
on race and on the formation of character.

Other studies of children's books are J. Merton England,
"The Democratic Faith in American Schoolbooks,
1783–1860," *American Quarterly*, 15 (1963), pp. 191–199;
John A. Nietz, *Old Textbooks* (Pittsburgh: University of
Pittsburgh Press, 1961); John A. Nietz, *The Evolution of
American Secondary School Textbooks* (Rutland, Vt.: C. E.
Tuttle, 1966); and Monica Kiefer, *American Children
Through Their Books, 1700–1835* (Philadelphia: University
of Pennsylvania Press, 1948).

The purpose of nineteenth-century American public schools was to
train citizens in character and proper principles. Most textbook writers
had an exalted idea of their function; almost all made statements such as
the following: "The mind of the child is like the soft wax to receive an
impression, but like the rigid marble to retain it." They were much
more concerned with the child's moral development than with the development of his mind. The important problem for nineteenth-century

American educators was to mold the wax in virtue rather than in learning. Noah Webster advocated the use of his book on the grounds that it would enable teachers "To instil into their [the children's] minds, with the first rudiments of the language, some just ideas of religion, morals and domestic economy." The textbook was to be a compilation of the ideas of the society. In 1789 he stated his purpose in writing a school book: "To refine and establish our language, to facilitate the acquisition of grammatical knowledge and diffuse the principles of virtue and patriotism is the task I have labored to perform." There was no doubt in the minds of the authors that the books used in public schools were important for the future of the Republic. They saw their function as the creation of an American nationality, the formation of a "National Character." Most of them believed that as European educators sponsored children's books which "are calculated to impress on their youthful minds a prejudice in favor of the existing order of things," so American educators must inculcate "American principles." The ideas taught in the nineteenth-century school were not necessarily universal truths, but national truths. It was the national prototype that was to be embodied in American school books. Dissent appeared in only one book, an 1832 reader: "The effort has been made to select such articles as men of a truly catholic spirit, in all countries may regard with approbation, rather than those of a patriotic or national character."

. . . .

The classroom method of the period made the textbook peculiarly important in the school. Because the teachers were relatively untrained, letter-perfect memorization without particular attention to meaning was the basic method of common, or public, school education. Few teachers outside of the large cities had much education beyond that of the schools in which they taught. When examined for the position their moral character was considered more important for teaching than any technical training. A nineteenth-century work on the theory and practice of teaching suggests that teachers be better prepared; the author believed that this could be accomplished if the teacher would read over the textbook before class. Apparently even this would have constituted a reform. The subject of professional training for teachers increasingly absorbed educational leaders from the 1830s on. In 1839 Massachusetts established the first public normal school, but by 1860 there were only twelve such schools in the United States. One half of these were in New

48

England; the others were distributed one in New York (1844), one in Michigan (1849), one in New Jersey (1855), one in Illinois (1857), one in Pennsylvania (1859), and one in Minnesota (1860). Four of the pre–Civil War normal schools were in one state, Massachusetts. These were reinforced by six private normal schools, but it is obvious that although the situation was improving, the day of the teacher trained for his profession was still in the future for most American schools.

. . . .

In many classrooms the memorization technique was reinforced by the monitorial system, whereby older students were designated to hear the recitations of the younger ones. It was a method attractive to taxpayers, since one teacher with the aid of monitors could handle an enormous class of many grades. But the monitor could be trusted only to see whether the student's memorization of the school book was letter-perfect. Questions given as teaching aids in the books themselves clearly expect this method. The typical form or question is: "What is said of . . . ?" Memorizing the sentiment of value judgment was quite as often required as memorizing the fact. For example, a textbook in the history of the United States requires that the child "Mention any other things in our national history which should excite our gratitude." A list of these "other things" appears in the text above.

Such classroom methods required absolute uniformity of texts to make mass recitation or recitation before an untrained teacher possible. This system remained in the realm of the ideal during the first part of the century, because the children used the school books of their parents, neighbors, or relatives to save money. In 1846 the state of Connecticut discovered that there were 215 different texts in use in its schools, although an official text had been chosen by each district board. But the method apparently conditioned the writers of textbooks effectively. Many of the books were written wholly in the catechism form. In order to assure boards of education that a new issue of an older textbook could be used in the same classroom with the original work, many of the Histories retained the old copyright date and added more recent material at the end of the book. A History ostensibly published in 1881 might include material through 1888. Many gave such assurance of stability as the following: "Teachers may rest assured, that all future editions of this work will be printed page for page with the present." This often produced strange anachronisms: the 1862 and 1865 editions of Mitchell's Geographies follow previous editions so closely that no word of secession or the Civil War appears, although both contain extensive treatments of the Southern states. When a revision of an older text was published, the publisher often made some such promise as the following: "This revision can be used in class with the older edition as the pages correspond throughout." As a result of this effort at uniformity the textbooks were singularly resistant to change.

Furthermore the basic material of many of the textbooks was in previously published school books; the essential method of composing a school book was often one of compilation and plagiarism. Throughout this study such similarities will be manifest; word order was left unchanged in many cases where no authority was cited, and where the last authority was clearly another textbook author. This is true even in the Geographies, where one would expect recent expert knowledge to be vital. The method of compilation itself, then, produced a startling similarity and time lag. It is well to keep in mind that experts in the particular fields did not enter the textbook-writing arena until almost the end of the century, and that even then they accounted for a very small minority of school books.

School books, central to the curriculum of the nineteenth-century school, offered both information and standards of behavior and belief that the adult world expected the child to make his own.

. . . .

The selections [in school readers] of every sort, whether prose or poetry, description or narration, are designed as much to inculcate virtue as to impart information. The statements or implicit assumptions of moral lessons are so universal that the slightest exception is startling, as when, in an 1867 Reader, one finds skating and sleighing described as just simple fun. Typical practice sentences in the Spellers are the following: "Aim to be good." "Abstain from evil." "Obey the law." "Remorse will haunt a guilty conscience." "Be on your guard against evil associates." "Abhor that which is evil." These are all found within three pages, interspersed with such other information as: "Bears lie dormant in the winter." "A sponge will absorb water." It is only near the end of the century that descriptions of natural phenomena are allowed to stand on their own merits. There are many direct strictures on individual behavior, ranging from the general precepts quoted above to simple matters of etiquette: "Belching, coughing, sniffling, sniveling, spitting, etc.

must be avoided as much as possible, especially in company and at table." But moral lessons are implicit in all of the material of these books. They advocate specific virtues no different from those that have elevated the great to their positions. The child is to be religious, industrious, thrifty, persevering, devoted to his parents, obedient to authority, charitable, and chaste; he must also learn to subdue his passions.

What will concern us here is not a reiteration of the virtues the child is to develop but the rationalizations offered to the child of why virtue is necessary and desirable. Why should he be good? As described in these books, the main religious duty of man is to cultivate moral behavior; indeed, religion is more nearly a system of ethics than of theology. That virtue is necessary for happiness is sometimes stated, and likewise its corollary: "Misery is indeed the necessary result of all deviation from rectitude." But evidently neither the teachings of the church nor conscience provide foundations solid enough for a sound superstructure of morality, for in additon the school books bombard the child with the idea, elaborately and richly illustrated, that virtue is rewarded and vice punished in an immediate and material sense. God does not wait for the afterlife to distribute rewards and punishments; He metes them out inexorably, not simply in pangs of conscience and remorse, but in things of this world.

God's hand is obvious in many of the earlier books. He threatens dreadful plagues (such as eye-hungry ravens) for those who do not reverence their parents and teachers. This reverence for elders requires silence in their presence unless directly addressed, nor should the child contradict them even if certain he is right. The future of the disobedient child is bleak indeed: "Soon she will be left an orphan; with neither friends nor home: and in ragged apparel she will be forced to beg from house to house." In another instance, divine punishment comes immediately to children engaged in teasing Elisha, when: "raging bears . . . tore them limb from limb to death, with blood and groans and tears."

But even when God's name is not specifically invoked, punishments for meretricious acts are His because His is the order of nature. The inevitability of earthly suffering for evil is abundantly illustrated. A story in several Spellers predicts the gallows for a boy who steals a book. In this instance punishment is directed both to the culprit and to his mother, who neglected her parental duties by not sufficiently punishing him for this first offense. Nature is in league against those not in accord

51

with moral laws, as in this practice sentence from a Speller: "A dog met a bad boy and bit him." Innumerable other stories and statements have the same theme: accidents happen only to those who deserve them. Such childhood misbehavior as playing hooky from school is always attended with dire consequences: one boy loses his leg in an accident while on such an unauthorized venture from school; another drowns. In the latter story the boy who fares worst is the only one of the group who could already swim and was not even trying to learn a practical skill in excuse for the expedition. His guilt is thus double; he has been idle as well as defiant of authority. The consequences of disobeying authority are further illustrated in the story of a little boy stung by nettles and covered with cold mud after disobeying his parents. The moral is: "And as it was with Jarvis, so will it be with everyone who acts disobediently. . . . To disobey your parents, your teachers, or any authority over you, be sure that a punishment awaits you if you do not resist it." In these incidents the penalty is related only to the fact of immoral behavior; it is not a natural consequence of the particular act. Such incidents clearly indicate the universal belief, firmly held and taught, that one cannot escape punishment on earth for evil deeds. Like modern psychiatrists, authors of nineteenth-century school books associate accidents with guilt. In the school books so-called accidents are really God's punishment exacted through nature. "The misfortunes of men [are] mostly chargeable on themselves."

Sometimes punishment grows directly and naturally out of the crime. Although the punishments are equally dire, they do at least bear a direct relationship to the nature of the misdemeanor. The boy who cruelly pulls the wings from a bee, or thrusts a stick into a hive, is sure to be stung. Another boy, habitually cruel to animals, is finally gored and tossed by a bull. Two boys disobey their father, one by playing with a gun, and the other by throwing stones; one loses a leg and one an eye. Another little boy teases a "crazyman" who finally hits him with a rock. In these instances the ensuing event is still regarded as punishment, but it is the natural result of a particular action rather than a mysterious blow from the heavens.

In a school book published in 1779 Anthony Benezet, a Quaker, complains that although children should be trained in tenderness, affection, humility, and self-denial, yet "our modern education is not of this kind, our Sons are generally exhorted to improvement from principles of covetousness or a desire of distinction." This was to be a valid criticism of school books for well over a century. The exhortation to virtue is most frequently backed by the certainty of material reward. The bad child would end up a miserable, poverty-stricken adult; the good child a happy and prosperous one. Every individual can regulate his life by virtue or vice, but the choice inexorably determines his fortunes in this world as well as the next. Dire physical punishments may await the sinner; lack of success in this world always pursues him. In this sense all men are self-made. Conversely, God allows affluence only to the virtuous man. Hence affluence is not only a reward but also a sign of virtue. The Social Darwinism of the late nineteenth century that saw morality in league with riches was simply reaffirming a Puritan lesson taught steadily throughout the period of this study. It is rare indeed to find such a statement as "There may be success in life without success in business."

. . . .

Combined with the assurances of material reward for virtue one finds an overweening admiration for the self-made man. Evidence is to be found in many sections of this study, and it reflects one of the most basic values in the nineteenth-century school book.

. . . .

Suffice it to say here that getting ahead is a moral duty enjoined on man by God; the Calvinist earthly calling is to be heard by all as clearly as the heavenly calling. In *McGuffey's Fourth Reader* in 1879, after one of the innumerable success stories, is the sentence: "And if you do not improve the advantages you enjoy, you sin against your Maker." This is further emphasized by the question at the end of the lesson: "For what are we placed in this world?" Spencer, Darwin, and the Social Darwinists were not the inspiration for this sentiment, for it has a longer history in school books. In 1810 it was put so: "Existence is a sacred trust; he who misemploys and squanders it away is treacherous to its Author." Since getting ahead economically by honest means is our primary moral duty, the virtues most helpful to that end are stressed *ad nauseam:* industry, thrift, frugality, perseverance, self-denial. These were, of course, Puritan values, as the end was a Puritan end. But they were also the virtues of the nineteenth-century American environment, necessary for survival on a frontier and useful to the expanding industrial economy. Geography and the economy had reaffirmed for the American those virtues already sanctified in the American tradition.

. . . .

The world created in nineteenth-century school books is essentially a world of fantasy—a fantasy made up by adults as a guide for their children, but inhabited by no one outside the pages of school books. It is an ideal world, peopled by ideal villains as well as ideal heroes. Nature is perfectly if sometimes inscrutably planned by God for the good of man, with progress as its first and invariable law. Nothing can hinder this march toward material and moral perfection, a movement particularly visible in the United States. Nature is benign, and the life close to nature inevitably a happy and healthy one. Individuals are to be understood in terms of easily discernible, inherent characteristics of their race and nationality as much as in terms of their individual character. Virtue is always rewarded, vice punished. And one can achieve virtue and avoid vice by following a few simple rules. Assuredly the adult world did not live by this pattern but elected to believe in it as what *should* be true, as the inhabitants of Samuel Butler's *Erewhon* believed in their "musical banks." Wishfully, adults in any age would like to proffer to their children a neatly patterned model of life, however mythical, which the child can accept and, following it, live happily ever after. But inevitably the growing child soon sees that life is not so simple: that the life close to nature may not only be a hard one but unrewarding and frustrating; that virtue is not always rewarded on this earth and that not even his school books can really know whether there is compensation for this after death; that progress in one area comes at great cost in another, that Catholics may be sincere, Indians gentle, Negroes intelligent, and Jews generous. To live in the real world the child would eventually have to abandon the simple model of his school books. And, with luck, he will develop experientially, and perhaps experimentally, a more adequate world view.

Perhaps the most fundamental assumption in nineteenth-century school books is the moral character of the universe—an assumption at the base of American culture in this period. Religion itself is rather a matter of morals than theology. Furthermore, all nature as well as man is invested with morality; animal and plant life both follow moral law. In school books, when ants store up food they do so as an act of moral responsibility rather than as instinctual behavior. Conversely, the grass-hopper's careless ways in not preparing for winter are his own fault, and his hunger in lean times is a richly deserved punishment. Whether a man succeeds in his business is not so much a question of the application of intelligence and energy to the problems of that business, but a result of good character. Success in business is viewed in school books largely as a by-product of virtue. It is to be sought not for material comforts it will bring, but as a sign of virtue, a status symbol if you will. Similarly, natural resources, location, availability of capital, and labor are minor factors in evaluating the decline and fall of nations; only a moral nation can achieve lasting power. The decline of Spain and the growth of the United States are illustrations of this. Everything in life is to be judged in moral terms. Nineteenth-century intellectuals might view nature as amoral, but the Puritan tradition still provided the basis of popular culture.

Unlike many modern school books, those of the nineteenth century made no pretense of neutrality. While they evade issues seriously controverted in their day, they take a firm and unanimous stand on matters of basic belief. The value judgment is their stock in trade: love of country, love of God, duty to parents, the necessity to develop habits of thrift, honesty, and hard work in order to accumulate property, the certainty of progress, the perfection of the United States. These are not to be questioned. Nor in this whole century of great external change is there any deviation from these basic values. In pedagogical arrangements the school book of the 1790s is vastly different from that of the 1890s, but the continuum of values is uninterrupted. Neither the Civil War nor the 1890s provide any watershed in basic values. There is no hint here of Darwin's natural selection from chance variations, nor of the Higher Criticism, comparative religion, William James's pluralism, nor of the neutral nature depicted by literary realists. Ethics do not evolve from particular cultural situations, nor are they to be developed by the individual from his own experience and critical thinking. Nor are they to come from his peers. They are absolute, unchanging, and they come from God. The child is to learn ethics as he learns information about his world, unquestioningly, by rote. His behavior is not to be inner-directed, nor other-directed, but dictated by authority and passively accepted.

Also in contrast to many modern texts, those of the nineteenth century, while ideologically simple, are not entirely bland. However glossed with sentiment, death and disease are a natural part of the world of the school book. Reality is portrayed not so much through the postman, fireman, and things familiar in the child's environment, but through the deeper reality of hardship, tragedy, passionate devotion to a cause, the satisfactions in overcoming obstacles. To be well adjusted the nineteenth-century child must be in harmony with the decrees of God and nature rather than with his peers. The life school books prepare him for is one of struggle and hardship in competition with his contemporaries. The horrors of failure as well as the glories of success are endlessly illustrated. While oversimplifying life to an extraordinary degree, his school books made the nineteenth-century child thoroughly aware that life is hard and full of natural and man-made pitfalls. It is his duty to strive for success, but he will struggle hard on the way.

Like the school books of other nations, those of the United States are bent on persuading the child that his nation is superior to all others. The development of American ideas and institutions is usually depicted without its proper world setting, and important forces in American life—such as freedom and the Industrial Revolution—are assumed to be creations of this hemisphere. Indeed, freedom is frequently discussed as a chemical component of the very air of America. In order to be a good American, the child must reject Europe and things European. Unfortunately this results in the repudiation of scholarship and the fine arts, associated in school books with an effete and aristocratic Europe. The child is, however, expected to develop a fervent faith that the American example will inevitably and gloriously save Europe from its present state of corruption and decline. America is to be a source for Europe, not Europe for America.

Each race and its subdivisions—nationalities—are defined by inherent mental and personal characteristics which the child must memorize. Individual personality is largely submerged in race and nationality. And these traits are used to determine the rank of each race and nation. In describing typical members of such groups the part must be substituted for the whole. The American, as the ideal man, is of the white race, of Northern European background, Protestant, self-made, and if not a farmer, at least retaining the virtues of his yeoman ancestors. As race becomes an increasingly significant way to think about human beings, the English are exalted to a position just below the Americans.

They misbehaved at the time of the American Revolution, but this was a temporary aberration. Essentially, racially, they are superior; to impugn the English character would degrade American stock. Yet the American population is not identical with the English because the American environment sieved the English population. The weak would not come, and only the pure in heart could survive. The American is a distilled Englishman.

Although school-book authors consider themselves guardians of liberty, they can be more accurately described as guardians of tradition. On social questions the tenor of the books is consistently conservative. The United States is always identified with freedom, but this freedom is best defined as that established in 1783 after separation from Great Britain. The nineteenth-century child was taught to worship past achievements of America and to believe in the inevitable spread of the American system throughout the world. But contemporary problems are conspicuously absent, and reform movements which would have profound social or political effects are either ignored or derided. While Jeffersonian and Jacksonian democracy agitated the adult world, the child was taught the necessity of class distinctions. Nor are Jefferson and Jackson ever ranked as heroes; their social philosophies provided new forms of Americanism in other circles, but in the schools Hamilton and Daniel Webster governed the minds of the children. Problems of the farmer after the Civil War are not mentioned; instead, farm chores are suffused with bucolic charm, and farming is described as the ideal life close to God and nature. The Industrial Revolution wonderfully increased American power, but it left no divisions in American society. The organization of labor does not appear at all until the late nineteenth century, and when it does it is identified with violence and property destruction carried out by irresponsible elements in American society. Women in the United States have already been awarded all the rational liberty suitable to their natures, and more than in other countries. Dissatisfaction with their status is both unwomanly and ungrateful. Always the child is shown an America serene and united. He must be tolerant of other religions, but he should not recognize them as equal to Protestantism on pain of subversion of both church and state. He should be moved emotionally by the inhumanity of war, but he should admire without reserve the exploits of military heroes and be happy to sacrifice his life in any war in which his country is engaged. Before the Civil War he may

57

pity the slave, but he must stay away from the abolitionist movement. After the Civil War he can look back to the evils of slavery now safely buried in the past, but he need not concern himself with the freedman; the latter quickly fades from the pages of his school books. He must revere values already established in American society by his school books rather than attempt to institute new ones or expand the old. Ironically their very efforts to present a united society prevent these school books from mirroring America as a whole; only the social ideals of the more conservative members of the society were offered the nineteenth-century child. It is these social ideals that nineteenth-century school books admit to the American tradition and hope to preserve.

By defining what they consider American, these school books perform a function required in few other societies. To be English, French, or German is usually taken for granted, but Americans have always worried about what "Americanness" is, and whether they have it. Perhaps their immigrant background explains this, but surely their mobility and the fact that they were building a new society also contribute to this strange but pervasive American phenomenon. Unlike the European, whose life was lived within a fairly settled pattern of society, the American had to set up social patterns afresh and find his place in them. These might be the same patterns of culture already developed by older societies, but he had to make conscious and unconscious choice of what he would use. Optimism and buoyancy, but also probably insecurity, resulted from this task. The American is not clear on who he is, and he tends to wear his Americanness like a cloak he puts on rather than a skin that grows with him. Most nineteenth-century school books include specific descriptions of the American character, but in a larger sense everything they teach the American child is part of this attempt to find out what the American is and should be. Whatever is good in ideas, behavior, and institutions they identify with the United States and its citizens. By selecting what they consider most essential to preserve in America, nineteenth-century school books offered to the broadest and most impressionable American audience an image of themselves as a guide to the future.

II
RACIAL TEACHINGS IN
NINETEENTH-CENTURY SCHOOLS
Ruth M. Elson

The century that produced the racist theories of Joseph Gobineau, Houston Stewart Chamberlain, John Calhoun, and George Fitzhugh showed increasing interest in shouldering the white man's burden and raised racism to the status of scientific doctrine. In the beginning of the century the cosmopolitanism of the Enlightenment had begun to disintegrate under the ideological implications and international activities of the French Revolution. Romanticism, with its stress on local color, particularity, and the national soul, saw the individual not as a specific form of universal man, nor even as a member of a particular class, but as a creature innately conditioned by his membership in a particular race and nationality group. If medieval man had found his milieu in a local manor and a universal Church, nineteenth-century man increasingly found his fulfillment as part of a race and nationality. The doctrine of race as a method of classifying men was singularly rigid: it assumed that biologically inherited traits—physical, mental, and moral—are immutable. Church and class affiliations are theoretically changeable, but biologically inherited characteristics are not. By the end of the century it was widely assumed that nature had conferred specific characteristics on each member of a racial group throughout historical time. Furthermore, races could be classified according to the desirability of their traits.

In the United States popular ideas of race and of the racial inheritance of the individual came to have far-reaching importance in the generations that decided the issues of the Civil War, Reconstruction, and the place of Negroes, Indians, and immigrants in American society. These concepts are latent in all the school books, in stories, descriptions, even arithmetic problems, and, most important of all, in the Geographies. Here the child was formally presented with the idea of race and with the various races of the world and their characteristics. In their surveys of each country the Geographies are often more specific about the inherent characteristics of the inhabitants as a group than about the natural resources of the country. In all but the most experimental schools of the time the child was generally required to memo-

59

rize such characteristics and the rank of each race in the accepted racial hierarchy.

Authors of nineteenth-century school books never questioned nature's division of mankind into separate unalterable races defined by inherent physical, intellectual, and spiritual qualities. "Nature has formed the different degrees of genius, and the characters of nations, which are seldom known to change." The original historical unity of mankind is also unquestioned. Throughout the century Adam and Eve, rather than any Darwinian progenitors, retain their identity as the common ancestors of men; with the dispersion of the sons of Noah, environmental factors and "other causes" created separate branches of the human race. "The great family of mankind—although descended from Adam and Eve,—by being spread over the surface of the earth and subjected to the varieties of climate, and from other causes, has been divided into several distinct races, differing in color, form, and features and in mental characteristics also." Differences in climate receive the most prominent etiological position, but just as invariably, mysterious "other causes beyond the reach of our investigation" are also mentioned. With an evolutionary foundation for the establishment of races, a hint of the possibility of future development might be expected. But the races are regarded as fixed for most of the past, the present, and the future. Guyot, one of the few authors of school books who was a professional geographer, agrees with the rest: "Certain physical features and mental characteristics . . . have remained unchanged from a time anterior to all history."

All of the Geographies divide mankind into distinct if increasingly elaborate racial categories. In the first half of the century the normal division is: Eskimo, Tartar, East Indian, Negro, American Indian, and European. In the latter part of the century the categories adopted are usually those of Blumenbach: Caucasian, Mongolian, Malayan, Negro, and American Indian. But whatever the racial subdivisions, throughout the century whites are ranked at the top and Negroes at the bottom. Guyot's is the most original theory to explain this hierarchy: in a section entitled "The White Race the Normal or Typical Race," he develops the idea that the typical man is to be seen "in the unrivalled works of the ancient sculptors." "A comparison of the different tribes and races of men, reveals the fact of a *gradual* modification of types, on every side of the central or highest race, until by insensible degrees, the lowest or most degraded forms of humanity are reached." The white is then the normal race from which others have deviated. The degree of degeneration from the typical race is directly dependent on geographical distance from the original habitat of the normal race: *"The degree of perfection of the type* is therefore proportioned, not to intensity of material agencies but to distance from the central or highest race irrespective of climatic conditions. The degree of culture of the races also varies in the same order. The central race is the race of culture and progress, both now and in all ages past." The perfect man from whom all others are deviants was the inhabitant of the mountains of Iran. All school books imply that the white was the original race and the pattern for all others; Adam and Eve were Caucasian.

The superiority of the white race is also taken for granted. Physically "they furnish the greatest number of beautiful figures." They are, in addition, "superior to all others in intellectual and moral development, and are the leaders of Christian civilization." Their initiative and energy are singled out as distinctive features. At the end of the chapter on race some question like the following is often asked: "Which is the most intelligent race?" When pictures are used to show a typical member of each race, the cards are usually stacked in favor of the whites. Guyot uses the idealized head of the Apollo Belvedere as an example of the white race, but quite ordinary specimens for the others. Other Geographies display the face of a lovely white woman with refined and delicate features surrounded by rather swarthy unpleasant types to exemplify other races. In the Readers, now and then, an imaginative piece of writing illustrates the superiority of the white race. One Reader at the end of the century includes an essay by Washington Irving, "Origin of the White, the Red and the Black Men": the Great Spirit first made black men, saw he had bungled, and so made red men. He liked red men better, but only when he had finally made white men was he satisfied. In the context of these books Irving's whimsy becomes an anthropological statement. Several books assume that the white race is superior in quantity as well as quality. In only one book does the white race as a whole assume the white man's burden: "To the Caucasian race by reason of its physical and mental superiority, has been assigned the task of civilizing and enlightening the world." But the child with a social conscience, influenced by any of these books, could easily be persuaded that white superiority requires the performance of such a task.

The concept of racial superiority leads to interesting and somewhat contradictory results when two races contend for the same land. The history of this contention in English America is presented as an illustration of "a well-established law of nature, that causes an inferior race to yield to a superior when one comes in contact with the other." In the earlier books, contemplation of this inevitable process is recommended to inspire a pleasing melancholy: "What can be more melancholy than their [the American Indians'] history? By a law of nature they seem destined to a slow but sure extinction. Everywhere at the approach of the white man they fade away." The manifest destiny of the superior race to conquer the inferior is an accepted axiom throughout the period, specifically and abundantly illustrated. Although they do not set it down as a law of nature, these authors clearly believe that a superior race is bound to degenerate if it does not maintain racial purity. As in most racist doctrines, the superiority of a race does not extend to its dilution; in any racial mixture the characteristics of the inferior race dominate. A 1900 Geography, noting that more than half of the population of Spanish America is made up of descendants of Spanish-Indian marriages, ascribes to this racial mixture the primary reason why Spanish America progressed less rapidly than English America: "These half breeds are an ignorant class, far inferior to the Spaniards themselves. . . ." In a child's mind, such strictures against intermarriage might be outweighed by the union of Pocohontas and a white man, from which "some of the principal families in Virginia are descended." This marriage is mentioned with approval in most books. Perhaps she was exempt from the ordinary laws of nature as a heroine of American nationalism who had saved John Smith, himself the savior of the Virginia colony. Washington and other heroes of American nationalism also found natural laws at times suspended in their favor. It is particularly interesting that a Southern history of the late nineteenth century includes the story of this marriage, and a similar complimentary comment on the ancestry of the eminent families of Virginia.

The child influenced by these books probably viewed any new acquaintance in the light of his race and its characteristics as memorized from his school books. As part of nature's law, progress is possible only with the conquest and subordination of inferior races; the child would question the wisdom of indiscriminate immigration to the United States; he would not expect the Negro to take an equal place in American civilization; he would expect race to be a determining factor in the development of the individual. Nor would he think the American melting pot capable of amalgamating racial traits into a homogeneous whole.

. . . .

From his description in all Geography books, the African Negro is clearly regarded as the most degraded of the races. Southerners, who by 1830 justified slavery on the grounds that the Negro was incapable of improvement, could find ample evidence for their attitudes in the school books used at the time in both North and South. The generation that decreed the abolition of slavery and the disposition of the freedman after the Civil War was educated in the belief that "they [Negroes] are a brutish people, having little more of humanity but the form"; or "their mental powers, in general, participate in the imbecility of their bodies"; or "Africa has justly been called the country of monsters. . . . Even man, in this quarter of the world exists in a state of lowest barbarism." At best Africa is distinguished as the land where "human nature is nowhere exhibited in a more rude and disgusting attire than in this portion of the globe." Negroes are described not as destitute of education but as "destitute of intelligence." In one story a schoolboy is indignant at being mistaken for a Negro: "Why, man, it would set our blood a boiling in December, to be mistaken for one of your West India negroes." His indignation arises at being mistaken not for a slave, but for a Negro. Throughout the century a direct correlation is assumed between darkness of color and weakness of intellect. In several books, whimsical tales of the origin of man, in addition to that of Washington Irving, show God in the creative process: He first made the black man, realized He had done badly, and then created successively lighter races, improving as He went along. To the white man He gave a box of books and papers, to the black a box of tools so that he could "work for the white and red man, which he has continued to do." In another, God gave the whites clothing, guns, and gunpowder, but to the Negro only cattle, rain-making, and inferior hearts. The only positive characteristics assigned to them are gaiety and, in a few books published after the Civil War, loyalty.

Slavery as an institution is condemned as a moral wrong in a majority of books, although there are some which mention it without value judgments. In books published before the Civil War most of the antislavery agitation is aimed not against slavery itself but against the international slave trade. Almost all of the Histories and Geographies and many of the Readers condemn the practice bitterly. Casual references frequently employ the adjectives "shameful," "unmerciful," or "abominable," particularly when describing the trade as one in which Christian nations engage. After 1807 agitation against the slave trade was no longer a demand for reform, since in that year the international slave trade was abolished for the United States. Hence the fulminations against it in American school books are essentially criticisms of other countries. Many indicate that the trade was foisted on English America by the Dutch before the achievement of independence, and fastened firmly by the English. Throughout the century the slave trade is considered a blot on Christianity and on civilized society. By 1832 the school books acknowledge that only France, Spain, and Portugal are still slave traders, but the fulminations are just as strong. The odium of the original enslavement is usually passed on to the Africans themselves by the observation that Africans enslaved each other before the Christians arrived.

In pre–Civil War school books whether the slave was treated well or ill was a matter of discussion, with some difference of opinion. There are several tales of slaves who defend their masters in time of peril in return for the kind treatment they have enjoyed in the past. At times contentment with his lot is ascribed to the well-treated slave because "many of the negroes, at the *present* day, work as easy, and live as comfortably, as any class of *labouring* people in the world." It is interesting to observe that these scattered examples of good treatment are all from the period shortly before the Civil War, when the question of slavery was most strongly agitated in the society. Apparently the question was approached in an increasingly conciliatory manner as it became a more hotly contested issue. One author illustrates this caution when he says: "For the honour of humanity, I trust that the stories we hear of the cruel treatment of slaves, are *exaggerated*; but the *slave trade* is clearly founded on injustice and oppression." The slave trade as a settled issue may be implacably opposed, but the institution of slavery must be approached delicately.

· ·

Three books before 1830 consider slavery to be inconsistent with the American tradition. One lists the ways in which the American people have been blessed above others, and then pleads with them: "Why, when thus happy, thus great, thus amiable, will you suffer the national glory to be tarnished, by the inhuman avarice of a worthless few!" The other two consider slavery contradictory to the principles for which America is preeminent: "The existence of slavery in this country is its greatest reproach. That slavery should be tolerated amongst free men, is in the most eminent degree disgraceful. . . . Genius of liberty! how long shall this detestable bondage continue to disgrace our country and remain a standing contradiction to all our professions and institutions?"

School books published after the Civil War accept without question the emancipation of the slaves, and with hindsight they condemn wholeheartedly the institution of slavery. Inherent qualities assigned to the Negro are the same unpromising ones accorded to him in the pre–Civil War period, and his future is still a matter for gloomy speculation. But slavery is universally condemned and its demise celebrated. The school books rejoice over the abolition of an institution "so repugnant to the principles of Christianity, and so fraught with danger to society, religion and the state." In post–Civil War books, slavery occupies a much more prominent position in American history. Just as they view all of colonial history as leading to the American Revolution, so American historians consider that the events after the Revolution develop toward the Civil War. In a conciliatory mood toward the South, they blame both sections for the establishment of slavery; it was fastened upon America "not less by the cupidity of the north which found its profits in the slave trade, than by the cupidity of the south, which found its profits in slave labor." Many authors specifically mention sentiment for the abolition of slavery in both North and South at the time of the American Revolution. But the invention of the cotton gin and factory-produced cotton goods ended that possibility. Only one book puts the whole onus on the South. A homely dialogue between mother and child ends with the child foreseeing the defeat of the South as retribution for the sin of slavery: "So I am sure the Virginia colony would have to suffer for it sometime." Most authors, far from assigning blame, would agree with Fiske, who sees the change in the sentiment to slavery as part of an evolution of the moral sense of man toward perfection:

Very few people in those days [the seventeenth century] could see any-
thing wrong with slavery; it seemed as proper to keep slaves as to keep
cattle and horses. . . . In our time nobody but a ruffian would have

anything to do with such a wicked and horrible business. Changes of this sort make us believe that the world is growing to be better than it used to be. But the improvement is very slow.

A post–Civil War book by a Southern author for Southern pupils takes much the same position; it observes that in the colonial period "the conscientious opposition to slavery had been stronger in the South than in the North," while the North monopolized the slave trade without scruple. The only visible difference between the Southern and Northern interpretations in school books is the greater stress in the Southern books on the constitutional right to slaves as property. The Southern book cited above also recognizes the importance of slavery to the economy of the United States: "However objectionable the system may now be generally regarded, no facts stand out clearer in American history than that the steady and directed toil of the Southern slave first placed the United States among the great commercial nations of the world. . . ." It also trained the Negro to do useful work.

. . . .

In a few books published after the Civil War the future of the Negro becomes a matter for brief speculation. Some of these apply their generalized expectation of progress to the Negro: "Many of the former slaves have become landowners, and are beginning to realize the duties and responsibilities of citizens." In a speech by the Goddess of Liberty another book supports Negro suffrage: "Shall color prevent an honest heart from the right of suffrage? God created all men free and equal. The black and the white man are subjects of his creation." And a Speller illustrating use of the words "concur" and "demur" would accept the Negro into American politics more readily than the Indian: "When the Judge says that the law gives the right to vote to negroes, I *concur*; but when he extends the provision to wild Indians, I *demur*." But most of the books, when they mention the subject at all, offer hope for the future of the Negro as an equal component in American civilization only if he has direct and careful guidance from the white. Unaided, he is now uncivilized and will remain so. This is a typical statement: "The negro race have, by themselves, made only the first steps in civilization and the great mass are still in the savage state. Where they have been brought up under the influence of cultured nations, however, they have shown themselves capable of a high degree of progress." Another view is less optimistic but more moralistic: "The negroes are doubtless happier now than when slaves, but in spite of the efforts to educate them on the part of the whites and of some members of their own race, many still remain densely ignorant. What shall be done for their elevation is one of the greatest problems of the present time. It should be remembered, however, that their ancestors were brought here against their will, and it is now our duty to help and improve the negro." This author also observes that whites are used in a cotton mill in Alabama in spite of the numbers of available Negroes, because the latter are generally believed to lack the intelligence for even such simple work. Interestingly enough a post–Civil War History written by a Southerner for Southern schools sees no need to quarrel with Northern predictions of the future of the Negro: "The systematic training bestowed upon him during his period of servitude, and his contact with higher intelligence have given to the negro an impulse to civilization that neither his inherent inclinations nor his native environment would of themselves bestow." Thus it is only through serious humanitarian efforts of the white race that improvement of the Negro race is possible, for the Negroes do not contain within themselves the seeds of cultural advance. And even with such help, most school books are dubious about their achieving equality with the whites.

The child influenced by these books would be unlikely to see the Negro as a participant in and a contributor to American culture. He would judge the abolition of slavery a righteous act that erased a serious blot on his civilization, a blot made by foreign nations before America had charge of its own destiny. Emancipation absolved the whites from any debt to the Negro as an equal. But the child would assume that some responsibility for the care of the Negro would necessarily devolve on the white, because the Negro was incapable of self-control and self-direction. The generations that made decisions about the Civil War, slavery, and Reconstruction, whatever they were taught about slavery, were thoroughly indoctrinated with the idea of Negro racial inferiority. It is interesting to observe that this inferiority consists in a lack of the very qualities—responsibility, industriousness, initiative—considered particularly valuable to an America "on the make." Their conspicuous absence makes the Negro a poor candidate for equality in American civilization.

It should also be noted that the image of the Negro is of the same gay, foolish, childlike creature who appeared in the writings of George Fitz-hugh and Thomas Nelson Page, as well as in the consciousness of the old Southern aristocracy, and finally in the minstrel show. It is not the bestial Negro in the writings of Thomas Dixon at the end of the century, nor in the thinking of the Ku Klux Klan and the Southerners who fixed a rigid and all-pervasive segregation of the race. The Negro of the school books must be cared for by the whites as one would care for a child; he is not vicious, nor is it necessary to quarantine him. His place in America's future is clear: he will assist the whites from his menial but useful position.

★ 5 ★

THE PATRICIAN SOUTH AND THE COMMON SCHOOLS
William R. Taylor

Much of the writing on the history of education has tended to obscure the differences among regions in the United States. Usually it is assumed that the inequities that are conceded to exist are merely matters of degree. The history of publicly supported and controlled education, for example, has been pictured as a procession with the New England states, particularly Massachusetts, in the lead and the rest of the states following along behind. All move in the same direction toward a similar goal. This essay reminds us of the importance of regional differences and of the distortions in the processional concept.

Numerous documents on Southern education before the Civil War are reprinted in Edgar W. Knight, ed., A *Documentary History of Education in the South Before 1860*, 5 vols. (Chapel Hill: University of North Carolina Press, 1949–1953). See also Clement Eaton, *The Mind of the Old South* (Baton Rouge: Louisiana State University Press, 1964).

During the 1830s, 1840s, and 1850s, the Southern states participated in a nationwide debate over the aims and instrumentalities of education. In the South, this debate began as a discussion of common schools, and these remained an important aspect of it and provided it with focus. It enlarged, however, to include all schools—public and private; collegiate, secondary, and primary. It also embraced in its terms—and sometimes in its specifics—educational institutions for society at large:

libraries, lyceums, and that *most* important educational institution for the nineteenth century, the Home. As the debate progressed, there emerged conflicting ideas about a very large theme: how the youth of the South were to be *nurtured* (to seize a term from the debate itself) and toward what ends. Finally, it was not simply the youth of the South that were under discussion but the society itself—its aspirations, its fears, and, in fact, its very attitude toward knowledge itself. This paper recounts that debate and tries to show how the terms and scope of it changed as time went on.

The debate began as a discussion of how to improve the educational level of society—both by improving the schools themselves, and by extending the benefit of education to more people. But between the thirties and fifties Southerners—not all Southerners, but a significant, articulate minority—appear to have changed their minds. The transformation in educational philosophy that appears to have overtaken those who wrote about the schools is not, of course, as crisp and clear as my analysis will make it seem. There were still Southerners in the late fifties who were speaking in the terms of the thirties about the need for universal free education and a system of schools, normal schools, and colleges that were to be directed to the needs of the whole population. But by the fifties they were lonely voices and they had taken on a note of despair.

What emerges is a definable tendency or trend that becomes apparent in the magazines and journals that saw fit to introduce and reintroduce the subject of education. This trend is away from a commitment to education as a matter of public responsibility, as a matter of general concern to the states in question, toward the definition of education as a private, or, at best, a local question. Insofar as a coherent educational philosophy continues to exist by the fifties, it has become a belief that the object of education is not, as earlier writers have insisted, to equip the population to guard its liberties and to place a check on those who ruled them, but rather to inculcate the Southern orthodoxies and to fend off the criticism being directed at the South from the outside. One can say with a good deal of justice that the prevailing view changed from regarding education as providing an electorate that could control the machinery of democratic government, to regarding it as providing an electorate that the machinery of government could control. Instead of seeing education as a means of controlling and guiding the workings of the society, writers speak increasingly of the need for education as a

70

means of social control and manipulation. Instead of conceiving of the educational process as the introduction of the young to a process of inquiry and questioning, these writings speak in increasingly strident tone about the urgent necessity of preparing the young to do battle for the very orthodoxies that it had become heretic to question or examine. Education, instead of being the palladium of the Republic that Jefferson had made it, became the shield and buckler of the slavocracy.

In the course of this transformation, many things that had preoccupied the writers of the thirties and forties were shunted aside and lost sight of. An inordinate distrust of all forms of education developed, a distrust of knowledge itself, and a distrust of the society, first of the North and, finally, of the South itself. As Southerners looked about for someone they could trust with the task of education, they turned first from Northern schools and colleges, from Yankee textbooks and Yankee schoolmasters, to the educational institutions of the South. These Southern institutions were themselves in turn viewed with increasing suspicion and seen as centers of subversion and of Yankee influence. Even the Southern women who had been urged as the logical (and economical) replacement of Yankee schoolmasters and Northern professors were viewed with suspicion—and for precisely the same virtues that had recommended them as teachers in the first place: their intuitive compassion and their abhorrence of cruelty and injustice. If the University of Virginia, as one writer put it, had not been sufficiently "cottonized," the Southern woman had, in her soft domestic isolation, not been sufficiently conditioned to the exigencies of the South's peculiar institution. In the last analysis, the influences of the Southern Home itself—as the nineteenth century called it—became suspect.

The question became: where was it possible to indoctrinate the young in beliefs that Southerners themselves held with increasing insecurity? The unanswerable nature of this question gives to much that was written about education after the mid-fifties its peculiarly unrealistic and utopian cast, as some of the writers themselves realized. Education, for these few who found time to discuss it, became an introduction into a world that never was, rather than a preparation for the situation young Southerners faced in a United States confused and divided over the question of slavery and states' rights.

The debate began, then, with a campaign to improve the quality of Southern education. A good example of this concern is an address given

71

by a young Virginia lawyer, Lucian Minor, in September, 1835, to an audience at Hampden-Sidney College. It was printed in an early issue of the *Southern Literary Messenger*, a journal published in Richmond with the explicit purpose of advancing the cause of Southern letters and Southern culture. The speech strikes a Jeffersonian note. This is apparent simply from the subtitle, "as connected with the permanence of our republican institutions." Given the complexity of republican government and the divisive forces at work in the country, Minor begins, the only security for Virginia lies in educating the people to monitor the complexity of the governmental system they have inherited. Rulers cannot be trusted with power, even in a republic with built-in checks. The only restraint on demagoguery and despotism lies in the vigilance of the electorate to the possibilities of the abuse of power. It is education and education alone that can preserve the liberties of free men. "If there is a remedy for the diseases that poison the health of liberty; the reason— that remedy—can be found only in one short precept—ENLIGHTEN THE PEOPLE!" It is clear from Minor's passing observations that his rhetoric should not be placed in a Jacksonian setting. He proposes no changes in the social system and he says not a word about education as an end in itself. Education is not discussed as a means of self-realization for the citizenry or as a way of assuring all men an equal start in the race. His emphasis is civic and his attention is focused, perhaps even somewhat narrowly, on the need to preserve the social order. This becomes apparent in an apostrophe:

> *Nothing—I scruple not to avow—it has been my thought for years— nothing but my reliance upon the efficacy of this precept (enlighten, etc.) prevents my being, at this instant, a* monarchist. *Did I not, with burning confidence, believe that the people could be enlightened, and that they may so escape the dangers that encompass them, I should be for consigning them at once to the calms of an hereditary monarchy.*

Minor then goes on to describe himself, quoting Jefferson, as a true Whig: "The sickly, weakly, timid man," he quotes Jefferson as saying, "fears the people, and is a tory by nature. The healthy, strong, and bold, cherishes them, and is a whig by nature." It is with this preface that Minor then proceeds to advocate universal common school education of the kind that was being developed in New York, Connecticut, and Massachusetts. In a journey to the New England states the year

72

before, Minor had been struck by the literacy and intelligence of ordinary people, and he had made a direct connection between common school education and the prevalence of newspaper reading, the use of libraries, and the comparative absence of tippling, crime, and vice. Calm reason seemed to him to operate on all deliberative questions, as for example in the matter of abolition. "Abolition," he observed at one point, "if not dead here, is in a state too desperately feeble to give us an hour's uneasiness. Of the many intelligent men with whom I have conversed on this subject in Massachusetts, Rhode Island and Connecticut, there is but a single one who does not reprobate the views of Messrs. Tappan, Cox, Garrison and Co. as the suggestions of the wildest, most pernicious fanaticism." And as for the explanation of this extraordinary civil discipline, Minor leaves no doubt of his own explanation. "Much, if not most of these virtues must be attributed to the system of *common schools.*"

Two things are worth noting about this early appeal. First, there is an unmistakable note of regional pride and a desire to create viable cultural institutions for Virginia—and, by implication, for the South. But the North, and especially New England, are not to be shunned but imitated. In a letter to a friend written after his tour of New England, in fact, Minor goes on to advocate that Southerners travel in the North and acquaint themselves with the real features of New England life. The second point is obvious from the allusion to abolition. The fact of slavery and opposition to it ought not to be construed as an argument against education. Reasonable men will always approach social problems reasonably. The best argument against demagoguery and social quackery is precisely the course the New England states have chosen to follow: the enlightenment of its citizenry.

As late as 1844, the discussion was still being carried on in the same terms. A proponent of common schools, for example, writing in New Orleans in that year, made a point that was to be made by a succession of others. Common schools were what he called the "cement" of a republic. "Educate the masses," he went on to say, "make men understand their rights, and you preserve their freedom, and make it worth preserving. . . . We insist that no unenlightened people can ever be a powerful people. We employ Lord Bacon's maxim, that 'knowledge is power,' as a kind of watchword; we maintain that public virtue is the offspring of salutary instructions impressed upon the mind in the opening period of life; and if told that corruption, proceeding by stealthy foot-steps . . . is sapping the springs of the body politic, and that the 'devil is unchained' in the midst of us, we exclaim . . . that the schoolmaster should be abroad to grapple with him." Indeed, the word *was* more powerful than the sword, as another proponent of common schools ob-served a few years later; but there were at least two ways of construing this claim.

The early interpretation was the kind advanced by a South Carolin-ian, Theodore H. McCaleb, then a federal judge in New Orleans, still in 1844. In a speech before the board of directors of the Second Munic-ipality of the city, McCaleb made the usual point. The board "knew that the clouds of prejudice must be dispelled; that inertness and preju-dice must be animated to a sense of moral responsibility." The means for doing this was the common school, and the certain result of an ex-tension to other parts of the state of the experiment then being con-ducted in the Second Municipality would be "Revolution," no more, no less; but by revolution he meant a transformation of a wholly benefi-cent kind. Through training in music, the animal in children would be subdued and their natures softened; through physical training their bod-ies would be made healthy and tough, resistant to vice and dissipation; through the total abolition of corporal punishment in the schools, pupils would be induced through acts of kindness and mutual respect to observe the rights of others. Through a simultaneous training of mind, body, and heart, the young would be led to an appreciation of the idea of freedom and of the limitations imposed upon freedom by mutual regard. What could possibly follow from this, if extended to the nation at large, but a firm knitting together of the Union itself? And here McCaleb allowed himself to proceed unchecked toward his utopia:

> Yea, that the whole South, yielding to the influence of our own bright example, may soon cause the pure and limpid waters of social exis-tence, which shall bountifully flow from the system we this day ad-vocate, to roll back upon their great Northern source, until our whole happy Union . . . shall pour forth a perennial flood of moral in-telligence.

The combination of local pride and ardent nationalism, the confu-sion of modes of freedom and determinism at play in this morsel of rhet-oric, exemplify the ambiguity that was working in the thinking of the most optimistic of Southern advocates of universal education. Who but a citizen of New Orleans would think of bottling up the Mississippi River at its mouth, tides and all, and sending it north to flood the Union with "limpid waters" of that city's "social existence"? Who but a stout Unionist would assume that such an inundation would necessarily be welcome when it reached the stony soil of New England, which, after all, had small but limpid rivers of its own? Who but an optimistic judge of the rationality of man would entrust the idea of moral intelligence to such an undiscriminating vehicle as a river turned upon its source and out of control? If the great central channel of moral intelligence could be imagined as flowing north, it took little imagination to see a tide flowing south, or more precisely, southwest from the "great Northern source" the judge had mentioned—as an increasing number of Southern opponents of common schools on the New England model took the occasion to point out. If moral intelligence could be released like well water, it mattered who manned the pump and who guided the flow at every point. If education, on the other hand, meant encouraging individuals to exercise their sense of what the judge had called "moral responsibility" by freeing them from "clouds of prejudice," then the consequences of education for the South might not be altogether predictable, especially in a society that lived in some uneasiness with an institution that even Southerners found it possible to refer to as "peculiar."

Men like McCaleb were, of course, unconscious of the implications their arguments contained. Like the judge himself, they were more often than not from what the South chose to call its aristocracy. Revolutionary lineage, private tutors, and education at Northern schools—McCaleb had attended both Exeter and Yale and studied law with Rufus Choate in Salem, Massachusetts—had provided them with a large view of American life. In the life of McCaleb, furthermore, other expansive forces had been at work. A Whig who could ingratiate himself with Democrats, a frequent host to traveling European dignitaries such as Thackeray, Tocqueville, and Chateaubriand, and a professor of admiralty and international law at the University of Louisiana, he could claim as broad a perspective as any of his American contemporaries. He surely must have felt that he exemplified the kind of moral intelligence that he advocated and that he owed his acquisition to the education he had received. Only the onset of the war managed to shake his faith, and

75

even then he held on to his judgeship and his chair in international law until after the fighting began. A lifelong Unionist who cast his lot with the South, he must have died with his dreams in some disarray when he succumbed at his plantation, "The Hermitage," in 1864.

But well before his death McCaleb's views had come to be held only by survivors from a previous generation. The debate was still argued from the same initial premises, but the conclusions drawn from these premises had indeed changed.

How the debate became transformed can be well traced through the correspondence received over many years by Horace Mann. Mann was the editor of *The Common School Journal,* and in this capacity received letters for many years from correspondents in several Southern states—Mississippi, Alabama, Georgia, Louisiana, South Carolina, and Virginia. From Virginia, in fact, he received a whole succession of letters from several correspondents that amount to a genuine exchange of ideas on educational principles and tactics.

Typically, these letters request the forwarding of pamphlets and addresses by Mann and others and put questions to him concerning all phases of education—college curricula, his defenses of female education, and organizational questions about the development of common school systems and centralized systems of state education. They unfailingly express great deference to Mann and admiration for the work that he is carrying forward in the North. Often, too, these letters contain acid critiques of the educational facilities in the correspondent's home state. The Grand Lodge of Odd Fellows of North Carolina in 1846 even sent Mann a bank draft of ten dollars "for much valuable information on the subjects of schools."

To all these correspondents Mann sent long and patient expositions of his educational philosophy and organizational ideas, along with the requested enclosures. To Southerners accustomed to thinking of school support in terms of county or parish taxation, Mann urged the creation of centralized state systems. With some deference, for example, to his own ignorance of the South, Mann recommended to a correspondent in Virginia the adoption of state rather than county taxation. "If left to the counties," he wrote, "I should fear that those which need an improved system least, would be the only ones to adopt it, while with those who need it most, their indifference would be proportionate to their need." Above all, he stressed the point made by Minor that education was a public trust and that civic order depended upon its improvement in every part of every state. If parts of the society were to remain in ignorance, the whole society could be expected to suffer, or, as Mann himself put it, "this punishment [is] inflicted upon the innocent quite as much as upon the guilty." From time to time, Mann allowed himself to philosophize upon the process through which the public was to be brought to an enlightened state. To the popular Southern argument that a priority should be placed upon creating a college-bred elite, Mann returned a spirited defense of the fundamental importance of beginning educational reform at the primary level:

> As to the relative importance of primary schools on the one hand, and colleges and academies on the other, you may depend upon it as a law of nature, that colleges and academies never will act downward to raise the mass of people by education; but, on the contrary, common schools will feed and sustain the academies and colleges. Heat ascends, and it will warm upwards, but it will not warm downwards.

Nor was this correspondence with Southern admirers terminated by the publicity given at the close of the forties to Mann's pronounced views against the extension of slavery and the Mexican War, and, in fact, one Southern correspondent, apparently a Quaker, appended a note of congratulation at the close of his letter. This correspondence with Mann and his co-worker in Connecticut, Henry Barnard, continued until almost the outbreak of the war. As late as 1856, Southerners were able to assure these New England advisers that their counsel would not be discredited because of their place of origin.

By 1849, however, a new and changed note had begun to creep into these letters from the South, and one begins to feel that letters sent after this date are designed to elicit sympathy fully as much as instrumental advice. The expected and hoped for changes within the South had not materialized, and Southerners who had devoted much of the forties to campaigns to advance the cause of the common school were beginning to lose heart and to despair of the result. Typical of this new tone of despondency was a letter sent to Mann early in 1849 by one of Virginia's most distinguished evangelists for public education, John B. Minor, a brother of Lucian. Minor, coming from a prominent Virginian family and having himself received the best and most expensive private education available in the state, was in many ways characteristic of the group

77

of men who had been active through the forties. He had also for a few years been the editor of the *Southern Literary Messenger,* which he made into a forum for the discussion of educational ideas. He was a Whig in his political affiliations, and his adult life was divided between the practice of law and a succession of teaching appointments. He had acted briefly as the principal of the Virginia Female Institute at Staunton, Virginia, and was, at the time of his letter, editing a journal for young women, significantly called *The Home School for Young Women,* and once again practicing law. In 1860 he was named president of the University of Missouri, and before his death was associated with at least three other educational institutions. His complaint must therefore not be construed as coming from a man of markedly radical views or from one only casually associated with educational reform.

> *Your sympathy, alone, had it been unattended by advice . . . would have been valuable, for the blended ignorance and indifference of our Countrymen to popular education makes such sympathy rare. The few who indulge in enthusiasm upon the subject, must cherish this fire in the seculusion of their own hearts. . . . We are now in a condition infinitely worse than you were then [in 1837 when Mann began his work]. The whole machinery of organization, & even the policy of public education is unknown to us, and with English conservatism, we distrust what is new and untried, & cling to usages that are hoary, whether they be the best, or the less good.*

In the balance of his letter Minor makes it clear that it is not only English conservatism, as he calls it, but ignorance, prejudice, and irrational fears among the ordinary citizens and planters of the counties that have prevented effective action in the state. And, for Mann's entertainment, Minor appended a whole list of "fables," as he calls them, being spread about the proposed system of common schools—that they mean socialism, that they represent an interference with the sanctity of family life and discipline, that they will lead to the indiscriminate mixing of both social classes and sexes. As a final item, Minor noted almost casually an ominous new objection that was to be heard with increasing frequency during the coming decade. "And a *very few*," he noted, "stand upon the forlorn ground that general education is unfriendly to virtue and good order!"

The thought that educational institutions and ideas, especially those of New England origin, were subversive and threatened the social order in the South was for the most part a discovery that Southerners made during the fifties, when "the very few" voices noted by Minor swelled to a chorus. In a sense, the change that was to overtake educational thought in the South was built into the premises of the earlier educational reformers themselves. Those who struck the Jeffersonian note in the thirties and forties had argued that universal education was a vital public concern, but not because the people deserved it, not, that is to say, as a good in itself or as a means of self-fulfillment. Rather it was because it seemed the only means of preserving the social order in a republic from disruptive influences. The assumption clearly was that enlightened public opinion was the sole means of preserving the social fabric. The people, if entrusted with the knowledge to do so, could be counted upon to act as a rational restraint upon the forces of demagoguery, fanaticism, and irrationality. New England in 1834 had provided Lucian Minor with an excellent example of precisely this kind of social self-discipline at work: drinking, gambling, crime, and a susceptibility to abolition rhetoric had been attenuated by the extension of common school opportunities to the general populace.

Two elements, therefore, existed in the thinking of these men. One was a faith in the rationality of men in general and a belief that the sources of irrational behavior could be eradicated through the kind of instruction administered by the schools. The other was the changing estimate placed upon the test case of New England. A remarkable feature of the evangelical writing produced in the South during the early part of the century was the high estimation in which the educational system of Prussia was held. Once Southerners began to need arguments against wider education and to examine what they took to be the results of universal education, Prussia was labeled with autocracy and New England with anarchy. If the same system of schools could foster social systems so diverse as to stifle liberty on the one hand and let it degenerate into anarchy on the other, what confidence could one have that the same system of education, if adopted in the South, would necessarily lead to or preserve social order?

It is in this connection that the earlier declaration of Lucian Minor—namely, that if his faith in the enlightenment of the people should fail, he would become a monarchist—seems most revealing of the turn that was to come in the fifties. If order was the end, then apparently any governmental and, presumably, educational means to that end was acceptable. It had been the strength of Mann's philosophy that education itself was interpreted as a form of government-through-understanding. In a work on European education that Mann published in the mid-1840s, he cites a German school book in which the student is led through a succession of readings that pertain to different kinds of order—order in the parental home, order in the town and society at large, order in nature and in the cosmos. Once one began to doubt the ability to instill a sense of order, or once the results of such training seemed not to carry over into political and social conduct, one was justified, given Minor's premises, in turning from Jefferson's Whig into Jefferson's Tory overnight, so to speak.

It was precisely a re-estimation of these two elements that seems to characterize the educational debate of the forties and fifties. New England on the one hand and the rationality of man on the other were subjected to close but not always very dispassionate scrutiny. If the declared end of education was the inculcating (to use a favorite word) of both public and private virtue, then who could be trusted with knowledge—and how much of it could be administered to the population in general without subverting the very thing it was intended to preserve? If the object of knowledge was to free men's minds from cant and superstition, to induct the young by stages into the meaning of order, then it was necessary to agree upon the meaning of order. On one thing all parties agreed. The schoolmaster was a pivotal figure in any society. So important was the cultural conditioning of a child in school considered, that one proponent of common school cited with obvious approval the German saw, "Show me your songs, and I care not who makes your laws." Or, as another put it, "Knowledge is Power." Thus it is scarcely surprising that increasingly Southerners began to wonder who could be trusted with such power as the schoolmaster held and who could be trusted to receive such power as knowledge conveyed. Could one entrust such power, for example, to the slave? The question, put in this fashion, would have seemed palpably absurd. Yet the question was raised in other ways, at least indirectly. So great was the imputed power of knowledge that Southern states in this period successively passed laws making it a crime to teach slaves to read and write. On the other hand, if maintaining the social order was the first concern of every society and knowledge was the means of doing so, then should not the slave receive some kind of education that would acquaint him with his place in the order of things? The question, as we shall see, was answered in a guarded affirmative. Unless one could agree upon a definition of order, however, every claim staked for the schoolmaster and for knowledge was a twoedged sword: it could defend the social fabric or it could cut it to shreds. There was thus, from the outset, an important ambiguity that played over the declarations of education's stoutest defenders.

One of the surprising features in the lives of those who took either side in the debate over the schools is the similarity of their biographies. Yet this similarity is somewhat less surprising when the common assumptions from which they operated are made clear. Often the position taken seems to be the result of where one enters the web of argument in a universe of discourse so finely and closely spun. Opponents seemed the obverse of the same coin, and one position led logically to another. The major point of difference lay in the question whether the schoolmaster alone could handle the problem, or, indeed, in the last analysis, whether the schoolmaster could be trusted at all. If, to revert to McCaleb's metaphor, the devil was actually unchained in their midst, it mattered terribly whether the devil and the schoolmaster walked hand in hand or met in combat, as the supporters of common schools assumed they would.

From the beginning of the debate it is possible to detect a thread of wholly understandable skepticism directed at the wholesale unloading of educational responsibilities on the schools. This skepticism, moreover, was for a time almost entirely free of sectional bias. What kind of society, it was asked, would assign such momentous responsibilities to outside agencies and assume purely mental training could not corrupt as well as buttress? What must have seemed an obvious point was made by a speaker before an educational convention held in Richmond in 1841. In all traditional societies, he observed, the most important training a child receives is in the home and family, where he is inducted into the values of the society he is about to enter. Is there some fundamental failure in Southern families that makes this function impossible to fulfill, and if there is, can schools possibly fill it? He then went on to make a point that was later made by others to somewhat different effect. What will be the consequences of this unusual emphasis upon sec-

81

ular and rational training? Is it not through religion that men are brought to see and accept their place in society? "Religion ought to teach man to know himself—to resign and reconcile himself to his lot—recognize and adore the hand of Providence, even in those social arrangements which might perhaps strike him as unjust and arbitrary." The consequences of neglecting the importance of religion, he felt, could be seen in the recent history of France. The consequences of decreeing that there was no God and of worshiping the false deity of Reason had brought on the most awful social upheaval in modern times.

As the sectional crisis increased in intensity after 1849 the same arguments were subtly transformed into the now familiar indictment of Northern schools, Northern textbooks, Northern teachers and tutors working in the South, and even of the evangelical benevolence of Northern churches. What has been lost sight of in accounts of this educational indictment of the North and its influence upon Southern youth is the problem that this indictment posed for the South itself, and some of the implications concerning the South that the exploration of this problem revealed.

It was one thing to advocate "educating Southerners at home," to use the popular slogan of the time, and another thing to do it. Where, for example, did the North end and the South begin? Even the most parochial prosecutors confessed their inability to draw the line. Not only was the University of Virginia finally suspect, but the nearest schoolhouse contained textbooks that openly attacked the institution of slavery. All knowledge seemed to bear the concealed watermark of its "Northern," Yankee origin; teachers, books, the gospel itself required careful scrutiny, and yet there was no other option. Only knowledge could produce the kind of educated Southerner, man and woman alike, that the times seemed to require. Yet so long as knowledge was conceived of as omnipotent it could neither be safely withheld nor freely administered.

Discussions concerning the education of the slaves that went on during the fifities illustrate the dilemma that had overtaken the South. If the slave were left in ignorance, he would fall prey to the teachings of Northern abolition; but how was one to educate him without giving him the lethal weapon—literacy—that might enable him to break his bonds? The answers given seemed contradictions in terms, and their phrasing reveals the uncertainty with which they were put forward. "It is most particularly to be remembered," one writer interjected, "that all the information necessary for them [the slaves] must be communicated *orally*. We do not say this merely because there is a law forbidding other instruction, or because we have the slightest apprehension of the evils to result from any other system. We say they must be instructed orally from the very *nature* of things. We do not believe in imparting knowledge in any other way to a laboring class." The writer concludes by pointing out that laborers in all countries are predominantly illiterate and lack the time to learn to read and write.

It was inevitable that someone would eventually put the same question concerning the South's poor whites, and within a few years a number of writers did. In the confusion that resulted, it becomes apparent how radically the idea of education had been transformed. White men who labor bodily, ran one version, must be educated with special care, so that "the man will not become submerged in the work." Only in this way could the white laborer be brought to see the dignity of his work and his solidarity with other white men, who seemed on the face of it his superiors. The white laboring man, ran another account, should be given only as much knowledge as he felt he needed and was willing to pay for. Knowledge by this reckoning is seen as a purely personal adornment and as a profoundly dangerous force, since it creates an appetite for leisure that the harsh realities of the world cannot provide to any but a favored few. The writer continues:

> If we lived in Utopia, and our numbers were few,—if we were not required to struggle, not only for the means of living, but for life itself, if the circumstances of every man were such that his necessary labors were only so great as to brace his nerves and his muscles for enjoyment during his hours of relaxation,—then would universal education be not only a sweetener of life but a necessity.

But what of the claim that "education is not only the palladium of our liberties, but the guide which is to lead us to eternal truth"? "Cant," replies this particular theorist, and he goes on to explain why:

> [*Education*] would be essential to the perfect development of Utopian life. But our world is one of fact. Life is a sober reality. In spite of the falsehoods which constitutions proclaim to the contrary, the privileged few must govern. To the mass of mankind the character of government

83

is a matter of indifference. The free-born peasant of England is not happier now, than was his ancestor, the born-thrall of his feudal lord. . . . Liberty is an instinct, not a principle.

Thus, in the dilemma concerning education, it seemed safest to withhold it from almost everyone, to disavow its civic purpose and make it a matter of the cultivation of one's leisure hours; and a succession of writers, in one way or another, made this point before the outbreak of war. To do so, however, it was necessary to secede not only from the Union but from history itself and to turn back the tide in quite a different fashion from that imagined by Judge McCaleb ten years before. To a society in full flight from the moral implications of its labor system, it became difficult to believe in education at all. Though derision of the North continued in article after article, it became clear that the real opponent was not the Yankee with his school book, but human knowledge itself. If liberty was an instinct, not a principle, knowledge became a luxury, to even one's self, and anyone who held to the contrary would bear watching. The scene had thus shifted from a society where the people watch the government, to a happy land where, as one writer put it, "the master's eye directs the work and watches the morals of his people, where the great and simple truths of Christianity are freely but *orally* taught to the slave."

★ 6 ★

THE EDUCATION OF NEGROES
BEFORE THE CIVIL WAR
Howard K. Beale

The history of the education of blacks in America largely remains to be written, despite recent interest in the subject. Whether slave or free, blacks have been a challenge to the sincerity of the often proclaimed American faith in opportunity for all through education. In antebellum America, the education of slaves was primarily used to encourage acquiescence in a subordinated economic and social position. Many of the white Americans most closely involved, however, were haunted by the possibility that any attempt at education would stimulate discontent and provide opportunities for its organization into rebellion. Education for blacks, then, meant many different things. It usually consisted only of primitive oral instruction in religion and social duties. Occasionally there were opportunities to learn to read and write, or to learn a trade.

Howard K. Beale discusses the history of the education of blacks in the South and the North before the Civil War. Other writings include Horace M. Bond, *The Education of the Negro in the American Social Order* (New York: Prentice-Hall, 1934); Leon Litwack, *North of Slavery* (Chicago: University of Chicago Press, 1961); and Carter G. Woodson, *The Education of the Negro Prior to 1861* (Washington, D.C.: Associated Publishers, 1915).

In the first place, teachers were generally not permitted to instruct Negroes. Difficulties first arose in colonial days, when missionaries sought to save the souls of Negroes. The Friends and emissaries of the Anglican Society for the Propagation of the Gospel were particularly eager to teach Negroes the elements of Christianity. Throughout colonial days these men clashed with masters who feared the effects of Christianity upon their slaves. In these early days it was believed by many Negroes and feared by many masters that conversion to Christianity would free slaves. There had once been an English belief that no Christian could be held as a slave. It was early abrogated, but even when it became thoroughly understood that Christians could be held in bondage, other difficulties remained. Admission that a Negro could be converted to Christianity implied that he had a soul. This might lead to regarding him as a human being. Holding a human being in bondage and maintaining that Christianity freed his soul but not his body raised implications that could be avoided as long as the slave was a savage pagan. Conversion, it was believed, developed ideas of religious equality, which made slaves dissatisfied and hard to manage. Recently arrived Negroes were savages regarded as little better than beasts. A Swedish traveler, Peter Kalm, reported masters afraid to see their slaves converted because equality at the communion table raised in them a pride dangerous to the social order.

Various methods were used to discourage the teaching of slaves. Mere social pressure usually sufficed. Many a minister who wished to teach slaves to read the Bible was deterred by fear of the displeasure of wealthy planters. Those who had the courage to face planter disapproval were apparently not molested. In 1680 Virginia prohibited meetings of Negroes in large numbers under penalty of "Twenty Lashes on the Bare Back well laid on." Maryland passed similar laws in 1695 and 1723. A teacher who gathered Negroes together was fined one thousand pounds of tobacco. Other colonies followed this lead, New York, for example, in 1702, and Georgia in 1765. These acts could be used to dissolve Negro schools—or churches, for that matter—but where no strong desire to suppress schools existed, these "insurrection laws" were not applied to that kind of gathering. South Carolina in 1740 and Georgia in 1755 enacted laws prohibiting all men from teaching Negroes to write. The South Carolina law laid a penalty of one hundred pounds upon any one "who shall hereafter teach or cause any Slave or Slaves to be taught to write, or shall use or employ any Slave as a Scribe in any manner of Writing, whatsoever."

Many Colonial masters, however, were eager to have their slaves converted to Christianity. It salved qualms of conscience about enslaving Negroes to feel that slavery was freeing them from the bonds of savage paganism and providing eternal salvation. Benevolence led many masters to seek Christian teaching for their house servants. Others found a Negro able to read, write, and figure a valuable asset. Therefore many slaveholders provided Christian teaching for some of their slaves and taught ambitious ones to read and write. The Friends, impelled by humanitarianism, were, however, the first to instruct slaves. Their efforts were resented in the South from the first, because they also preached abolition of slavery. In New Jersey, Pennsylvania, and New York, however, they met less opposition, and it was there that men first enjoyed the privilege of teaching Negroes. The Society for the Propagation of the Gospel made a still more systematic attempt to instruct slaves and early sent out not only clergymen but schoolmasters. That a few colonial slaves could read and write is evidenced by the advertisements for runaways.

. . . .

While these Negro schools were exceptional, it is important that in colonial days men who taught Negroes were frowned upon rather than punished. Toward the end of the colonial period, the spread of eighteenth-century liberalism through the South provoked contradictory reactions. Some men were impelled by it to grant greater privileges to Negroes, to encourage or provide teachers for them, and to talk of freeing them. Other men became alarmed at the effect Locke's and Rousseau's views would have upon slaves who were able to read them. On the whole, however, the years of Revolution and Jeffersonian liberalism provided the greatest freedom ever enjoyed under slavery by teachers of Negroes.

Indeed, during the first decades of the nineteenth century, before the slavery issue fixed racial prejudice upon the South, one Negro, at least, conducted a school in North Carolina that white boys attended. He was John Chavis, who had acquired his education in part by unofficial study at Princeton under President Witherspoon of that institution. Among the pupils of this cultivated Negro were such prominent white North Carolinians as United States Senator Willie P. Mangum, Governor Charles Manly, Abraham Rencher, congressman and governor of New Mexico, the Reverend William Harris, and two sons of Chief Justice Henderson.

The discovery of the cotton gin, the increasing economic importance of the slave system, the beginnings of abolition criticism from the North, the Nat Turner insurrection in 1831, a gradual realization that the slave section was falling far behind the free states in population and economic power, and the new slave philosophy that the South built up as a defense mechanism against world humanitarianism's indictment of slavery, combined to intensify the struggle. With the widening of the suffrage in the half century following the Revolution, the alarm of a newly vocal non-slaveholding white group desperately afraid of free Negroes was added to the slaveholders' desire to maintain the slave system. Until about 1830 the South was divided about slavery. Gradually criticism died away. Belief in slavery came to be a mark of Southern patriotism.

The religious leaders, who had been numbered among those most eager to teach Negroes, gradually ceased to oppose and came to support the slave philosophy. Formerly religious instruction had involved learning to read and write. Now the various evangelical sects contented themselves with oral instruction in religious beliefs. The Catholics and Friends alone continued to try to teach Negroes to read and write, and they were not numerous in the South.

After 1830 Southerners felt more and more keenly the dangers of allowing Negroes to be taught. The poor white feared the competition of educated Negroes. The slaveholder felt that education of slaves menaced the whole slave system. Slavery was justified partly upon the theory that the Negro was uneducable and therefore capable of nothing better. The slaveholder inwardly feared that this might be disproved if men were allowed to try to educate Negroes. More serious, however, was the fact that with the growing effectiveness of escapes, ability to write enabled the slave to make out passes and, if questioned, to establish his freedom by proving he could write. Worst of all, reading would give a Negro "dangerous ideas," which would destroy his contentment and happiness, make him restless, and unfit him for slavery. As abolitionist literature increased in volume, fear of literate Negroes grew. "Instead of reading the Bible," wrote De Bow, "slaves would have placed in their hands those 'other documents, books, and papers' inculcating insubordination and rebellion, and thus placing the lives of our families in imminent peril. If with the ability to read you could impart true religion, or even a desire or disposition to read the Bible, the danger would be largely diminished. But if a judgment may be formed from the known conduct of white readers, we may reasonably conclude that the majority of blacks would prefer other books than the Bible. Is there any great moral reason why we should incur the tremendous risk of having our wives and children slaughtered in consequence of our slaves being taught to read incendiary publications?" Ability to read and write made the communication of plots of insurrection easier. An "incendiary" publication of one Walker of Boston seeking to arouse Negroes to improve their condition was a large factor in the passage of the North Carolina law forbidding the teaching of Negroes. The Nat Turner insurrection led to the immediate exclusion of all Negro children from white Sunday schools in Washington.

Teaching of Negroes was, then, vigorously forbidden throughout the South. Berry declared in the Virginia House of Delegates in 1832, "We have, as far as possible, closed every avenue by which light might enter . . . [the slaves'] minds. If we could extinguish the capacity to see the light, our work would be completed; they would then be on a level with the beasts of the field, and we should be safe. I am not certain that we would not do it, if we could find out the process, and that on the plea of necessity." A Virginia law of 1805 forbade overseers of the poor to require black apprentices to be taught reading and writing. Another in 1819 prohibited the teaching of Negroes or free mulattoes and provided for the punishment of the teacher, black or white, with a fine of three dollars and costs or twenty lashes on the bare back. In 1831 the fine was increased to a maximum of one hundred dollars. In 1800 South Carolina forbade the teaching of Negroes "in a confined or secret place of meeting, or with the gates or doors of such place of meeting barred." An 1834 enactment allowed a white teacher of free Negroes or slaves to be punished with a fine as high as one hundred dollars and six months' imprisonment, a free Negro teacher with a fifty-dollar fine and fifty lashes on the bare back, and a slave teacher with fifty lashes. A Savannah ordinance of 1818 punished the teacher with a fine of thirty dollars if white and thirty dollars plus thirty-nine lashes if black. In 1833 the penalty was increased. In 1829 Georgia imposed a fine and a whipping upon Negro teachers and a five-hundred-dollar fine and imprisonment upon white teachers. In 1818 and again in 1829–1830 the North Carolina Legislature rejected an anti-teaching bill. But in November, 1830, it forbade teaching slaves "to read or write, the use of figures excepted." The punishment for a white teacher was a fine of one to two hundred dollars; for a free Negro teacher, a fine, imprisonment, or a whipping; for a slave, thirty-nine lashes. In 1832 Alabama enacted a fine of two hundred fifty to five hundred dollars for any teacher of free Negroes or slaves. In 1833 this law was modified to allow any one licensed by the mayor of Mobile to instruct children of "free colored Creoles" in Baldwin and Mobile Counties whose ancestors resided there when Louisiana was purchased from France in 1803. Missouri passed an anti-teaching act in 1847. Louisiana in 1830 penalized teaching slaves by one to twelve months' imprisonment. Tennessee, Kentucky, and Maryland were the only slave states east of the Mississippi where teachers could lawfully instruct slaves.

Yet in spite of these rigid laws some men did teach Negroes. In New Orleans, the private schools of Negro Creoles were tolerated "because of the freedom, wealth, respectability and light color of the parents, many of whom were nearly white, and by blood, sympathy, association, slaveholding, and other interests, [were] allied to the white rather than the black." Virginia had a few Negro schools despite the prohibitory law. In Alexandria, then a part of the District of Columbia, a freedman named Parry conducted a night and later a day school despite a local anti-assembly ordinance. When arrested, Parry pleaded his good reputation but to no avail. The Mayor declared that his consent for teaching Negroes would never be given though the teacher were "as pure as the Angel Gabriel." Then the Mayor proceeded to wink at Parry's teaching, and Parry took the precaution of hiring a white man to be present at his night school. Tennessee had a few Negro schools. Kentucky had more. Lexington, Richmond, Maysville, Danville, and Louisville each possessed at least one school where masters permitted their slaves to be taught. In Baltimore slaves occasionally went to school with white children; one large community center for Negroes housed several schoolrooms; a Catholic order of colored women conducted a school for colored girls.

Nevertheless, openly conducted schools for Negroes were exceptional. Negroes were usually taught privately by masters or clandestinely without the masters' knowledge. A master occasionally found it useful to educate slaves trusted with responsibility and slave children who were constant companions of the master's children. It was a New Orleans custom for a master to send illegitimate children by slave mothers abroad or to the North for a good education, but they received their elementary training at home. Often the master himself taught the slave. Sometimes it was a kind-hearted mistress; sometimes the master's children, while they were themselves studying. Occasionally Negro children were allowed to sit in on the lessons of the white children. Many Negroes learned to read or write at Sabbath school. Stonewall Jackson, for instance, taught a Negro Sunday school while a professor in Lexington, Virginia. Nat Turner got his education in Sunday school. Abundant records evidence a not uncommon practice of privately teaching certain household slaves. Planters apparently regarded the laws as applying not to themselves but to non-slaveholders or Negroes or Northerners who wished to teach their slaves.

More often the teaching was done clandestinely. Frederick Douglass's white playmates were his teachers. One slave obtained a spelling book with a ninepence a man gave him for holding his horse, studied in the hayloft on Sundays, and got white children to hear his lessons. Sarah Grimké as a girl in South Carolina taught in the colored Sabbath school, but was allowed to instruct the Negroes only orally. She longed to teach them to read, but argue and plead though she did, this was forbidden. Therefore, "I took almost malicious satisfaction," she wrote, "in teaching my little waiting maid at night, when she was supposed to be occupied in combing and brushing my long locks. The light was put out, the keyhole screened, and flat on our stomachs before the fire, with the spelling-book under our eyes, we defied the laws of South Carolina." In 1851 Fredrika Bremer reported two Negro schools in Charleston. In Savannah the Union army found a Negress named Deveaux who for thirty years had conducted a school undetected.

Regular schools were frequently conducted surreptitiously. A District of Columbia mulatto named Mrs. Peake taught a school secretly by night in her cabin. A Fredericksburg Negro named De Baptiste turned his home into a school, where his children and relatives were taught first by a Negro and then by a Scotch-Irishman. The police became suspicious and watched the home but were never able to get evidence sufficient to take action. Two English women in Fredericksburg who ran a secret school kept on hand a supply of splinters and a match preparation so that, if any one surprised them, the children could be learning to make matches.

More often, however, teaching of Negroes was discovered and stopped. The experience of the future Negro bishop, Turner, in South Carolina was typical. He managed to buy a spelling book and got a white boy to teach him to spell, but the boy's brother learned of it and forbade it. Turner then employed a white woman to teach him on Sundays, but her neighbors learned of it and prevented her continuing. Finally he went to work for some lawyers who allowed him to use their books and taught him to read and write. Frederick Douglass's mistress began to teach him to read the Bible, but when his master heard of it and explained the dangers of educating a slave, she not only stopped the instruction but thereafter watched Douglass's every movement and rushed at him in wrath and took away his book or newspaper whenever she caught him reading. When it was discovered that Mrs. Caroline Hill, then a slave nursemaid in Tennessee, was learning from memory the lessons her charges recited, she was kept apart from them while they were studying or reciting.

In Charleston, schools conducted by clergymen for free Negro children were closed. While in that city, an English traveler named Benwell who went to a meeting in the home of a prosperous free Negro to discuss the organization of a school for Negroes was warned by the proprietor of his hotel that he had been shadowed because of interest he had expressed in the school and that it was known he had attended the school meeting. He was urged for his own safety to write a letter to the press repudiating all interest in the matter. When he refused, the proprietor "related several instances of mob law, which had been enacted within the twelve months preceding, which, he said, were quite necessary to maintain Southern rights." The school was opened but "the virulent conduct of the constables, supported by some of the citizens and the civil authorities," forced it soon to close.

In North Carolina, where public opinion had once been favorable to Negro education, a Sunday school run by two Friends, Levi and Vestal Coffin, was attacked in 1821 as dangerous. Slaveholders were persuaded to withdraw their slaves. Finally the school was forced to close. In a few more years the "patrols" were ordered to search every Negro house in the state for books and prints, particularly Bibles and hymnals.

. . . .

Violence was sometimes used. By this method, the school of an Ohio free Negro was broken up in Halifax County, North Carolina, and Frederick Douglass's Sabbath school for fellow Negroes was twice dissolved. Once Douglass was helping a white man conduct a Sabbath school in the home of a free Negro when a mob of white church members armed with sticks and missiles rushed in and drove them away. One of them accused Douglass of trying to be another Nat Turner and threatened that he would share Turner's fate if he did not desist. Another time his secretly teaching a Sabbath school under a large tree was discovered by a mob with missiles. Douglass and his pupils were threatened with flogging if they met again.

But violence or the threat of violence was not usually necessary. Even the laws prohibiting teaching were important chiefly as evidence of overwhelming popular sentiment. Public opinion completely dominated by the slave psychology was the really effective restriction against the teaching of Negroes. That this was effective is abundantly proved by the testimony of Negroes like Booker T. Washington and Frederick Douglass who wanted an education, and by the dense ignorance men confronted in the Negro population when, after emancipation, they set out to establish a system of Negro education.

So thoroughly did the slavocratic psychology possess the country that even in the North there was strong opposition to teaching Negroes. This was based partly upon unwillingness to spend money upon them, partly upon a feeling that a Negro school was not quite respectable and would ruin a community, partly upon the belief that education spoiled a Negro if it did not make him dangerous, but, more than anything else, upon the fear that allowing Negroes to be educated would bring an influx of them into the community. Northerners were not fond of Negroes. Ohio, Illinois, and Oregon enacted laws forbidding the migration of free Negroes into those states. Other state laws discouraged it. Public opinion frowned on anything that would encourage them to come. Most Northern states had no law prohibiting teaching them. Yet a year after Alabama imposed her two-hundred-fifty- to five-hundred-dollar fine for teaching Negroes, Connecticut forbade the private teaching of out-of-state Negroes or the admission of out-of-town Negroes to any school without the consent of the "civil authority" and "the select-men" and provided a fine of one hundred dollars for the first violation, two hundred for the second, and four hundred for the third. Ohio in 1829 forbade teachers and school directors to admit Negroes to the public schools. The African Colonization Society opposed education because it would encourage Negroes to refuse to be colonized back to Africa. Even in Canada escaped slaves found opposition to their being educated. In rejecting a proposal in 1853 in the Indiana Legislature for the education of Negroes, the opposition insisted that it was "better for the weaker party that no privilege be extended to them" since education "might . . . induce the vain belief that the prejudice of the dominant race could ever be so mollified as to break down the rugged barriers that must forever exist between their social relations."

In the North resentment toward the teaching of Negroes led to forc-ible closing of schools, driving out of teachers, and burning of build-ings. In Cincinnati, Augustus Wattles, who resigned a professorship at Lane Seminary to teach Negroes, and four young women who volun-teered as helpers "were daily hissed and cursed, loaded with vulgar and brutal epithets, oaths and threats; filth and offal were often thrown at them as they came and went; and the ladies especially were assailed by grossest obscenity, called by the vilest names, and subjected to every in-dignity of speech which bitterness and diabolism could frame." Room-ing houses in which they lived lost other tenants, and landladies, on learning their occupation, set their trunks upon the sidewalks. No one had "accommodations for nigger teachers." Finally they had to club together, rent a house, and board themselves. They were threatened with violence. They received letters enclosing pictures of hearts thrust through with daggers, bloody tongues hanging from mouths spouting blood, decapitated heads, or cut throats. Now and then their schools were closed entirely by mob violence.

Elias Neau, a missionary of the Society for the Propagation of the Gospel, established a Negro school in New York City in 1704. At first opposition forced him to go from house to house to teach his pupils, but soon he was able to gather them at night into his own home. For four years the school prospered. Then a group of Negro incendiaries tried to burn the city. Neau was accused of complicity. The Governor visited his school and gave it his full sanction. Neau was cleared of all suspicion in the trial that followed. The guilty slaves were found to be those whose masters had forbidden their education. Nonetheless the council passed an ordinance prohibiting Negroes from being out after dark without lanterns or candles. Since Negroes could not afford these, the school was henceforth seriously handicapped. When in 1790 another Negro school was opened in New York, prejudice was so great that it had difficulty surviving. After the New York School Society in 1834 took over the Negro schools formerly under the Manumission Society, they were badly neglected.

But New England, the heart of abolitionism, provided the most famous cases of suppression of freedom to teach Negroes. In Canaan, New Hampshire, Noyes Academy was founded in 1834 with a constitution admitting colored pupils. Undeterred by the threat of a town meeting resolution barring intercourse with anyone who taught blacks, the school opened in 1835. Another town meeting then appointed a committee to remove the Academy. A mob of several hundred men and nearly a hundred yoke of oxen dragged the seminary to a swamp, left it there in ruins, and drove the teacher from town. Then the town meeting solemnly voted: "The Abolitionists must be checked and restrained within constitutional limits, or American liberty will find a speedy grave." Apparently this was not accomplished without criticism because Kate Brousseau in a French treatise quotes the New Hampshire *Patriot* as caustically reporting "qu'on le déposa intact à l'angle près duquel était située la maison de réunion des Baptistes, où il se dresse aujourd'hui, non pas comme le monument de Bunker Heights, élevé à la mémoire des héros disparus, qui combattirent et tombèrent dans la lutte pour la liberté, mais comme un monument élevé à des vivants qui combattent pour détruire ce que nos pères ont conquis." Yet no one was punished and no property restitution was made. In fact, this violence was ordered by formal town meeting vote of the "best citizens."

In 1830 the First Annual Convention of the Colored People of the United States, meeting at Philadelphia and aided by Arthur Tappan and the Reverend Simeon Jocelyn of New Haven, decided to erect a manual labor college for Negroes at New Haven. The citizens of that city in alarm gathered and resolved: "That the founding of colleges for educating colored people is an unwarrantable and dangerous interference with the internal concerns of other States, and ought to be discouraged"; that the establishment of such a college in New Haven "is incompatible with the prosperity if not the existence of the present institutions of learning, and will be destructive of the best interests of the city"; and that "the Mayor, Alderman, Common Council and Freemen will resist the establishment of the proposed college in this place by every lawful means." The plan was finally abandoned.

In the village of Canterbury, Connecticut, in 1831, Sarah Harris, daughter of a respectable Negro farmer, asked admission to the school of Prudence Crandall. Miss Crandall, knowing the sentiment of the town, hesitated but was finally impelled by her Quaker conscience to admit the girl. Her pupils apparently did not object, but some of the parents and many of the townspeople did. The opposition was led by a wealthy Democratic politician and later judge of the United States District Court, Andrew T. Judson, whose house stood next to Miss Crandall's school on the village green. Warning was given that if Sarah was not dismissed, the white pupils would be withdrawn. Miss Crandall, knowing that it probably would mean loss of property and ruin to her school, finally decided to keep Sarah and to advertise in the *Liberator* for Negro girls. She was interviewed, argued with, threatened, insulted. When this failed, a town meeting on March 9 passed resolutions condemning the school and appointed a committee to persuade Miss Crandall to abandon the project. The resolutions protested that the school would "collect within the town of Canterbury large numbers of persons from other States whose characters and habits might be various and unknown to us, thereby rendering insecure the persons, property and reputations of our citizens." Mr. Judson declared, "The colored people never can rise from their menial condition in our country; they ought not to be permitted to rise here. They are an inferior race of beings, and never can or ought to be recognized as the equals of the whites. . . . The Constitution of our Republic . . . settled forever the status of the black men in this land."

In April fifteen or twenty Negro girls arrived. An attempt to frighten the pupils with an old vagrancy law imposing a fine and ten stripes on the naked body failed. Nonintercourse aggreements were made. No one would sell to Miss Crandall. She bought her supplies in neighboring towns. The stage-driver refused to carry her pupils. Boys threw filth into her well and her neighbors refused her a pail of water. Stones and rotten eggs were repeatedly thrown at her home. She and her pupils were insulted and threatened whenever they appeared on the street. Finally in

May, an act of the Legislature made it a punishable offense for her to teach Negroes. In June she was arrested, confined in the common jail in the cell just vacated by an executed murderer, and in August brought to trial. The judge put aside the defense arguments and declared the law constitutional, but the jury disagreed. In a second trial in October Miss Crandall was convicted. She appealed, and in July, 1834, the highest court evaded a decision on the constitutionality of the law by quashing the indictment on a technicality. The infuriated citizens of Canterbury then set her house on fire at daybreak. She and her pupils persisted in their school. Finally, late one night, a mob of men attacked the house with heavy clubs and iron bars, broke in all the windows and doors, and seriously damaged the first floor. Then the school was abandoned. The most significant feature of this whole episode is that the attacks on Miss Crandall were inspired and led by the wealthiest and "best" citizens of the town.

Even in the nation's capital under the federal aegis a teacher was not free to instruct Negroes. In 1835 mobs of white men attacked the Negro schools of the District, demolished several of the buildings, destroyed the furniture in the others, threatened the white teachers and leading Negro residents, and ransacked the homes of Negroes. Nearly all of the teachers—white women—abandoned their teaching after this. One of them, Miss Miner, when warned by one of a mob that her school was about to be destroyed, asked, "What good will it do to destroy my schoolroom? I shall only get another and go right on." Her school continued for many years. About 1843 the school of John H. Fleet was burned. In 1845 a Georgetown ordinance was passed, but never rigidly enforced, forbidding all meetings of Negroes except for religious instruction by whites. In 1858 two teachers from England and five white supporters of their schools were expelled from white churches of Washington and insulted; their schools were burned; and finally they were driven from the city. In 1860 Miss Miner was again threatened by a mob but again defied it. Finally her school was set on fire, though she escaped.

★ 7 ★

MODEL ZIONS FOR THE AMERICAN INDIAN
Robert F. Berkhofer, Jr.

Since the earliest settlements by Europeans in the New World, solicitude for the welfare of American Indians has been expressed. Most whites, however, were more interested in lands and furs than in the Indians' minds and souls. Consequently, warfare and trade instead of learning and religion have been the dominant modes of contact. But as Indians became less of a threat to white control of the continent, they won a greater claim on educational and religious philanthropy. It was generally agreed that education should aim at assimilation, specifically at encouraging conversion to Christianity and the adoption of the prevailing ideals of social and economic individualism. The resources devoted to this ambitious task of cultural transformation were never adequate. They amounted only to the establishment of scattered missionary and government agencies and schools and the admission of a few Indian youths to predominantly white schools. In the late nineteenth century, with the elimination of Indian resistance, the federal government established off-reservation boarding schools; Carlyle, in Pennsylvania, a former military post, was the best known. During the New Deal of the 1930s the assimilationist ideal fell out of favor with the government officials responsible for Indian educational policy, but attempts to initiate alternatives met with only limited success. In his essay, Robert F. Berkhofer discusses the emergence of the manual labor boarding school for Indian youth prior to the Civil War—and finds a wide significance in his topic.

A general survey of Indian education is Evelyn C.
Adams, *American Indian Education: Government Schools
and Economic Progress* (New York: King's Crown Press,
1946).

Ever since the days of Frederick Jackson Turner historians have argued
whether the cultural baggage carried westward by American settlers or
the frontier environment itself was more important in shaping western
institutions. An analysis of the evolution of the manual labor boarding
school as an agency of missionary activity among the Indians shows the
development of one frontier institution in relation to this question. Developed by Protestant missionaries after a century and a half of experience with the Indians, the institution was formed more by cultural assumptions prevalent in the East than by aboriginal contact in the West.

From John Eliot's Indian towns of the mid-seventeenth century to
the late eighteenth century when pietism flowered in a proliferation of
local and state societies, a few missionaries had labored alone and in
scattered locations among the Indians. Colonial efforts had been confined to the establishment of villages of converted Indians like the Ven-
erable Eliot's and the Moravians' or to the location of a solitary missionary in a savage settlement. In either case, the missionary hoped by
example and exhortation to convert the heathen to his brand of Protestantism and the godly life. Although these colonial efforts were respected by the pious of the new Republic, they deemed them failures.
Sharing the optimism of the early nineteenth century, the founders of
the new national societies, with their large treasuries and staffs, looked
forward to the immediate mass conversion of the American Indians,
and so the managers sought a new method of missionization. The manual labor boarding school seemed the answer to their prayers.

The idea of such an institution originated in colonial times. The first
exposition of it occurs in a small pamphlet published in 1743. Its long
title suggests its aim: *A Letter from the Revd. Mr. [John] Sergeant of
Stockbridge, to Dr. Colman of Boston; Containing Mr. Sergeant's Proposal of a More effectual Method for the Education of Indian Children;
to raise 'em if possible into a civil and industrious People; by introducing
the English Language Among Them; and thereby instilling in their
Minds and Hearts, with a More lasting Impression, the Principles of
Virtue and Piety.* Sergeant proposed to accomplish this in a school on

99

the Stockbridge Reservation where youths ten to twenty years old would board. Two masters would direct their duties: "One to take the oversight of Them in their Hours of *Labour,* and the other in their Hours of *Study;* and to have their time so *divided* between Study and Labour as to make one the *Diversion* of the other, that as little time as possible may be lost in Idleness." A farm attached to the institution would both provide the place to labor and sustain the scholars. Sergeant believed this new approach to Indian education, based on Irish charity schools, would succeed where other plans had failed. If this plan had been realized and elaborated, it would have provided a model Christian community in the wilderness, but Sergeant's death ended the experiment.

Rather than locating an establishment among the Indians as Sergeant had proposed, Eleazar Wheelock, the founder of Dartmouth, planted Moor's Charity School in the wilderness away from any savage influence. There he hoped to train young Indian boys in learning and industry and send them back to their tribes as missionaries. Girls were to be instructed in the "Female Part, as House-wives, School-instructresses, tayloresses, &c." to accompany the boys back to the tribe, where they would maintain a proper household for the Indian missionary so he would not relapse into savagery and where they would "recommend to the savages a more rational and decent manner of living. . . ." According to this plan the actual station in the field would be staffed by a man and wife who preached, taught school, farmed, and kept house. As such they would have been a model for Christian family life in the wilderness. Although the training program was of the new type, the end product was the model family idea, which resembled a prevalent form in colonial missionization.

Not until the nineteenth century did the model community plan come into its own in missionary work. When missionary Joseph Bullen of the New York Missionary Society returned from the Chickasaws he brought the request of the principal chief for farmers and mechanics to teach the tribe agriculture and trades. Since the Society believed in the importance of civilizing the Indians, it permitted Bullen to gather a company of twenty-two, including a saddler, a blacksmith, a shoemaker, with their families, as well as a farmer and a schoolteacher, who were willing to instruct the Indians. The Society resolved "that the formation of a small religious society of such characters among the Indians might be of great importance of subserving the interests of the Society." The plan was never realized for lack of funds.

Abortive as Bullen's efforts were, his example was not lost on Gideon Blackburn, who first developed the boarding school located within the Indian tribe. In the mid-1790s Blackburn, aware of previous mission failures, set about devising a plan that could combat "*ignorance, obstinancy,* and strong prejudices," without having the Indians "dogmatically instructed on the most exalted subjects that can occupy the mind of the most enlightened man." He soon concluded:

> I knew that the operations of God in the hearts of men were not confined to means. Yet even in religion cause and effect have been in the order of events without any deviation. I conceived it therefore indispensable to prepare the mind by the most simple ideas, and by a process which would associate civilization with religious instruction, and thus gradually prepare the rising race for the more sublime truths of religion, as they should be able to view them.

Thus the Indians, "if rightly managed," eventually would "become American Citizens, and a valuable part of the Union." The plan was based on a school because he believed "that after the habits are formed, the only way to reduce them is by the influence of the children." In the Tennessee Presbyterian's opinion, instructing the unsocialized children would "not only rescue the rising race from savage manners, but also . . . light up beacons, by which the parents might gradually be conducted into the same field of improvement." In essence this was the child-training theory upon which the model Zion was built.

Blackburn sought financial backing for his ideas in 1799, but his frontier presbytery was too poor to support the ambitious project he proposed. In 1803 he gained the funds from the Presbyterian General Assembly. In presenting his plan to accomplish a "revolution in the habits of the Cherokee nation," so strongly did he urge the necessity of thoroughly preparing the way for the Gospel by civilization, that the standing Committee on Missions stated definitely that the station was "intended as an introduction to the notice of the Indians, to conciliate their friendship, & to prepare the way for extensive usefulness among them at a future day." The Committee considered the whole affair an experiment. Eagerly and prayerfully Blackburn returned south. On his journey home he discussed his plans with President Jefferson and received letters of recommendation from the secretary of war. In October, 1803, he laid his plan before the Cherokee chiefs. After a few days of deliberation, they consented to his proposal and fixed a site for the school near the Hiwassee River in a part of the tribe most unlikely to be civilized.

Immediately Blackburn set about establishing the institution. In the spring of 1804 the school opened, and by the end of the first week twenty-one children were enrolled. Two buildings, the schoolhouse and the teacher's house, doubled for boys' and girls' sleeping quarters at night, with the schoolhouse serving as dining hall as well as its nominal function. To maintain steady attendance at his boarding school, he persuaded the chiefs to rule that any child leaving school without permission or remaining home beyond ten days after vacations forfeited the clothing given him by the mission. The chief of the child's district bound himself to return the delinquent's clothing to the school, or Blackburn had the privilege to deduct the clothing's value from such chief's share of the annuities.

Since in Blackburn's opinion success lay only in training children in white ways before savage habits formed, not an aspect of their small lives was to go unwatched and unchanged. "The mode of dieting, clothing, and instructing them, and even their recreations was important." For this reason he purchased all the table provisions and hired a cook who prepared the "victuals in American style." He furnished a large table around which the red scholars

> could decently take their seats; and after the master had looked up for a blessing, during which time they all devoutly attended, they were taught ettiquette [sic] of the table. It was indeed particularly pleasing to see how emulously they strove to excel, and how orderly they would wait for a dismission by the returning of thanks: A conduct which might put to blush many of our coxcomb would be infidels. . . .

Meals were regular, the diet wholesome (and "American"), and the preparations neat and clean in light of contemporary custom. The children were dressed in American clothes and cleanliness of person strongly encouraged. The school also furnished the blankets for the scholars to sleep on, because Blackburn discovered the use of beds was unknown to the tribe. To complete this process, each red scholar was given a name "thought proper," that is, an American name.

The school day was as strictly controlled as the environment. Early in the morning the children rose, prayed, and washed. School opened with scripture reading and public prayer, after which the children engaged in lessons. Breakfast interrupted their studies, and then an hour of recreation. At nine o'clock they returned to lessons for three hours, followed by a meal and two hours of play. Lessons then claimed their attention until evening. In the summer between sundown and dark and in the winter between dark and nine o'clock, the children said their spelling lessons. The long day closed with hymn singing and a prayer by the master. Just before going to bed, the children prayed upon their knees. During the instructional periods singing and lessons alternated to keep the "mind open to truth"—or perhaps awake. To develop proper study habits a prize was awarded at each public examination to the child exhibiting the greatest progress.

After three and a half years of work Blackburn concluded that his schools, for by then he had established a second, were no longer an experiment but successful proof of his plans for educating the savages. He no longer doubted "the strength of Indian genius, even in those parts of literature which do not depend on mechanism." In his plans he looked confidently to the future. If funds were available, his first school should become a center for higher learning, gathering scholars from smaller schools scattered about the Cherokee Nation. Such an institution would excite the small-school pupils to strive for advanced training, which in turn would fit them to assume leading roles in the tribe. When the scholar graduated from school he should be provided with a small library for further study. If funds were only available, enough Christian teachers could be hired to provide all the education desired and in "a few years would raise in the forests civilized families and magnificent Churches. . . ." At this stage of progress the tribe would assume the support of the schools. Funds were not available and these roseate dreams never materialized in Blackburn's time.

During the same period that Blackburn pursued his experiment, Joseph Badger instituted the first manual labor boarding school. That the Western Missionary Society established such a model community resulted from Badger's ultimatum: "the only condition, on which I was willing to enter the field of missions among the Wyandots, was, that domestic and civil improvements should be united with religious instructions." For the first time since Sergeant's plan, Badger's idea was "to unite religious and moral instruction, schooling of children, in the English language, and agriculture, so as to render them auxiliary to each other." As a result the station possessed, in addition to the usual school facilities and equipment, two teams of horses, two yokes of oxen, plows, chain, and laborers who instructed the Indians in fencing, plowing, raising corn and other grain, and building houses. The farm raised vegetables for the mission family and scholars and also served as a demonstration project to the Indians. The Society planned to add a blacksmith's shop and a horse mill to make the mission even more self-sufficient, but the Shawnee Prophet's hostility and the outbreak of the War of 1812 destroyed the station.

Blackburn's plan, and perhaps Badger's, influenced the American Board of Commissioners for Foreign Missions' first endeavor. Cyrus Kingsbury, the originator of the Board's enterprise among the Cherokees, claimed his plans were patterned "as to all its important parts" after Blackburn's in the tribe, but the emphasis on the model farm suggests Badger's influence. In extending to the Cherokees "the distinguished blessings which we enjoy," Kingsbury, like his Presbyterian predecessor in the tribe, believed no measure was "so likely to succeed, as to begin with the instruction of the rising generation."

In two articles in the *Panoplist* in the spring of 1816, Kingsbury outlined his proposals. In the first article, whose title—"What are the Motives Which Should Produce the Churches in the United States to Attempt the Conversion and Civilization of the Indians?"—reveals its contents, he prepared the American Board's supporters' minds for the new enterprise. He suggested in the second article, "Sketch of a Plan for Instructing the Indians," the general plans for his enterprise. He argued the feasibility of boarding schools located inside the tribe. If these institutions were taught on the Lancastrian plan, one school would suffice for "several hundreds of children." In the classroom the Indian youths would learn the "rudiments of the English language, and the branches of learning usually taught in common English schools." Adjacent to the school were to be a workhouse, a large garden, and fields, where the children "might occasionally be instructed in the most useful mechanical arts, and in agriculture. This will afford them a pleasant and profitable amusement, during a part of the time when they are out of school." The teachers and farmers at these stations, with their families, would be a model of Christian home life. Kingsbury well realized the greater expense of these establishments compared to the model family type, but thought within a few years the children could do much to support themselves.

Soon after the publication of these articles, the Board asked Kingsbury to begin a Cherokee mission. On his way south Kingsbury visited Washington, D.C., and related his plans to the Secretary of War. The President authorized the Cherokee agent to erect a comfortable schoolhouse, a teacher's house, and a boarding house, and to furnish two hoes and six axes to aid in introducing civilization to the pupils. Furthermore, he promised a loom, six spinning wheels, and six pairs of cards whenever a female teacher was hired to teach the girls how to use those implements.

After discussions with the Cherokee chiefs and influential Tennesseans, Kingsbury elaborated and systematized his plans for the station. Since the aim of the establishment was to make the native children "useful citizens, and pious Christians," the instructors must "form them to habits of industry, and . . . give them a competent knowledge of the economy of civilized life," as well as a common English education to accomplish these aims successfully.

The children should be removed as much as possible from the society of the natives, and placed where they would have the influence of example, as well as precept. This can only be done by forming the school into one great missionary family where they would be boarded by the Missionary and teachers, be entirely under their direction and have pious[,] orderly & industrious example constantly before them.

To the impecunious missionary society, financing was always important. The resourceful Kingsbury pointed out that if the Board furnished the tools and horses to work the free land and employed the students to do much of the work, then the establishment would be self-sustaining. All expenditures for stock and equipment would increase the value of the station. In addition it would afford every facility to instruct the children in agriculture, "and give them habits of industry, in such a way as directly benefit [sic] the institution."

The ground plan of Brainerd, as the station was named, exemplified in wood the abstractions of Kingsbury. Over thirty buildings were required to shelter its many functions. In the center was the two-story mission house occupied by the superintendent and the other missionaries. Behind it was the dining hall and the kitchen and flanking it was the girls' schoolhouse. On the edge of the clearing stood the boys' school, which was capable of holding one hundred scholars; on the Sabbath it doubled as a church. At the other end of the lane on which the buildings stood was the grist mill and a sawmill. In between, other buildings served as barns, storehouses, and dwellings for the laborers and students. Surrounding the little community were a garden, an orchard, and several cleared fields, mostly fenced, constituting in all about fifty acres. Though small in extent, the sight of the little community, as one observer expressed it,

> *being in the midst of a wilderness, whose deep forests appear on every side, presents to the beholder a scene of cultivation and of active and cheerful life, which cannot but inspire him with pleasure. To the Christian, who contemplates the moral wilderness by which it is surrounded, it presents a prospect more delightful than tongue can express.*

Here at last were realized all the principles of the manual labor boarding school. The institution was a self-contained community in the wilderness. The children were removed from their parents into a totally controlled environment. This physical separation deemed so essential here is also demonstrated in other stations in even so small an item as a fence to keep the non-scholars out of the scholars' play yard in order to avoid contamination by savage customs. The varied instruction required a large number of laborers who exemplified Christian and civilized life in the controlled environment. The products of student labor were both economically rewarding to the society and educationally beneficial to the child. The parents were attracted to view the establishment by their offsprings' presence and they too learned by the demonstration project. Yet the school could not be located too near the Indians' habitations for fear of contamination; instead the adults must travel to the controlled environment.

A minister jubilantly declared that the plan had been "visibly owned by the Holy Ghost," and the new national missionary societies of the various denominations rapidly adopted the model community in hope of reaping the aboriginal fields that had lain barren so long. So sure were the missionaries and their patrons of the merits of the manual labor boarding school that one society in 1823 proclaimed the results of the experiment before it was fairly tried: "that the American Savage is capable of being both civilized and Christianized, can no longer be questioned. The problem is already solved. Successful experiment has placed the subject beyond doubt." Further impetus was given the movement by the federal government's espousal of the method, backed by assistance from the funds appropriated annually since 1819 for civilizing the Indians. This financial blessing, plus the enthusiasm of the missionary directors, meant most of the schools founded in the 1820s were of the new type, but size and staff varied considerably among them. For example, in 1828, forty mission schools, or almost all those in operation, received government aid. The largest establishment had twenty-seven members, but several were staffed by one person or a single family.

In terms of the mental climate of the period, it is easy to understand the mission societies' optimism. At last they thought they had found a certain method of accomplishing their chief end—the propagation of the Gospel. That this was their task as they conceived it rested upon the basic Protestant tenet of the acceptance of the Bible as the sole standard of faith. To the Gospel was ascribed "a miraculous power of producing conversion which is inherent in the word." But was no human agency necessary? In the missionary directors' opinion the task's accomplishment among frontier *white* settlements destitute of religion reduced simply to collecting sufficient funds to have Bibles printed, distributed, and expounded. But what was needed for the savage? The Word could be conveyed by preaching, but in that situation the listener depended upon the authority of the speaker. Should not the convert be able to determine for himself matters of doctrine by reference to the Supreme Source as revealed in the Holy Scriptures? Was not literacy required and did not this necessitate the founding of schools? Furthermore, did not the Indians need an economic system that would support the requisite schools and churches? In short, was not civilization as well as religion necessary to the establishment of scriptural self-propagating Christianity? As one writer said:

the Gospel, plain and simple as it is, and fitted by its nature for what it was designed to effect, requires an intellect above that of a savage to comprehend. Nor is it at all to the dishonor of our holy faith that such men must be taught a previous lesson, and first of all be instructed in the emollient arts of life.

In fact, in viewing the actual operations of the manual labor boarding school, we have seen civilization inextricably combined with Christianity in every attempt. The question now becomes: what meaning did the words "civilization" and "Christianity" possess in the minds of the missionaries and their supporters in the early nineteenth century that inevitably made them link the two concepts together? An answer to this question will reveal the assumptions that determined the form of the manual labor school.

Civilization as conceived in this period meant an upward unilinear development of human society and America was its highest incarnation. The concept was composed of a complex of related ideas: progress, fundamental law, the free and responsible individual, manifest destiny, and faith in America as the best embodiment of civilization in the world's history. To the missionaries as to most Americans, Protestantism was an inseparable component of the whole idea of civilization.

As the missionary shared his fellow countrymen's evaluation of American civilization, so he shared their image of the Indian. That nineteenth-century Americans could not observe the aborigine without measuring him against their own society has been demonstrated by Roy Harvey Pearce in his book *The Savages of America*. A certain type of cultural relativity and moral absolutism combined in this view to show that though white and red man were of the same biological mold, the Indian possessed customs that fitted him perfectly to his level of development in the history of man, but the level was far inferior to that of the white European. The savage was the zero point of human society. As Pearce remarks,

One would thus be evaluating not so much the qualities of an individual as those of a society; and one would be placing that society in relation to one's own in such a way that history, and the idea of progress which gave meaning to history, would solve the problem of evaluation. The idea of history made it possible fully to comprehend the culture earlier as morally inferior. . . .

Therefore, seemingly objective observations on Indian character were always normative analyses of what the Indian should be in terms of nineteenth-century American society. Persons engaged in the missionary movement particularly viewed the objects of their benevolence in this manner, because moral evaluation was their stock in trade.

Thus the concept of civilization both set the goal and explained the object of benevolence, for the missionary was, of course, a member of his culture, holding its basic values and attributes in common with his fellow participants. Like other Americans he dressed, possessed but one wife, believed in abstract justice, ate certain foods in certain ways, and favored a specific economic system. Yet as one anthropologist has pointed out, missionaries "represent a subculture within western culture," for they "stress theology and the moral taboos more than their fellow-countrymen." They adhered more rigorously to the sexual code, were more honest (or were supposed to be), propounded the theological system more seriously, and were intensely concerned with the minor taboos of our culture, tobacco, drink, and the verbal prohibitions against obscenity, profanity, and blasphemy. As convinced adherents of their culture, they imparted literacy, science, a certain technology, and the other facets of white life in the form of school curricula, adult instruction, and other conscious methods. They also held "certain basic attitudes which [were] not part of the essential ethic of Christianity or the useful cultural technologies" which they transmitted. "These attitudes manifested themselves in unsystematized but nevertheless consistent reactions to situations." Some of these behavioral patterns are the reaction to the exposure of the human body, open discussion of sexual matters, and practice of certain rituals of social intercourse. Such behavior frequently reflected certain social class values in the culture, for example, attitudes on drinking and profanity. Missionaries were representatives of middle-class society. To utilize the anthropologist's summary, "a missionary [was] thus a member of his society, characterized by the culture of his society, and differing only from other members of his society by emphasis on particular aspects of his culture."

For all these reasons Christianity and civilization were unified in the minds of the missionaries, and the version of their culture which they propagated may be called, as some termed it, "Christian Civilization." The only good Indian was a carbon copy of a good white man, or as a Methodist missionary wrote, "in school and in the field as well as in the kitchen, our aim was to teach the Indians to live like white people." In spite of varying emphases in missionary work, the future Indian utopia envisaged by the directors of the societies was the same—a mirror of their world. Such was the vision of the Board of Managers of the United Foreign Missionary Society.

Let then, missionary institutions, established to convey to them the benefits of civilization and the blessings of Christianity, be efficiently supported; and, with cheering hope, you may look forward to the period when the savage shall be converted into the citizen; when the hunter shall be transformed into the mechanic; when the farm, the work shop, the Schoolhouse, and the Church shall adorn every Indian village; when the fruits of Industry, good order, and sound morals, shall bless every Indian dwelling; and when, throughout the vast range of country from the Mississippi to the Pacific, the red man and the white man shall everywhere be found, mingling in the same benevolent and friendly feelings, fellow citizens of the same civil and religious community, and fellow-heirs to a glorious inheritance in the kingdom of Immanuel.

Thus both Indian institutions and Indian "character" had to be transformed. The institutions needed by the Indians were just those already possessed by Americans. As a Presbyterian missionary remarked, "It is to make these [savage] abodes of ignorance and degradation, as happy, as gladsome, as the happiest and most gladsome village in our peaceful land." The arrogant savage was to be turned into a man of humility who implicitly believed "industry is good, honesty is essential, punctuality is important, sobriety is essential. . . ." This new man abhorred idleness and considered labor good for the body and "not unprofitable to the spirit." The Christian Indian was to manifest "tenderness of conscience, a docility, and a desire for further instruction" in the great mysteries. Many missionaries also wanted him to show "Yankee enterprise—go ahead determination."

What was the method required to achieve these goals? If a savage merely lacked knowledge of the more advanced condition to which human society had evolved, then a missionary had but to point out the way and the savage would adopt it. Field work, then, was a simple matter of instruction to be quickly accomplished—if the Indian, like the white man, was rational. Fundamental to this idea was a belief in the similarity of "human nature" along the evolutionary continuum of human society. Not thinking in terms of cultures as social scientists do today, but in terms of "human nature," the missionaries and their patrons assumed the same system of basic values was held by savage and civilized man alike. In the missionaries' eyes any right-thinking savage should be able to recognize the superiority of Christian civilization when shown him. Thus, in regard to secular knowledge, the New York Missionary Society Directors instructed their laborers among the Tuscaroras to "persuade" that tribe "by every rational motive to the practice of civilization, & to relish the enjoyments of domestic society" by calling to their attention that the whites increased in population because they farmed.

This argument will operate on the feelings of the patriotic Indian, and will serve to establish with convictive energy the arguments adduced from self-interest, so clearly evinced in the diminution of bodily fatigue, in the alleviation of mental anxiety, & improvements of domestic comforts & will strengthen & confirm the more powerful & weighty motives derived from the obligations of Religion.

Likewise with Christianity, since Protestantism embraced the highest evolution of morals, the missionary had only to explain its superiority over savage degradation to secure mass conversion. Since conversion to Christ and civilization was conceived simply as an instructional problem, schools were established. There the Indians would be "persuaded" by "right reason" to adopt the white religion and ways, and would learn how to pray, farm, and behave. Such plans meant, of course, a large establishment to show the full complexities of American life. In effect, they were model communities which sought to catch the children before native custom did and to serve as demonstration projects for the adult Indians.

Not only were the goals of mission societies prescribed by the sponsoring civilization, which is only to be expected, but even the method used to achieve these aims developed in line with a preconceived image of the Indian rather than through field experience. In other words, the evolution of the manual labor boarding school was determined less by the second party in the contract situation than by the stereotypes prevalent among the white population at that time. Reality on the frontier, as in the East, was only seen through the perceptual framework of the culture. The activities of missionaries were determined in main outline before they ever arrived in the wilderness.

★ 8 ★

THE EDUCATED WOMAN IN AMERICA:
CATHARINE BEECHER AND MARGARET FULLER
Barbara M. Cross

Women in America have never had equal educational opportunities with men. In colonial times elementary education for girls was often available in the "dame schools" and other local private institutions. It was considered good for young ladies to learn to read and write, but they needed no formal instruction beyond these primary skills. Girls were not admitted to the colonial grammar schools that prepared boys for college, but were often allowed to attend the private academies that sprang up early in the nineteenth century. Then a few secondary schools for women were established and a few colleges began to admit females. At first the colleges that welcomed women set up separate courses, but occasionally women were permitted to take the same classes as men and to qualify for the bachelor of arts degree.

In view of the limited opportunities for advanced schooling, it comes as no surprise that most of the highly educated women of the times were taught by tutors, friends, or family at home. Whether educated at home or at school, they faced a difficult question: what were they trained to do? What social role would the educated women fill? In this essay Barbara Cross describes the paths followed by two American women of the nineteenth century, Catharine Beecher (1800–1878) and Margaret Fuller (1810–1850). Other works on women's education are Mabel Newcomer, *A Century of Higher Education for American Women* (New York: Harper & Bros., 1959), and Thomas Woody, *A His-*

tory of Women's Education in the United States, 2 vols. (New York: Science Press, 1929).

Catharine Beecher was . . . the oldest and favorite child in a family of thirteen; she enjoyed the publicity and importance accorded a minister's daughter. During her childhood she saw her father, Lyman Beecher, become famous as a revivalist and preacher. His "constant companion," she considered him her "playmate" and counted on his indulgence. She was poetess and dramatist for the family; her role was to make them laugh and to show her pluckiness when her father swung her out of an attic window or suddenly pushed her head into a basin of water. The Litchfield school she attended did not count for much in the nervous, frisky household, where Lyman Beecher frolicked, fiddled, danced in his stocking feet, and won souls for the Gospel; where his beloved wife, Roxanne, painted flamboyant flowers on her carpet, read Maria Edgeworth, Sir Walter Scott, and *The Christian Observer,* and was adored as the sole example of "disinterested benevolence" her husband had ever known; and where Catharine "did little else but play." As Catharine grew older, she and her mother shared her father's "elevated thoughts" on the unique Edwardsian virtue of benevolence and on the duties of temperance, Bible reading, conversion, and missions. If she was not pretty, she impressed the family with her cocky wit and compelled admiration even if she did not always inspire love.

But death interrupted and deflected her jauntiness. When Catharine was sixteen, her mother died, and the young girl, left to a "dark and dubious night," assumed the responsibilities of womanhood. She made the clothes for the younger children; prepared the doughnuts, grog, and all the "fixings" for the minister's wood-spell; and composed the stiff letter with which the children greeted their elegant new stepmother a year later. So the young Catharine adjusted to her loss through labor and responsibility; she kept her intimacy with her father, and she regained her high spirits. When she was eighteen, the "soft and perfumed air" around Boston made her so "*mad* with delight" that she "climbed on the rocks and *shouted* for joy"; at the age of twenty-one, she was exchanging "queer" letters, full of "spunk," with a young Yale professor, Alexander Metcalf Fisher. In 1822 an engagement was arranged, to Lyman Beecher's glee, and Catharine saw herself headed for an honored domesticity as the wife of "the greatest mathematician and philosopher in the country!"

As she stood on the verge of a new life, however, Catharine was again balked by death. In 1823 her fiancé was killed in a shipwreck. Neither Catharine nor her father could find evidence that Fisher had known saving grace; and Catharine faced a grim, more final loneliness, as she arraigned her father's God and prepared herself for spinsterhood. The Calvinist economy made the death appear as a providential judgment upon her happiness and as a tocsin for change. "I am not what I was," she wrote accurately; "I never shall be again." She turned her liveliness to habits of command; people no longer associated her with "a constant stream of mirthfulness." Yet, even as an old lady, she kept the childish corkscrew curls that incongruously framed her heavy features and her sallow skin. A vociferous and bossy guest, bent upon a public service of impersonal benevolence, she lived chiefly in other people's houses. She worked incessantly, haranguing, planning, repeating herself, spending her income on her philanthropic projects, fighting for other women luckier than herself. Only periodic breakdowns, when the performance of any duty brought "extreme pain and such confusion of thought as seemed like insanity," interrupted her resolute service. She elected the costly virtue of renunciation, doing always "what, as to personal taste, I least wished to do." Like her father, who published his letters to his bereaved daughter as a model of New England divinity, Catharine plucked her experience for the instruction of others. As she shoved privacy and joy behind her, she set herself, her loss, and her convictions upon the public stage; in deliberate repudiation of the personal, she made her memories serve her cause and turned her nostalgia into a program for the nation.

So Catharine Beecher set about finding the widest "sphere of influence" available to a single woman. In 1824 she opened a girls' school in Hartford, which austerely limited its curriculum to "the most necessary parts of education" and charged extra fees for music and dancing. Though the school grew rapidly, by 1832 Catharine was glad to join her family in a move to Cincinnati, where her father hoped to build a bulwark of evangelical Protestantism and where she headed the Western Female Institute. But she soon went after bigger game. To her father and to herself, Fisher's death finally seemed a sign that she had been reserved for some special mission, and she devised a strenuous gospel from the past she could never recover. Though the process of moral publicity emptied the past of its insouciance and warmth, she fastened the more fiercely upon her useful memories. Echoing her father's note of apocalyptic urgency, she called upon American women to save their nation and the world by honoring their peculiar womanly duties as nurses, teachers, and mothers. Her program sprang from indignation at a society so awry that "to be the nurse of young children, a cook, or a housemaid is regarded as the last and lowest resort of poverty"; and she tartly recalled her readers to the era when women were judged by their "faculty" and intuitively knew the cheapest, healthiest, and tastiest foods.

Miss Beecher had circulated a questionnaire among middle-class wives, and the responses convinced her that most of them suffered from invalidism, spasms, backache, or neurasthenia. She found that the agonies of childbirth, nursing, and motherhood made women despair at the birth and marriage of daughters; and she worked to replace the languishing, corseted lady of wealth, the worn, extravagant housewife, and the "fainting, weeping, vapid, pretty plaything" of society with an energetic and enlightened figure, clad "in the panoply of Heaven and sending the thrill of benevolence through a thousand youthful hearts." Her concern was always the restitution of a home where work, health, and frugality ensured immediate and eternal happiness and where family comforts were never sacrificed to elegance, nor space for kitchens and nurseries to "expensive piazzas." She demanded that the dark, isolated kitchen be replaced by a large sunny room, where both cooking and family life could be enjoyed and where women might be dressed gracefully for both housework and society. In her household blueprints, the entire first floor was given over to the "Family Room" and the "Home Room," while parlor and library were squeezed together on the second floor. Since her idyll of domestic life could not accommodate "coarse and vulgar" immigrant servants, who lived in the cellar and slept in the attic, who ruined food in the kitchen and children in the nursery, she tried to get such strangers out of the home and to replace them with diligent children and coping wives.

Imbuing home and mother with a holiness that would have appalled her Presbyterian father and her Puritan ancestors, Catharine Beecher helped her century invest the more matter-of-fact domesticity of the past with a sacred terror. For though Cotton Mather, Jonathan Edwards, and Lyman Beecher had taken their duties as heads of households seriously, they had characteristically thought in terms of family government, not family beatitude. Only in the nineteenth century—in the rhetoric of gift books and best sellers like *The Mother at Home*, in popular manuals on home building like Andrew Jackson Downing's *Architecture of Country Houses*, in the arguments of ministers like Horace Bushnell and educators like Catharine Beecher—did the family emerge as the *imago dei*. To Catharine Beecher, the family seemed the incarnation and the seedbed of Christian virtue. For the family was founded on the law of sacrifice, and within its economy the wife and mother engaged in the continual humiliation, service, and selfless love that had constituted Christ's work and command. Accepting the lowliest, least prestigious tasks—serving the weak, the ill, and the young—woman made her life an imitation of Christ: "Her grand mission is self-denial." For the many Americans instructed in New England Calvinism, the injunction possessed an august exigency; from the time of Jonathan Edwards, Presbyterian and Congregational theologians had discovered in such selfless benevolence the distinguishing mark of the elect. Though educators like Mary Lyon and Emma Willard shared her conviction that woman's profession was one of service, only Catharine Beecher incorporated this imperial vision of woman's role into books of recipes, household hints, and physiology.

Miss Beecher based her grand claims for the wife and mother upon the psychology of the Scottish common-sense realists, which dominated nineteenth-century American texts in moral and mental philosophy and which taught that childhood associations between particular sensations and the experience of pleasure or pain largely determine character. Like Horace Bushnell, Horace Mann, and the authors of many best sellers on child care, Miss Beecher announced the power of nurture, which could make "the ill-natured amiable, the selfish regardful of the feelings and rights of others, the obstinate yielding and docile." She joined this doctrine of childhood plasticity to other theories which stressed the supreme powers of the mother but which assumed that these powers were based upon physiology. All future "feelings, thoughts, and volitions" were determined by the food particles that passed through children's brains. Able to regulate the air, the clothing, the food, and the hours of the family, the mother was "sovereign of an empire." Whether their children went west to farm or cityward to prosper, the many readers of Miss Beecher's books could comfort themselves with the thought that no child would ever lose the imprint of his mother's enlightened goodness. Thus the sanctification of the bourgeois home served a nation of wanderers. In the 1830s, de Tocqueville noted that Americans had "no adolescence," since "at the close of boyhood the man appears and begins to trace out his own fate." The confident love of mothers who always knew the "right thing" to do could give a sense of stability to children soon on the move; and in the loneliness of their freedom, these boy-men might find security and constraint in the memory of their mothers' tireless sacrifices.

Miss Beecher spoke, too, to the dread and grief of bereaved parents in a time of high infant mortality. The literature of the gift annuals might assuage the grief through the rhetoric and iconography of sentiment, but Miss Beecher set about to eradicate the dread through know-how. *Hearth and Home*, *Physiology and Calisthenics*, and *The American Woman's Home* bristled with moralized information that could turn the diffident housewife into a formidable authority. The popularity of the books suggests that there had been some lapse in the training of the young and that faced with arranging *petits soupers* for hundreds, with Irish servants, and with the strangeness of the city or frontier, young wives were both disturbed and baffled. Printed substitutes for domestic apprenticeship, the books tutored women in a new self-consciousness. Graphically exposing the structure of the body—"the twenty-eight miles of perspiration tubes," the "delicate and sensitive parts" made ulcerous by corsets, the "poisonous effluvia" of the skin—they described a world so scary that the guardian woman, standing between her brood and insanity, sickness, or death, was indeed awful and resplendent. Small bedrooms and airtight stoves were "poisoning more than one-half of the nation"; excessive study, which drew the blood from the organs, was creating mentally disturbed children; babies were being killed by medicine and ignorant nurses. Patently the housekeeper mattered: it was up to her to provide the "hogshead of pure air every hour" that would save her family from "sleeplessness, nausea, apoplexy, and even death"; to ensure that teething infants escaped convulsions; and at the same time—though thus constantly threatened by ruin and mortality—to preserve her "good temper." For the Christian household had to be not only efficient but regenerative as well.

118

Catharine Beecher spent the income from her books on educational projects that would implement her convictions. Certain that the former schoolteacher made the best wife, she worked to establish colleges where women could be trained for their intricate duties as nurses, housekeepers, and teachers. Through the Board of National Popular Education, founded in 1846, and the American Woman's Educational Association, founded in 1852, she collected Eastern funds with which to send to the West teachers armed with her own *domestic economy*. She founded a permanent college in Milwaukee and two short-lived institutions in Iowa and Illinois. With shrewd ardor she fought for higher pay for teachers, institutional acknowledgment of the "discipline" of domestic economy, and recognition that society had to honor woman's "profession" if women were to do their work without humiliation and bitterness.

Catharine Beecher's books on domestic duties went through many editions. Other writers of best sellers shared her faith in the saving power of a mother's love; the popular gift books continually rhapsodized over motherhood. But Miss Beecher provided sentiment with a schedule, a program, and a confident self-righteousness. Erudite and handy, her American woman would know "how dampers and air-boxes should be placed and regulated, how to prevent or remedy gas escapes," and how to manage "ball corks and high and low pressure on water pipes." With such knowledge and through unflagging service, women would redeem the family and finally institute a "Pink and White Tyranny more stringent than any earthly thralldom." Without effusing over "the heart," Catharine Beecher defined a woman's love as the care of others and assigned her to a vigilant and informed protectiveness. Refusing to discount any necessary work as mere drudgery, she concerned herself with the lives the majority of women were called upon to lead and attempted to convert the fearful wife or mother into a learned and faithful steward of many talents.

But though Miss Beecher's books were read, female institutes continued to offer numerous courses in "elegant accomplishments," and schools for domestic science and teacher training were not widely established until the twentieth century. Harriet Beecher Stowe's Little Eva, not George Eliot's Mrs. Poyser, held the American imagination. Forced to witness the irrelevant, nerve-racking curricula of Smith and Vassar and the pointless agitation of suffragettes, Catharine Beecher kept on fighting; and at the age of seventy-eight, in the year of her death, she lectured to Elmira College students on "The Adaptation of Woman's Education to Home Life."

Even in her own time, Catharine Beecher's ideal seemed restrictive and ignominious to younger women raised in different traditions. Though Margaret Fuller, ten years Miss Beecher's junior, briefly deplored stale air and corsets, such matters bored her. Like the young men with whom she conversed and corresponded, Margaret Fuller was born "with a knife" in her brain, a "tendency to introversion, self-dissection, the anatomizing of motives." Her critique struck always inward; she lived in the glare of analysis, setting before herself and her small self-conscious circle the instructive mystery of feminine genius. "We have had no woman," Bronson Alcott testified, "approaching so near our conception of the ideal woman as herself." The role was taxing and was itself a kind of career. So for her contemporaries and for the future, Margaret Fuller's writings counted less than her personality, which she ruthlessly probed, arraigned, and publicized.

For Margaret Fuller, the first step in education was the achievement of self-knowledge. She maintained that the classical education which her father had forced upon her as a child had only muffled her true self "under the thick curtain of available intellect," and throughout her life she resented the nightly recitations to him, which had left her sleepless and hallucinatory. If as an adult she labored at books as hard as he could have wished, she did not settle for erudition alone but avidly pursued the secret of herself—her motives, her grandeur, her privation. Upon consideration, she found no intellect in New England equal to her own; yet, at the age of thirty-six, she delighted in being called "a fool, little girl," by her elusive beloved, James Nathan. A troubled, ambiguous knowledge of herself informed her sense of the feminine, and her severe perceptions made the genial generalizations of an earlier generation seem glib.

Margaret Fuller found the ideal of sacrifice that had inspired Catharine Beecher too constraining to be moral. "I have been too much absorbed today by others," she complained at Brook Farm. "It has almost made me sick." She saw in renunciation not a "piercing virtue" but a dreary waste; a middle-aged woman who had spent her maturity caring

120

for her decrepit mother depressed her as a "bloodless effigy of humanity." She demanded total fulfillment, though she—who had early decided her lot was to be "bright and ugly"—knew at first hand how hard it was to achieve such fulfillment. Her habit of "incessantly opening and shutting her eyelids," her nasal voice, her "arching and undulating neck" repelled acquaintances; yet she requisitioned deference and craved love. Somehow the "wild beasts and reptiles" of her "great nature"—the childishness and the arrogance—had to be tamed. Like Catharine Beecher, she assumed that intellectual activity was at odds with true femininity: the "Woman in me," she decided, "kneels and weeps in tender rapture; the Man in me rushes forth but only to be baffled." So she required integrity and knew division, until life seemed to her a process of mutilation. "A tone of sadness was in her voice like the wail of the ocean," Emerson recorded. "And from my earliest acquaintance, I had a feeling as if someone cried *Stand from under!*"

Rejecting the Christian terminology by which Catharine Beecher, Mary Lyon, and Lydia Sigourney had defined the ideal woman, refusing to see with "common womanly eyes," Margaret Fuller elected the role of genius and sibyl; and with all her harsh, nervous flamboyance, she set out to be the American Corinne. Still, she found herself sick to faintness at the sight of the savage bosom of Michelangelo's sibyl and knew it was an evil fate to have "a man's ambition" and a woman's heart. Desperate for the tenderness she knew she repelled, she accepted her exclusion from the usual woman's lot with an extravagant and bitter pride. The depressions and three-week migraine headaches seemed the price of her genius, the exactions of her betrayed sexuality. "This ache is like a bodily wound. . . . When I rise into one of those rapturous moods of thought . . . my wound opens again."

A small group of New England intellectuals offered her the categories and attitudes that enabled her partially to order her divided nature. Emerson first awakened her to the "inward life," and with him and the "stiff, heady, and rebellious band" that gathered around him, she found a way to be. She joined Alcott, Emerson, Thoreau, the Ripleys, Theodore Parker, and Frederic Hedge in an ardent revolt against everything that limited the human spirit. Though they did not consider themselves a party, to their enemies and to posterity they were transcendentalists; they shared the certainty that man's greatness outpaced his history and that once he was transfigured by a divine quickening, he would be free.

Their vague and lofty presumptions, their exacting pieties, their watchful intimacies appealed to Margaret. "I wish, I long to be human," she announced to James Nathan, "but divinely human." In the dedication of these "fanatics in freedom," she found a vocation for herself and for all those worthy of being women. Though "blighted without," she had found "all being" at the center of herself; the inner world, with its majestic simplicity, was the only thing that counted. Writing to Channing from Europe, Margaret did not bore him with descriptions of famous people and "magnificent shows." "All these things are only to me an illuminated margin on the text of my inward life. I like only what little I find that is transcendently good."

For the "bright and ugly" young girl, the high-minded obliviousness of the transcendentalists provided a certain security; yet their resolute spirituality could be harassing. The transcendentalist genius could not brook drudgery, and Margaret saw the "low neutralizing cares" of maternity, babies, and housekeeping as impertinences to the spirit. At first she dismayed Emerson by making him laugh at her satiric gossip; but she learned the high transcendentalist note, and her comic bent was duly curbed to New England's willed and censorious innocence. "I look to Concord as my Lethe and Ennoe after this Purgatory of distracting petty tasks," she wrote to Emerson after the failure of Alcott's experimental school, where she had been teaching; "I am sure you will purify and strengthen me to enter the Paradise of thought once more." Accountable for high seriousness, for solitary joys, and for penetrating originality, the transcendentalists checked up on themselves and on each other. In 1843 Emerson was gratified to discover that Margaret had risen to a visibly "higher state" since their last meeting; she, on the other hand, accused him of being always "on stilts." There were many pitfalls: Margaret felt guilty for her chronic apathy toward spiritual subjects; yet she had to guard against the "intoxication" of Emerson's presence, which made her giddy and dependent.

Margaret Fuller began her career as disciple of the transcendentalists' strenuous idealism, and in 1844 she set forth her program for women in *Man and Woman: The Great Lawsuit*. She had found that her own law was "incapable of a charter," and she urged her sex to a similar emancipation. Her fundamental argument was that every conventional limitation upon woman betrayed her, since spirit knew no sex. Woman could learn her sacred independence and develop her latent powers only in liberty. The "weakening habit" of dependence had to be broken, for it had led to an "excessive devotion," which destroyed love and degraded marriage. If a wife was subordinate to her husband, her slavery would twist the lives of both. At present, there was "no Woman, only an overgrown child." The privileges granted women were insults, and their powers were corrupting. By controlling daily comforts, by relentless chattering, by exploiting the weapons of the servile—"cunning, blandishment, and unreasonable emotion"—women could subjugate their husbands. But Margaret Fuller's long exposure to her own buried motives made her mistrust the gentility of a "Pink and White Tyranny."

Though the popular literature of the time celebrated the sanctity of the family, Margaret Fuller described the bourgeois household as bleak and dreary. She saw desperate "good wives" trying to escape their boredom and their families by attending "balls, theaters, meetings for promoting missions, and revival meetings." Convinced that the primary crime was interfering with the flow of creative energy, she announced that the central evil of her society was its sexual code. Many were forced to celibacy; yet she found spinsters and bachelors repulsive, "inhuman and inhumane." Taught that passion was revolting and that their husbands' lust had to be quickly gratified, young women inevitably became disturbed and squeamish wives. The women of genius—a Mary Wollstonecraft or a George Sand—were turned into outlaws by society's restrictive sexual code, but Margaret Fuller saw George Sand's many love affairs as the necessary expression of her great nature. Her attack was radical and arrogant, the work of one who could announce that she did "not believe in society." Secure in the queer high freedom of mid-nineteenth-century New England, she—unlike Catharine Beecher and M. Carey Thomas—dared relate woman's happiness to her sexual fulfillment.

While Catharine Beecher began her analysis with woman in society, Margaret Fuller started with an antecedent, prescriptive meeting between the individual spirit and the Muse. Woman's proper education began with a return to her original freedom. Only in separation could she recover her relationship to the sacred central energy from which her obligations sprang. Appropriating Emerson's vision of true manhood, Margaret made a feminist war cry of it; woman, like man, was the "channel through which heaven flows to earth," and she had only to claim her privileges. The encounter with the Muse, like antinomian faith, freed the initiate from bondage to convention. By hastily assuming the role of wife, housekeeper, teacher, or nurse, woman betrayed the freewheeling divinity that was the source of true life. The primary duty of women was to attune themselves to the discoveries of solitude; then "let them be sea-captains."

All Margaret Fuller's pedagogical theories sprang from her faith in the freed intelligence. Though she read "at a rate like Gibbon's," though she mailed Emerson more volumes than he bothered to unwrap, she saw her studies only as a means to becoming an "*Original Genie.*" For children, she recommended an education that followed, rather than preceded, their experience. Rather than being moralized or "monotonously tender," children's books should present the facts of history and nature with provocative directness, thus instilling in their readers a sense of "vast mysteries." Memorization and too much reading hindered the emergence of the passionate individuality that was each child's birthright.

Harassed throughout her life by the necessity of earning money, Margaret Fuller for a time, and with some reluctance, tried out her theories in the classroom. She taught languages at Alcott's Temple School and in 1837 became a principal teacher at the experimental Greene Street School in Providence, where she omitted many things customarily thought indispensable in education but slowly taught her sixty pupils to walk in "new paths." She insisted that her students "*talk* as well as *recite*," puzzled them with a definition of poetry full of terms like "imagination" and "ideality," cut them "up into bits," scared, perplexed, and inspired them. Yet despite her students' worship, she hated the schoolroom, which made her feel "vulgarized, profaned, forsaken"; and despite her need for money, she quit after a year and a half. "I do not wish to teach again," she wrote to Channing.

Teaching had distracted Margaret from her primary duty of self-education, and her next occupation joined more closely her inner and her public callings. For the transcendentalists, the central ordeal was not parenthood, childhood, marriage, or education, but friendship, which made even the language of love seem "suspicious and common." The subject was obsessive for them all, and throughout the 1840s Emerson and Margaret made the concept an occasion for inquisition. Both knew how precious and exacerbating the relationship was. "The other night I found myself wishing to die because I had friends," Emerson wrote. Yet only the meetings between friends could bring a fleeting illumination and a brief release from solitude; marriage reduced the Elysian tables of friendship to fragmentary confidences "not worth picking up." The delicate equipoise of friendship proved the soul. Perhaps Margaret was too importunate; perhaps Emerson was disabled by his "porcupine impossibility of contact with men." Margaret accused him of turning their friendship into "trade." But neither would accept defeat. "I am no usurper," Margaret protested; "I ask only my own inheritance." In 1841 Emerson analyzed the austere offices of friendship in the *Dial*. "The solidest thing we know," friendship thrives where there is no "touching and clawing" but only the stark and sacred election of soul by soul. Friendship requires a prickly autonomy, and it does not bend to infirmities. "It treats its object as a god, that it may deify both." It was as the friend of chosen men and women that Margaret Fuller played her part and made her living in the Boston-Concord world. Presumptuous, rude, needy, she found a critical discipline in the role.

By common testimony, Margaret Fuller had an oddly magnetic power; younger women revered her and told her "the most jealously guarded secrets of their lives" with an alacrity that irritated husbands like Hawthorne and Greeley. Sophia Peabody Hawthorne addressed her, in a series of sonnets, as "A Priestess of the Temple Not Made with Human Hands." Elizabeth Peabody kept a journal on her; Anna Ward "idolized" her. What Margaret Fuller offered the women who clustered about her was a stern lucidity. She did not traffic in the conventions that made Sophia Hawthorne a "dove" to her Nathaniel; she instructed the most benevolent of her friends with scathing candor. Thus she informed the philanthropic and good-hearted Elizabeth Peabody that her "suffocating" friendships made her repulsive. With her piercing glance and "rudely searching words," she complimented women by bothering to "find them out." She made them feel that she knew their sad limitations, and they repaid her discrimination with devotion. Elizabeth Hoar told Emerson, who was bemused by Margaret's eventual romance, that any one of the "fine girls of sixteen" she knew would gladly have married her "if she had been a man," for she "understood them." With both men and women she insisted on a harrowing intimacy, which brought ecstatic "fusions" and abrupt recoilings. Emerson thought her too passionate, so she tried to repress her extravagant love, only to find herself even more "prodigal." Still, she and Emerson eventually agreed that she had risen above the "search after Eros," and by 1843 her friendship with him made his relationships with others seem like "trade." Whatever needs made her overweening, her conscious effort was always toward the achievement of true friendship, which would confer upon each friend a "clue to the labyrinth" of his being. As a friend, she detected the "Immortal under every disguise in every place" and inspired everyone with a fine discontent. As a friend, above all, she talked.

The medium of friendship was conversation, and the little circle of friends set about conversing with resolute pride. Like the journal and letter, conversation could capture the quick play of the spontaneous spirit. It was for her talk that Margaret Fuller was noted, admired, and feared. Alcott thought her the best "talker" of the age; Orestes Brownson praised her conversation, in *The Quarterly Review*, as "brilliant, instructive, and inspiring"; to Emerson, her talk seemed the most entertaining in America. When Rufus Griswold wrote up "Sarah Margaret Fuller" in *The Prose Writers of America*, he praised her for her mastery of this form, which mid-nineteenth-century Americans prized.

Margaret's talents and society thus enabled her to devise a new form of pedagogy. In 1839 she decided to offer a series of "conversations," which would afford an interested circle of women the chance to inquire earnestly: "What were we born to do? And how shall we do it?" She had never taken to solitude; ravenous always for the human encounter, she had a bent for dialogue, and in nothing perhaps was she more American than in her incorrigible faith in high talk. Though Elizabeth Barrett Browning could not quite grasp the genre of a paid conversation, a businesslike high-mindedness made sense to Bostonians. If the conversations cost as much as lyceum lectures, they reached more deliberately after the soul. Twenty-five of the wives and daughters of ministers, professors, merchants, high school teachers, and physicians of the Boston area paid their fees. Many of them—Lydia Maria Child, Eliza Rotch Farrar, Eliza Buckminster Lee, and Ellen Hooper, among others—were themselves authors. Through the conversations, these educated women were to avoid the vain "display" of learning and begin to build "the life of thought upon the life of action." Planning to make "heroes" of them all, Margaret required that these friends risk the ridicule of society, give up haziness and "coterie criticism," and forage after truth itself. Above all, they had to talk, for she would feel paralyzed by "general silence or side-talks."

For five winters, from 1839 to 1844, Margaret Fuller held her "conversation parties," in which about a third of the group took an active part. Desiring a topic "playful as well as deep," "serious" but not "solemn," she chose Greek mythology for the first subject, since she was after the game of intellect, not a provincial partisanship. The tone was set by Margaret, who was coquettish, scolding, arch, or oracular. She opened each conversation with an outline of the subject under discussion; after her presentation, the group speculated and listened. It was not always easy going. At first, she had trouble getting the ladies to discuss beauty—"they would not attend to principles, but kept clinging to details"—and for a time she let beauty "drop." Caroline Sturgis might prepare for a snooze, or Elizabeth Hoar might find the evening theatrical. But Margaret was pleased to have evoked "the tone of simple earnestness."

Except when the presence of Emerson and other "untrained gentlemen" disturbed the "poetry" of the occasion, Margaret dominated the discussion, leaving her students impressed by her "beautiful modesty" and by their private discoveries. Sophia Peabody kept a record not of what was said but of her "impressions"; and in *Margaret and Her Friends*, a book reporting one season's meetings, Caroline Healey recounted her own unspoken thoughts as meticulously as she recorded the comments of Margaret, Emerson, and Alcott. In all the available accounts of the meetings, two people are central, Margaret and the writer. Margaret's techniques encouraged the ladies to heroic generalizations, and their dogged and blithe inquisitiveness gave the meetings a kind of spectral liveliness.

In their gaudy moralizing, the ladies combined the exotic and the homely; and Bacchus, Ceres, Apollo, and Prometheus took on the more familiar shapes of Geniality, Productive Energy, Genius, and Pure Reason. No reading was required, for moral intuition provided a short cut to knowledge. Margaret announced that the puzzling marriage of Venus and Mercury must be an interpolation, since there could be "*no* affinities between love and craft." She moved quickly to the largest view and recapitulated the gist of a talk with vigorous finality. Thus she summed up an evening conversation: "The Indomitable Will had

127

dethroned Time, and acting with Productive Energy . . . had driven back the sensual passions to the bowels of the earth." A few members risked skittish parallels with Christianity. Subjects that touched on the controversial or contemporary—creeds, women, Catholicism—proved unsuccessful. Yet the little band managed to tackle topics at once puzzling and obliquely germane. To one participant, the conversations suggested Platonic dialogue; for another, Margaret Fuller exposed "the book of life." "Whatever she spoke of revealed a hidden meaning. . . . I was no longer the limitation of myself," Ednah Dow Cheney recalled, "but I felt the whole wealth of the universe was open to me."

Though the excitement of the conversations often left her sleepless, Margaret found the work "sweet." Swept by a power "higher than her own," she saw herself as a prophetess, who turned the humdrum material of her students to her own ends and flashed such transfiguring "rays of truth" upon the familiar that her "startled" audience went "on their way rejoicing in the slight glimpse" of wisdom they had caught. If her hopes for her pupils were thus modest, she felt that she herself had at last enjoyed a "real society." By and large, her friends approved of her experiment in learning. To Emerson, the "conversation room" seemed, in the dreariness of the time, "the search of the best after the sun."

Pleased with her efforts, Margaret Fuller did not stop holding conversations, even after the Boston meetings had ended; and she saw her other work during the 1840s—as co-editor with Emerson of the *Dial* and as contributor to Greeley's New York *Tribune*—as similar to conversations. For, like talk, journals and newspapers spoke to the moment; they were impressionistic, volatile, accessible. The introduction to the *Dial*, written by Margaret and revised by Emerson, promised that the magazine would provide not the multiplication of books but a report on life: "Our resources are therefore not so much the pens of practised writers as the conversation [later changed to "discourse"] of the living and the portfolios which friendship has opened to us." Thus Margaret Fuller continued her effort to open an urgent human colloquy and to grace it with the magnanimity of the impersonal. Emerson spurred her on, praising her article on the drama as elevated above ordinary writing and rejoicing that "the hardened sinners will be saved for your sake, O living friend!"

In the last stage of her education, Margaret Fuller found herself again at the beginning. In 1846 she traveled to England and the Continent.

Like Henry James's American pilgrims, she first discovered through Europe how imprisoning a self-conscious rectitude might be. Unlike her contemporary, Nathaniel Hawthorne, who maintained a wary propriety in the labyrinth of Europe, Margaret Fuller proved herself capable of radical experience. Though Florence, which reminded her of Boston, struck her as "still and glum as death," Rome strangely illuminated "the whole bright house of her exposure." What she discovered was simply, as she informed Emerson, that she had wasted her life among "abstractions." Thus she dismissed her past—Emerson, friendship, conversations, and introspection—and with characteristic violence set about educating herself in reality. Though she no longer rehearsed the standard transcendentalist complaints about America's materialism, her tone toward her native country was newly acerb. While in Rome she decided that Americans were destitute not of spirituality but of passion, and she duly warned the conscientious American pilgrim that he could never understand the city. For it required something her compatriots lacked—the capacity for abandon. She took up the cause of Mazzini, finding in the Italian struggle for freedom an idealism absent in her own country. The headiness she had indulged to "save her soul alive" in the "unpropitious circumstances" of America was no longer necessary; at last, she had discovered a propitious place and time. As correspondent and as head of a hospital for the wounded, she wrote in 1848: "If I came home at this moment I should feel forced to leave my own house, my own people, and the hour which I always longed for."

All her earlier extravagance of passion and discipline had come to seem "useless friction." Incredulous, Emerson heard of lovers: an Italian wanted to divorce so he could marry Margaret, and Mazzini had proposed. In 1848 she had a child and was secretly married. Yet her final emancipation did not bring happiness; the division between her past and present life was too sharp, and she could scarcely now obliterate some twenty years of New England virtue. Her husband, Ossoli, was an impoverished Italian, with tenuous claims to nobility. He was ten years her junior, and she doubted that he would love her long. Incapable of speculating "about anything," ignorant, and without any "enthusiasm of character," he was in no way a "friend." When Margaret "conversed," he left the room. She knew that to her Boston circle her marriage would seem a curious betrayal, based, as Hawthorne sneered, on an attraction "purely sensual" and revealing that she was in the end only a woman, "strong and coarse." To Emerson, she knew, Ossoli would be "nothing." As for herself, she no longer planned on great achievements but made her "plea" with the Magdalen, that she had "loved much."

In Rome, Margaret Fuller learned the extent of her earlier ignorance. Of maternity and experience she had known nothing, and her letters reiterate her abrupt and baffled humility. When her child was asleep beside her, she had the only hours of happiness she had ever known; she chronicled his smiles, his kicking, his feeding, his weight. But she could find no place for the woman she had become. Her husband's love, "in which there was all tenderness but no help," seemed inadequate. She planned to write a book on the birth of her child but had to stop, for it seemed to her that "he would die."

In Italy, the republican cause had failed; there was nowhere to go but to America, where Margaret would have to support her husband and child. "With this year, I enter upon a sphere of my destiny so difficult that I, at present, see no way out except through the gate of death," she wrote to Caroline Sturgis. Her "tuition on this planet" now seemed complete. In 1848, with premonitions of death and praying only that she, her child, and her husband might live or die together, Margaret Fuller Ossoli embarked for America. The ship sank within sight of the New Jersey coast, and she apparently did not try to save either her own life or that of her family. Yet if Margaret—faced with a return to friendship—courted death in anticipation or act, her friends were loyal to the woman they thought they had known; when she died, Emerson felt he had lost his audience.

In her program for women, as in her life, Margaret Fuller had relied solely upon the private sensibility, which recorded the lessons of analytical friendships, rash passions, and a harrowing self-consciousness. If she paid for her individualism by often seeming foolish, her life, with all its extravagance, finally achieved an exemplary seriousness. "What spoke unto the best among the years 1838 to 1842," Emerson mused on her death, "was the spontaneous and solitary thought." Yet, he added bitterly, her friends could conceive of no better use for the "most educated woman" America had produced than that married and impoverished, she should die "to save her board."

AMERICAN PROTESTANTISM'S
TEACHINGS TO YOUNG MEN
Clifford E. Clark, Jr.

Since many young Americans drew their deepest beliefs from Protestant Christianity, the changes that were wrought in the Christian message in the nineteenth century are an indispensable aid in understanding the formation of social outlooks and values. Manuals of advice on behavior, manners, and the means of success, aimed at youthful audiences, were a popular literary genre of the times. Most of these works were written by ministers, and no minister was more widely known than Henry Ward Beecher, son of Lyman Beecher and younger brother of Catharine. In this essay about Beecher's *Seven Lectures to Young Men*, Clifford E. Clark, Jr., discusses the changing emphases in Beecher's application of Protestant teachings to the problems and decisions facing young men. Notable themes developed in this analysis include the transformation of spiritual into secular values and the stress on personal internalization of social restraints and controls.

The changing American conception of success is the subject of John G. Cawelti, *Apostles of the Self-Made Man* (Chicago: University of Chicago Press, 1965), and Irvin G. Wyllie, *The Self-Made Man in America* (New Brunswick, N.J.: Rutgers University Press, 1954). See also the extensive set of documents reprinted in Moses Rischin, ed., *The American Gospel of Success* (Chicago: Quadrangle Books, 1965).

The outlook of American Protestantism underwent a marked change in the middle decades of the nineteenth century, a change from an otherworldly perspective to a largely uncritical acceptance of the status quo. Various aspects of this transformation have been carefully explored, including the influence on the churches of the Civil War, the rise of the city, and the creation of a "New Theology," but historians have generally overlooked the internal dynamics of this change and have sometimes misunderstood the normative role that religion played in late-nineteenth-century American life. One may gain a better insight into the changing nature of Protestantism at mid-century by examining the career of Henry Ward Beecher and focusing on his popular book *Seven Lectures to Young Men*.

Henry Ward Beecher's book is clearly not the work of a great mind, but it reveals the assumptions and values of a clergyman who was generally regarded by his contemporaries as the most popular preacher in America. As minister to Plymouth Church in Brooklyn from 1847 until his death in 1887, Henry Ward Beecher attracted an enormous following. "Probably no man in the country is more generally known, or regarded with a more personal affection and enthusiasm," declared *Harper's Weekly* in 1858. "Whenever and wherever he speaks, vast crowds assemble. . . ." "No minister in the United States is so well known, none so widely beloved," stated a writer in the *Atlantic Monthly*. James Parton, a contemporary historian, agreed and added enthusiastically that his church was simply "the most characteristic thing of America."

Because of his immense popularity, Henry Ward Beecher exerted a strong influence on the religious outlook of his day. Through his extensive activities as newspaper editor, lyceum lecturer, and preacher, he spoke to thousands of Americans and helped shape their views on a variety of religious and social questions. The successive editions of *Seven Lectures to Young Men* are important, therefore, because they document the process by which Protestantism became more secular and lost its distinctive identity during the middle decades of the nineteenth century.

Henry Ward Beecher's lectures, with their ethical injunctions and puritanical attitude toward amusements, clearly reflected his background and training as a revivalist. The eighth child of one of New England's most prominent church leaders, Henry Ward Beecher had been frequently troubled in his youth by the fact that he had not been saved. At the age of twelve he had written to his older brother George to say: "I have been seeking after God but have not found him as yet. . . . I have been a little wretched before but never felt my lost condition [so strongly]. . . ." Several years later, after much hesitation and worry, he finally underwent the conversion experience. From that time on he was determined to become a minister.

Although Henry Ward Beecher shared his father's intense interest in revivalism, his approach to that subject was less impetuous and energetic. An easygoing, warmhearted man who was gifted with an infectious sense of humor and a colorful imagination, he spoke of salvation not as the last resort for sinful mankind but as a new road to happiness and self-fulfillment. The effectiveness of his approach first became evident during his ministry at a small church in Lawrenceburg, Indiana. After trying for several weeks without success to gain new church members by preaching about God's moral government, he decided that a different tactic was necessary. As he confided to his journal, "He is sure of popularity who can come down among the people and address truth to them in their own homely way and with broad humor—and at the same time has an upper current of taste and chaste expression and condensed vigor."

Henry Ward Beecher's efforts soon added new members to his congregation and in the spring of 1839 he came to the attention of Samuel Merrill, the treasurer of the state, who was visiting the town on business. Merrill was a deacon of the Second Presbyterian Church in Indianapolis, which was looking for a new minister. The church had already extended a call to two other clergymen and had been turned down. Now the congregation was becoming somewhat anxious. At Merrill's invitation, Henry Ward Beecher traveled to Indianapolis, delivered a trial sermon, and received a call. After some hesitation, he accepted the offer, explaining his reasons in a letter to his father:

Ohio and Illinois is [sic] safe. Indiana, a richer state than Illinois and determined to rise very high—is in nobody's hands. Her capital is her centre—geographically, commercially and morally. It is the key of the state. That held, will be an advantage not easily equalled at any other point in the state—the old school [the conservative wing of the Presbyterian Church] know it—are aiming at it. . . . The Churches are en-

terprising—will be wealthy—are influential—will publish *what is well written—and from this point it can be diffused by Representatives and business men over [the] whole surface of [the] land.*

Henry Ward Beecher's new preaching style became even more effective as he perfected it during his first years in Indianapolis. Despite frequent bouts of malaria, or the "chills and ague," as it was called, he managed to start a revival. In 1843, after a year of hard work, he proudly informed the General Assembly of the Presbyterian Church that 210 new communicants had been added to his church. That same winter he delivered the lectures that were to make him famous.

The *Seven Lectures to Young Men* developed out of his concern with the unstable social and economic conditions in Indianapolis. Like many other settlers who wished to plant traditional social and religious ideals in the West, he was upset by the fever of land speculation and the mania for internal improvements which swept the nation in the 1830s. The same boom psychology which attracted the new population threatened to destroy the social values that many settlers were striving to maintain. The lectures, therefore, not only documented Henry Ward Beecher's own beliefs but also reflected the outlook of many middle-class citizens who were conscious of their position in society and eager to preserve their respectability.

The two main themes in the lectures were the dangers that lay in wait for young men in cities and the "universal derangement of business" caused by speculation and gambling. Everyone, even those in rural districts, had need of these lectures, argued Henry Ward Beecher: "We are such a migratory, restless people, that our home is usually everywhere but at home; and almost every young man makes annual, or biennial visits to famous cities," the dwelling place of that "flash class of men" who were the most dangerous.

The lectures on moral dangers ranged in theme from a discussion of gambling and gamblers to a warning about prostitutes—"the strange woman." In effect, they were sermons rather than lectures, built around the exegesis of passages from the Bible. Following the approach that he had developed in his studies of preaching, Henry Ward Beecher simplified each question and presented it as a sketch of a character type—the wit, the libertine, the demagogue, and the party man. In each case he

134

argued that once the first step was taken, the youth would be committed to a life of degeneracy and sin.

The lectures were immediately popular. Part of their appeal undoubtedly derived from the selection of topics. To introduce a lecture on prostitution required a great deal of courage and a good bit of tact. While Henry Ward Beecher condemned the "false modesty" and the "criminal fastidiousness of the community" that prevented a discussion of this subject, he was careful to present his lecture in the form of an allegory. Yet, though he avoided the coarser aspects of his subject, he compensated by using lurid language. Typical of the allegorical discussion was his imaginative description of one of the rooms in the house of prostitution—the ward of disease.

Ye that look wistfully at the pleasant front of this terrific house, come with me now, and look long into the terror of this Ward; for here are the seeds of sin in their full harvest form! . . . Here a shuddering wretch is clawing at his breast, to tear away that worm which gnaws his heart. By him is another, whose limbs are dropping from his ghastly trunk. Next, swelters another in reeking filth; his eyes rolling on bony sockets, every breath a pang, and every pang a groan. But yonder, on a pile of rags, lies one whose yells of frantic agony appall every ear. Clutching his rags with spasmodic grasp, his swoln [sic] tongue lolling from a blackened mouth, his bloodshot eyes glaring and rolling, he shrieks oaths; now blaspheming God, and now imploring him.

The gruesomeness of this account, designed to deter a youth from entering a house of prostitution, had an attraction of its own for a western audience, for whom entertainment of any kind was scarce. The greatest appeal of the lectures, however, derived not from the vividness of the descriptions or from the strictures on moral dangers but rather from the advice on how to succeed. What made the lectures unusual was the way in which Henry Ward Beecher used the major tenets of the New School revivalist theology to support his arguments.

Central to his views about success was his attitude toward human nature. Like the New School theologians, he argued that although all men have a tendency to sin, they also have the ability, if they wish, to save themselves. "I do believe that man is corrupt enough," he declared, "but something of good has survived his wreck." This optimistic view of human nature, when carried over into the gospel of success, became the basis for his belief that anyone could become successful if only he worked at it. But Henry Ward Beecher also retained an element of the Old School view of original sin and argued that "the children of a sturdy thief, if taken from him at birth and reared by honest men, would, doubtless, have to contend against a strongly dishonest inclination."

Like the revivalist theology, Henry Ward Beecher's version of the gospel of success emphasized the individual, but not to the extent of ignoring his social responsibility. "Satisfaction," he wrote, "is not the product of excess, or of indolence, or of riches; but of industry, temperance, and usefulness." He considered it essential that the individual contribute to the public good by "private usefulness" and a "record of public service." The individual was to be both self-reliant and socially responsible.

Success, like salvation, moreover, was the result of conscious choice, fervent dedication, and unremitting toil and effort. Like salvation, it was available to all. Henry Ward Beecher went out of his way to emphasize that luck had no influence. "A good character, good habits, and iron industry," he declared, "are impregnable to the assaults of all the ill luck that fools ever dreamed of." Success, like conversion, would bring with it other benefits. "Experience has shown," he wrote, "that the other good qualities of veracity, frugality, and modesty, are apt to be associated with industry."

Henry Ward Beecher further argued that the object of success, like that of conversion, was the development of character. Riches were more of a hindrance than an asset. Only if they were gained gradually as the result of hard work could they be considered the "gift of God." As he declared, "if the taste is refined, if the affections are pure, if conscience is honest, if charity listens to the needy, and generosity relieves them; if the public-spirited hand fosters all that embellishes and all that ennobles society—then is the rich man happy." Later advocates of the gospel of self-help were to confuse material gain with moral worth in a way that was very different from Henry Ward Beecher's intention.

Still another parallel between the conversion theology and the gospel of success was drawn in his remarks on suffering and hardship. Just as tribulation and setbacks frequently made sinners aware of their faults

136

and more willing to be converted, economic hardships were beneficial because they taught the value of thrift and frugality. "Adversity," he wrote, "is the mint in which God stamps upon us his image and superscription."

It was natural for Henry Ward Beecher to use the basic tenets of revivalist theology to support his version of the gospel of success because both sets of beliefs shared a common objective. Both were designed to develop self-reliant, independent individuals who were motivated and controlled by internalized sets of beliefs rather than by legal or institutional forms of coercion. The object of revivalism, as seen in the act of conversion, was to internalize the religious beliefs of the individual so well that he would be able to maintain his faith even at times and in areas where the church was poorly organized, feebly supported, and without a minister. Similarly, those who advocated the gospel of success wanted to internalize a sense of ethical norms so that those who participated in the open atmosphere of the marketplace would do so fairly and equitably. Both sets of beliefs were thus part of a rearguard action—a defensive move designed to strengthen the churches and to improve the conduct of business at a time when both infidelity and cheating seemed to be on the increase.

By using the assumptions of revivalist theology to support his version of the gospel of success, Henry Ward Beecher helped to modify the conception of success that had been popularized by Benjamin Franklin. Franklin's image of the self-made man now became the image of the middle-class American whose goal in life was not the accumulation of wealth or the gain of social status, but rather the development of character. Franklin's suggestion that proper behavior in public was more important than personal rectitude in private was in a similar fashion no longer considered adequate advice. "Moral dishonesties practised because the LAW allows them," Henry Ward Beecher argued, were still sins. To develop character, the individual had to adhere to the basic standards of Christian morality in both his public and private life.

Henry Ward Beecher's interest in self-help and success, conversely, had an important influence on revivalist theology. By emphasizing ethical behavior rather than spiritual dedication, he helped to blur the distinction between religious and secular issues and to change the focus of religion from the world-to-come to the present. By stressing the ability of the individual to save himself in both spiritual and economic terms, he also helped reduce the importance of the church to that of an outside adviser. And, by using the basic tenets of revivalism to support his version of the gospel of success, he created an internal dynamic within evangelical theology that helped to change it from a distinctive religious outlook into an apology for the status quo. In this way, he contributed to the secularization of Protestantism that was taking place at mid-century.

Although Beecher's lectures can be read as a self-help manual, what is particularly striking about them is not their advocacy of success but rather their preoccupation with failure. Instead of giving practical advice on how to get ahead, the lectures dwell on the dangers and pitfalls that await the unwary young man once he leaves home. The warnings about indolence, idleness, laziness, haste, selfishness, and vain amusements are so incessant, in fact, that the concern for them seems almost hysterical.

The intensity of these warnings, which seem today to be far out of proportion to the real dangers of the time, raise important questions about the fears and anxieties of middle-class Americans. Why, for example, did such relatively harmless pastimes as idleness or inactivity appear to be so threatening? Why did the interest in recreation or the pursuit of leisure create so much fear? And what did Henry Ward Beecher propose to do about these apparent excesses? To answer these questions is to gain an insight into the ways in which Protestantism at mid-century was changing.

Inactivity in any form, Henry Ward Beecher believed, was harmful because it frequently was the cause of crime. "Indolence as surely runs to dishonesty, as to lying," he warned. "Society precipitates its lazy members, as water does its filth; and they form at the bottom, a pestilent sediment. . . ." Inactivity was also dangerous because it led to a search for entertainment at the race track and the theater, which were patronized by "gambling jockeys and jaded rich men."

What made these activities appear particularly harmful was the apparent weakness of many of the basic institutions of society. The national missionary and benevolent societies, for example, that had been created in the 1820s and 1830s to reform the drunkard, free the slave, and spread the gospel, had been considerably weakened by disagreements over tactics and by the schism within the Presbyterian Church in 1837. They no longer seemed to be an effective instrument for national reform. "To all this," Henry Ward Beecher warned, "must be added a manifest decline of family government; an increase of the ratio of popular ignorance; a decrease of reverence for law, and an effeminate administration of it." The vision of a Christian America that had inspired the earlier church leaders now seemed seriously threatened by the breakdown of social institutions and the increase of dishonesty and crime.

To meet the threats created by rapid social change, Henry Ward Beecher argued that the traditional role of the minister needed modification. Ever since the debates over the separation of church and state in the constitutional conventions of the 1820s, the correction of social problems had been considered less important than the conversion of individuals, and ministers who spoke out of these problems had been frowned upon. Alexis de Tocqueville acknowledged this point when he wrote of the clergy: "They keep aloof from parties and from public affairs"; and of religion: "It directs the customs of the community, and, by regulating domestic life, it regulates the state." The chief spokesmen of this view, Lyman Beecher and Charles G. Finney, had justified the approach by arguing that once the individual was converted, he would abstain from vice and thus social problems would automatically be solved.

By delivering public lectures on such controversial subjects as speculation, prostitution, and public amusements, Henry Ward Beecher was consciously trying to modify the traditional conception of the minister's role. "Allow me, first of all," he stated at the beginning of one of his lectures, "to satisfy you that I am not meddling with matters which do not concern me. . . . Religion is called a nun, sable with gloomy vestments; and the Church a cloister, where ignorance is deemed innocence, and which sends out querulous reprehensions of a world, which it knows nothing about, and has professedly abandoned. This is pretty; and is only defective, in not being true. The Church is not a cloister, nor her members recluses, nor are our censures of vice intermeddling." The proper role of the minister should not be simply to convert the individual, he argued, but to root out and publicize evil and to create and mobilize public opinion.

Henry Ward Beecher's insistence that the clergy should concentrate their energies on public issues rested upon the fundamental assumption that the private lives of individuals should be controlled and regulated primarily by their families. Because the basic norms and values of society would be instilled in the child by the family, the clergy could spend less time instructing the children and devote more of their efforts to speaking out on pressing social problems. The family, in his analysis, provided the key support for the efforts of the clergy and was the basic institution of social control.

Henry Ward Beecher frequently emphasized this theme in his lectures. As he describes it, the family's strength lies in the home, which is run by the mother. It is a protected and isolated world, full of creatures of purity and refinement. Even the home of the prostitute or "strange woman," for example, which today might be characterized as one in which something went wrong, is pictured as an idyllic environment. "Was not her cradle as pure as ever a loved infant pressed? Love soothed its cries. Sisters watched its peaceful sleep, and a mother pressed it fondly to her bosom! . . . [P]urity was an atmosphere around her." The young woman became a prostitute because of the influence of evil men who came in contact with her *after* she had left the home, not because of a flaw in the way that she had been brought up. The family and the home thus were the sphere where women dominated—women who invariably were patient, good, sweet, pure, and kind.

The image of the family as a cloistered retreat dominated by females was in part a reflection of his own family background. Although his mother died when he was three, in later life he always insisted that the memory of her had been an important influence in his life. His older sisters, Catharine and Harriet, shared this conception of the family and described it forcefully in *The American Woman's Home: or, Principles of Domestic Science*. Henry Ward Beecher's attitude toward the family was in part also a reflection of a new view of the family that was developing in the 1840s and 1850s.

Central to this new view was the belief that certain kinds of excitement were bad for young people. All aspects of a youth's life had to be controlled at all times, preferably from within. "Is it *safe* to accustom yourselves to such tremendous excitement as that of [horse] racing?" he asked the young men of Indianapolis. "There can be no industrial calling so exciting as the Theatre, the Circus, and the Races," he declared at another time. "If you wish to make your real business very stupid and hateful, visit such places." Once the first step was taken, moreover, the end was near. "So well am I assured of the power of bad men to seduce the erring purity of man," he warned, "that I pronounce it next to impossible for man or woman to escape, *if they permit bad men to approach and dally with them.*" The only way to avoid moral dangers, therefore, was for the young men or women to isolate themselves completely from such evil influences.

This restrictive attitude toward life outside the family, so clearly reflected in the lectures, was shared by many nineteenth-century Americans. It was supported, moreover, by the Protestant attitude toward original sin that Henry Ward Beecher had expressed. All men, though they had within themselves the power of improving their life and gaining salvation, still retained the seeds of original sin. Thus young men, who had been carefully guided by the family during their childhood, were particularly prone to err when they were forced to face the vicissitudes of life in the outside world.

The pervasiveness of a restrictive attitude toward youth is easy to document but more difficult to explain. It is perhaps best seen as a response of a society in which traditional social values and the means of social control appeared to be inadequate. In the chaotic America of the 1840s and 1850s, where the restrictions on young people once they left the family seemed ineffectual, it became important to develop some sort of restraint on the individual from within. This need was fulfilled by the self-help literature which repeatedly stressed the need for *self*-control and *self*-discipline. *Seven Lectures to Young Men*, as an early example of this literature, thus became one of the models for the vast number of books on how to succeed that appeared later in the century.

The publication of Henry Ward Beecher's lectures in 1844 had an important effect on his later career. Not only did it interest him in the possibility of becoming a lyceum lecturer but it also brought him to the attention of a new generation of merchants who had become successful in New York and moved to the nearby suburb of Brooklyn, where they wished to start a new church. Impressed by his emphasis on the middle-class virtues of industry and thrift, honesty and piety, they soon became convinced that the young preacher would wage an active campaign against the vices which tempted young men in Brooklyn. In the winter of 1846, therefore, they wrote to him and offered to establish a new church for him if he would come to Brooklyn. After some hesitation, because moving meant giving up the cause of revivalism in the West, he accepted the call and went to Brooklyn.

Henry Ward Beecher's interest in maintaining traditional social values had a particular appeal for the people of Brooklyn. Swollen by foreign immigration and the influx of people from New York, the population of Brooklyn grew in only twenty years from 30,000 to 295,000, creating a variety of economic and social tensions. Faced with the large foreign immigration, the older and wealthier citizens of the city began to move to Brooklyn Heights and the neighboring area. They were joined there by a new class of business and professional men who had made their fortunes recently and wanted to improve their social position. Disliking the new Irish and German immigrants and feeling guilty about their newly acquired wealth, the Protestant merchants wanted desperately to find a convincing rationalization for their own behavior. Many of them feared that the immigrants, with their unusual social customs and Catholic faith, might destroy traditional American values and ideals. More than anything else, they wanted to demonstrate that they were socially responsible and had concerns other than the pursuit of wealth.

That Henry Ward Beecher himself gradually accepted the outlook of these men is clearly reflected in the revised edition of his lectures that appeared in 1873. He had changed during his two decades in Brooklyn from a rough backwoods preacher into a polished urban minister and popular lyceum lecturer. Now earning more than $40,000 a year as a public speaker, newspaper editor, and minister, he was no longer as concerned with the pitfalls which lay in wait for the unwary youth. Instead, the first of the new lectures in his revised book concerned "the relations which the young of both sexes sustain to their parents, their employers, to themselves, and to the community or country in which they live." He was now careful to stress the complete subordination of the employee to the employer. Even if the employer treated the young man unjustly, he had no excuse for acting "peevishly or unfaithfully." The only possible excuse for refusing to follow instructions was when the instructions asked him to perform an unethical act. As he expressed it: "Never wrong your employers; neither do wrong for them."

But his interest in the maintenance of discipline between employer and employee was less important to him than his concern for the dangers which lay in wait for the rich and the affluent. Some of these warnings echoed sentiments from the earlier lectures. "When men are surrounded by all that wealth can give them,—by position, by circumstance, by plenary physical blessings,—how, after all, do they long for more! How piteous it is to see them!" But even in his discussion of riches there is some modification of his earlier views. In his previous lectures, riches were, more often than not, the outward manifestation of an inward corruption. Now, though they were potentially harmful, they could serve as a balance to other failings in character if they were used properly. Men who build up society and "associate their names with foundations . . . ," he wrote, "are noble men. A multitude of faults and failings do not detract from the grandeur of such natures."

Nevertheless, if Henry Ward Beecher extolled the virtues of those who used their wealth properly, he was far from justifying the activities of the robber barons who gained their money by speculation and fraud. Indeed, he went out of his way to emphasize the value of honesty, hard work, and thrift, as he had done in his earlier lectures. Happiness, he wrote, could only be obtained by "the creation of the noblest character."

Henry Ward Beecher was thus a spokesman for the status quo; but he was a spokesman with a particularly middle-class orientation. Although in his later lectures he spoke of relations between employer and laborer, and about the dangers of riches, he was still more interested in establishing those "character traits" which he had extolled in his lectures before the Civil War. As he declared in his lecture on "Practical Hints," "do not be a man of integrity just because it is profitable. I would not like to put moral qualities up at auction as merchantable things."

In the final analysis there was an ambiguous quality about Henry Ward Beecher's lectures. Read one way, they seemed to justify the outlook of the men of wealth in the 1880s; but, read in another, by calling attention to social problems and by insisting that each man be socially responsible, the lectures paved the way for the social gospel. Washington Gladden, one of the early social gospel leaders, acknowledged Beecher's importance for the social gospel movement when he wrote to Henry Ward Beecher that "I find it in my heart to tell you just now, how grateful I am to you for the good that you have done me—for the truth you have taught me,—for the noble and better views of this life and the life to come that you have opened to me." Gladden and the other leaders of the social gospel, like Henry Ward Beecher, combined an emphasis on the development of character with a call for social action.

Henry Ward Beecher's outlook, with its ethical injunctions and its emphasis on close contact between employer and employee, gradually became dated in the 1870s. The economy based on small businessmen and merchants that had existed in America before the Civil War had by then been transformed by the industrial revolution into a larger, more complex and impersonal system. The younger generation no longer turned to him but to another minister, Horatio Alger, for advice on how to succeed. Where Henry Ward Beecher had spoken to the sons of middle-class Americans, Alger now dramatized the lives of the poor— orphans, newsboys, and shoeshine boys. Unlike Henry Ward Beecher, Alger placed a strong emphasis on the importance of having a clean personal appearance, good manners, and proper dress. He was, in short, largely concerned with vertical mobility, the change in social status from rags to riches; whereas Henry Ward Beecher was primarily interested in horizontal mobility, the movement of middle-class Americans from the farm to the city.

Nevertheless, though Henry Ward Beecher's version of the gospel of success appears to us now as having been out of touch with the realities of the 1870s, it still had a real appeal to the older generation of Americans that had grown up before the Civil War and lived on into the latter part of the nineteenth century. At a time when new forms of organization, trusts, pools, and corporations were disrupting communities and changing the face of America, this generation of business and professional men wanted desperately to know that if they played the game by the traditional rules, they would eventually become successful. Henry Ward Beecher supplied this generation with reassurance by stressing the moral and ethical norms of the antebellum period.

Yet, in the process, he so blurred the distinctions between the dogmas of the church and the ethical injunctions of the self-help theory that the differences became practically indistinguishable. By sacrificing a concern for theology and a preoccupation with conversion to the urgency of speaking out on social and political issues, he contributed to the transformation of Protestantism that was taking place at mid-century. If American Protestantism before the Civil War still retained an otherworldly perspective, by 1880 the process of secularization had become virtually complete.

★ 10 ★

BUREAUCRACY AND THE COMMON SCHOOL: THE EXPERIENCE OF PORTLAND, OREGON, 1851–1913
David B. Tyack

The prevalence of bureaucratic institutions in modern American life has led historians increasingly to the study of earlier bureaucratic responses to social issues. There are few areas of American life that have been more frequently accused of exemplifying the bureaucratic mentality than the world of education. It is probably true that here, as in so many spheres of American concern, education is being made the scapegoat for processes in which the entire society shares. Yet, as David Tyack so clearly shows in the article printed below, the accusation reflects one of the realities of the history of education. In his study of the Portland, Oregon, schools he delineates a bureaucratic system which must have had few peers in American life. Probably only in the military could one have found a more centralized and authoritarian direction of human lives.

Tyack shows that bureaucracy originated in an effort to reform education by removing it from politics, raising standards, and introducing greater uniformity into the school experience. But why it was free to go to the lengths it did is less clear. Apparently Americans felt freer to experiment with new means of social control in education than in other institutions. Perhaps because they found few regularities in adult experience, they sought to impose many on children.

Important studies of bureaucratic processes include Raymond E. Callahan, *Education and the Cult of Efficiency* (Chicago: University of Chicago Press, 1962); Michael B.

145

Katz, *Class, Bureaucracy, and Schools: The Illusion of Educational Change in America* (New York: Praeger Publishers, 1971); and Robert H. Wiebe, *The Search for Order, 1877–1920* (New York: Hill & Wang, 1967).

"The most fundamental principle observed in the present conduct of the Portland school system is the maintenance unchanged of a rigidly prescribed, mechanical system, poorly adapted to the needs either of the children or of the community." So concluded a team of educational experts led by Ellwood P. Cubberley of Stanford in a 1913 study of the Portland Public Schools. "Because of lack of opportunity to exercise initiative," they observed, teachers and administrators were "carrying out a system in whose creation they had little or no part. The result is a uniformity that is almost appalling." Administrators were mere inspectors, certifying or compelling compliance with rules. The curriculum was "vivisected with mechanical accuracy into fifty-four dead pieces." Children trotted on one stage of the treadmill until they could advance to the next by passing an examination. "School board and superintendent, as well as principals, teachers, and pupils, are victims of the system for which no one is primarily responsible." The origin of the bureaucracy was a mystery; pride, ritual, and fear maintained it.

Cubberley and his colleagues were describing—with some caricature—a social pathology which had afflicted urban schools for decades. In 1880 Charles Francis Adams, Jr., blasted school superintendents as "drill sergeants" and described their schools as "a combination of the cotton mill and the railroad with the model State-prison." In a series of articles in the *Forum* in 1892, Dr. Joseph M. Rice attacked regimentation in city schools of the East and Midwest. That same year President Charles W. Eliot of Harvard denounced mass education, which "almost inevitably adopts military or mechanical methods, . . . [which] tend to produce a lock-step and a uniform speed. . . ." Inflexible routine degraded the "teacher's function. . . . There are many persons who say that teachers in the graded schools ought not to serve more than ten years at the outside, for the reason that they become dull, formal, and uninteresting; but, if this be true, it is certainly the fault of the system rather than of the teachers."

During the mid-nineteenth century most American urban school systems became bureaucracies, though schoolmen did not use that term.

They developed elaborate rules to govern the behavior of members of the organization, and a great premium was placed on conformity to the rules; they created hierarchies of appointive offices, each with careful allocations of power and specified duties; and objective qualifications governed admission to the various roles (whether "superintendent" or "third grader"). The schools, like other organizations, were trying to cope rationally with large numbers of heterogeneous pupils. Indeed, schoolmen commonly thought bureaucratization essential to progress. In 1890 the Committee on City School Systems of the National Education Association quoted Herbert Spencer on the value of "a differentiation of structure and a specialization of function," and concluded that urban schools needed not only "combination and unification for general purposes" but also specialized administrative structures "with well-defined functions and powers." In the actual organization of the schools, however, schoolmen of the nineteenth century tended to favor simple military or industrial bureaucratic models in which uniformity of output and regularity of operation took precedence over functional differentiation. Thus in practice they often created a curriculum which was identical for all children, preferred teaching methods which promised standardized results, and based the hierarchy more on a distribution of power than on specialized expertise.

The educational statesmen of Horace Mann's generation had tried to create system where they saw chaos. Urban school bureaucracies institutionalized this quest for standardization. Reformers believed that in order to unify the people they must first unify the common schools. They were dismayed by the heterogeneity of typical public schools: teachers untrained, mostly young and inexperienced, lacking a sense of professionalism; curriculum haphazard, textbooks miscellaneous; classes composed of students of wildly varying age and ability, irregular in attendance and unruly in behavior; buildings rough and messy, serving as general community centers for church services, lantern-slide lectures, social occasions, and political assemblies. The rural school was especially subject to the caprice of the community, the tyranny of the tribe which Edward Eggleston describes so clearly in *The Hoosier Schoolmaster*. In the small district school, authority inhered in the person, not the office, of the schoolmaster; the roles of teachers were overlapping, familiar, personal rather than esoteric, strictly defined and official (the same teacher in a rural school might be brother, suitor, hunting com-

147

panion, fellow farm worker, boarder, and cousin to the different boys and girls in the class). Normally the only supervisors were laymen, school board members, or ministers who dropped in from time to time on the local school. The school played a relatively small and often unpredictable part in the total socialization of the young.

Reform, then, meant standardization. Schoolmen sought to grade classes, to prescribe a uniform curriculum and textbooks, to train teachers in approved methods, to give them a sense of vocational identity and spirit, and to appoint officials to supervise the schools. Such bureaucratization was easiest in cities (where the population was concentrated and the tax base adequate). Urban residents were familiar with bureaucracies arising in manufacturing, commerce, transport, the military, and government. Posing the rhetorical question "Why the expense and machinery of a superintendent?" one school administrator replied:

> In industrial establishments, as well as in enterprises requiring unskilled manual labor, employers insist upon abundant supervision. A great railroad company places one man to boss three or four. Every factory, large or small, has its foremen and its bosses. Experience has taught that such an arrangement pays financially. The conclusions are quite as reasonable in the conduct of schools; where even a small aggregation of schools is, there an able superintendent can be profitably engaged.

Increasing ease of transportion and communication, together with the migration of teachers and administrators, spread the new patterns of organization. Richard Wade has observed that the new cities arising by the banks of the Ohio and the Mississippi—St. Louis, Cincinnati, and the rest—emulated the educational systems of "the great cities across the mountains" even though they were "freed from . . . old restraints and traditions." Louisville sent a new principal to study Eastern schools to eliminate the need for "expensive errors and fruitless experiments." Similarly, Portland, Oregon—a fir forest in 1840—had organized by the 1870s a school system based on Eastern models. By copying the most recent organizational reforms such cities could skip earlier, piecemeal stages of bureaucratization.

In 1874 leading American city and state school superintendents and college presidents signed A *Statement of the Theory of Education in the United States*, written to explain American educational practices to Europeans. In this outline they justified bureaucratization in matter-of-fact rather than crusading language. "The commercial tone prevalent in the city," they said, "tends to develop, in its schools, quick, alert habits and readiness to combine with others in their tasks. Military precision is required in the maneuvering of classes. Great stress is laid upon 1) punctuality, 2) regularity, 3) attention, and 4) silence, as habits necessary through life for successful combination with one's fellow-men in an industrial and commercial civilization." They seemed to accept employers' specifications as to the ideal character of workers. They saw the school as "a phase of education lying between the earliest period of family-nurture . . . and the necessary initiation into the specialties of a vocation. . . ." Because "the peculiarities of civil society and the political organization draw the child out of the influence of family-nurture earlier than is common in other countries," the American school had "to lay more stress upon discipline and to make far more prominent the moral phase of education. It is obliged to train the pupil into prompt obedience to his teachers and the practice of self-control in its various forms, in order that he may be prepared for a life wherein there is little police-restraint on the part of the constituted authorities." Therefore urban schools must socialize children to take part in an increasing bureaucratic society: the new size and complexity of "corporate combinations . . . make such a demand upon the community for directive intelligence that it may be said that the modern industrial community cannot exist without free popular education carried out in a system of schools ascending from the primary grade to the university."

Across the nation urban school bureaucracies won acclaim. The best teachers and administrators flocked to these systems in search of higher pay and prestige. But the reformers' very success became an affliction, as is often the case when reforms become institutionalized. Orderly grooves became ruts. In 1903 Charles B. Gilbert, the superintendent of schools in Rochester, New York, warned that large institutions tend "to subordinate the individual. . . . This is particularly true in great school systems. . . . The demands of the organization itself are so great, it requires so much executive power to keep the machine running, that the machine itself attracts undue attention and we are in danger of forgetting that the business of the school is to teach children." He knew, he said, superb teachers who were "driven from the school system because they did not readily untie red tape." Worst of all was a "shifting of conscience" from teaching to pleasing pettifogging superiors. "I know of cities in which supervisors go about from schoolroom to schoolroom, notebook and pencil in hand, sitting for a while in each room like malignant sphinxes, eying the terrified teacher, who in her terror does everything wrong, and then marking her in that little doomsday book." A school is not a factory, he said, "with a boss, sub-bosses, and hands." Like Charles W. Eliot, Gilbert looked back with nostalgia on "the small unpainted schoolhouse in the remote country district" as a place where the individual child, the individual teacher counted, where flexibility flourished. When the urban school bureaucracy turns children into robots and "grinds out the power of initiative from the teacher," said Gilbert, "then it is time to smash the machine; and there are countless machines all over this land that need to be smashed."

Just such a machine was the Portland school system when Cubberley and his colleagues arrived in 1913. There they found all the dysfunctions which Robert Merton describes in his essay on "Bureaucratic Structure and Personality." What had originally been a thoughtful response to problems of disorganization in mass education became archaic ritual. "Passive, routine, clerical"—these adjectives described "the attitude of principals and grammar school teachers toward their work," said the investigators. "And the attitude of the pupils is inevitably the same." With the exception of one lesson, they "heard not a single question asked by a pupil, not a single remark or comment made, to indicate that the pupil had any really vital interest in the subject matter of the exercise. . . ." Like experienced enlisted men, teachers "feared to advocate anything out of the routine, for that would mean more work, and more work—with its intended accomplishment—in one part of the system, would threaten other parts of the system with a like affliction!" The system was bound by rules which had so long outlived their usefulness that no one could recall their origin or state their rationale.

"There is no study," Charles Bidwell has observed, "of the prevalence or incidence either of bureaucratic structures or processes in school systems. . . ." This oversight is not coincidental. As Marvin Bressler has pointed out in his essay on "The Conventional Wisdom of Education and Sociology," scholars in education have tended to stress individual volition, broad social needs, and a "credo of unlimited

150

hope." Reformist and optimistic in temper, many educationists have written from an individualistic psychological perspective. They have often represented teaching styles and philosophies of education as if they were options independent of organizational patterns. The behavioral effects of institutional structure have more often been taken for granted than examined, while tacitly it was assumed that a teacher could choose to be "progressive" or "traditional." But the experience of Portland up to the time of the Cubberley survey suggests that the rigid bureaucratic system had an internal momentum and influence which largely shaped the conduct of teachers, administrators, and students. The persistence of this system in the face of major social and intellectual changes cannot be explained simply by conventional categories of individual intent, rational adaptation, or psychological or social needs. Although the founders of the bureaucracy knew the reasons for their actions, before long the structure of the organization began to produce in its members what Veblen called "trained incapacity" and what Dewey deplored as "occupational psychosis." People acted the roles which the institution demanded with little thought about the purpose of education.

So it was with the Portland bureaucracy. While this essay deals, perforce, with the individuals who built the system, the bureaucracy itself is the central subject rather than the actors. The essay will also explore the relevance of bureaucracy to "progressive education," in the conviction that this reform movement was a "revolt against formalism" quite as much in educational organization as in educational thought.

When the Rev. Thomas L. Eliot, a public-spirited Unitarian minister in Portland, became superintendent of schools in Multnomah County in 1872, he was convinced that Portland needed the kind of educational system his father had helped to build in St. Louis. "Economy of power and efficiency in our schools," he wrote in his annual report in 1873, "depends in great degree upon a proper division of responsibilities. As in the army, so here; and I have suggested to the Directors [of the Portland schools] some steps looking towards a more thorough supervision by the Principals of their subordinates." The next year he welcomed the appointment of a city superintendent (Eliot worked only part-time as county superintendent and his territory was far too large to supervise adequately):

151

This measure was . . . dictated by that common sense which sees the need of a head to every organization consisting of diverse and complex parts. Our 25 schools, like so many separate units, or "feudal baronies," were governed by as many systems and precedents as there were teachers. The grades were, indeed, supposed to be defined, but were in a decidedly nebulous state. It was not, nor could it be, expected of the Directors to spend their whole time in the details of school methods, discipline and examinations. It remained . . . to follow . . . the example of other cities throughout the country where Superintendents or visiting principals are appointed.

The early days of public education in Portland had a certain rustic charm: the first teacher, bearing the unfortunate name of John Outhouse, unloaded ships and built roads when he was not teaching school; a successor "graded" her ninety pupils by ranking them on steps in the old loft which served as her classroom; one dapper teacher went for his certificate to the home of a minister who was serving as county superintendent, found him at the washtub, and smartly answered his questions while the minister was drying himself and rolling down his sleeves; a canny class of children persuaded their teacher not to use the rod by threatening her with a roomful of mice.

But for Eliot and his predecessor as county superintendent, the Reverend George Atkinson, such haphazard schooling had grave flaws: how could such teaching render the next generation "homogeneous in habits of thinking, feeling, and acting"? Atkinson was a pioneer Yankee Congregationalist minister who taught for a while in the Oregon City schools. He patterned the system of grading and examinations in Oregon City on the Boston plan, and when he moved to Portland, he sought to standardize its schools as well. Eliot agreed; graded classes and strict examinations brought healthy uniformity, hard work, and moral indoctrination. "As a field of clover, well rooted, admits no weeds," he wrote, "so the mind of a child, thoroughly employed and interested, has little room for the culture of low imagination and vice . . . an ill-regulated school system will bear fruit in the lack of self-control, punctuality, order, perseverance, justice, truth and industry, in its citizens." Eliot believed that well-run schools could counter "the pitiful fallacies which plunge nations into years of social misery and political disorder. . . . The barest knowledge of political economy, widely diffused,

152

would prevent the notion of sumptuary laws, communism and interference with trade and circulating media, which even now delude the minds of large portions of the people." Immigration, immorality, class conflict, corruption—these threats demanded efficient schools.

These two ministers, architects of the Portland school system, borrowed freely from Eastern educational ideology and structure. The product of the schools was to be the homogeneous good citizen—sober, moral, industrious, one who would preserve rather than question the social and economic system; the means of production was to be prescribed curriculum and a semimilitary bureaucracy. Atkinson and Eliot were educational strategists: they saw the schools as only part of a total process of socialization and civilization, and they worked as well to establish libraries, churches, colleges, and a host of other stabilizing institutions and associations. But many of the schoomen who followed them were not strategists but drillmasters who mistook bureaucratic means for social ends.

When Samuel King, first city school superintendent, took office in 1874, Portland had about ten thousand residents, 1,168 of whom were enrolled in the public schools. A consummate bureaucrat, King believed that children's behavior must be precisely controlled, reliable, predictable. Regular attendance and punctuality—surely necessary prologues to schooling—became an obsession with King. His war on irregular attendance, also waged vigorously by his successor Thomas Crawford, made Portland students in a few years the most punctual in comparable cities across the nation (by 1881 only .04 percent were reported tardy). Superintendents continued well into the twentieth century to report attendance and tardiness statistics down to the second and third decimal point. In 1876 the school board adopted a policy of suspending any student absent (except for sickness) or tardy four times in four consecutive weeks. King and his successors also publicly reported the tardiness of teachers, and fined principals for not opening schools at 8:30 A.M. sharp. "A school with an enrollment of fifty, daily attendance fifty and none tardy," King wrote lyrically in 1876, "is a grand sight to behold in the morning and afternoon." So great was the stigma of tardiness, and so keen the competition among schools for a good record, that children sometimes hid all day to avoid coming into class late and teachers sometimes sent children home to avoid marking them tardy.

153

Sometimes Crawford complained of teachers who had "overdrawn the evils of tardiness"; but he set the style by patrolling the streets to spot absent or late children. And Crawford proudly listed in a roll of honor the names of children who had perfect attendance from one to six years.

Getting the children and teachers to school on time was only the beginning. King and his principals worked out a "system of instruction and a division of school labor" which included a uniform curriculum, primary, intermediate, and grammar departments divided into six grades (further subdivided into A and B sections), and a plan of written examinations to ensure that the children had been "thoroughly drilled in the work assigned." As a Yankee who believed that "a perfect system of school management is indispensable to the welfare of our Public Schools," King paid examinations the supreme compliment: "System, order, dispatch and promptness have characterized the examinations and exerted a healthful influence over the pupils by stimulating them to be thoroughly prepared to meet their appointments and engagements. Next to a New England climate, these examinations necessitate industry, foster promptness, and encourage pupils to do the right thing *at the right time.*"

The results of the first round of examinations might have dismayed a heart less stout than King's. In seven classrooms out of a total of twenty-one, none of the children passed. Only in six classrooms were more than half of the children promoted. But King maintained that the operation was a great success, though most of the patients died. Not surprisingly, in the next examinations teachers and pupils improved somewhat: this time between 13 and 75 percent of the children were promoted (in some of the classes, though, fewer than three-fourths of the students got up nerve to take the test). King published the results of the examinations in the newspaper, with the child's score and school next to his name. Parents could draw their own conclusions about the diligence of the child and the competence of the teacher, and they did. Incensed and anxious, the teachers joined irate parents to force King's resignation in 1877.

The new superintendent, Crawford, promptly abolished the practice of publicizing the test results. He wrote in his report in 1878 that "incalculable injury has been done, both to the teachers and to the pupils of our free schools, resulting from a spirit of rivalry on the part of the teachers." Some teachers had gone to great lengths to protect their reputations, urging children to withdraw from school shortly before the examination and even advising the superintendent to suspend slow students for trivial offenses so that they wouldn't drag down the percentage of promotions. The system of publicity had led, he said, to cramming, "bitter animosities," and "unpleasant wranglings, over arbitrary standards in marking papers." Yet Crawford was no Paul Goodman; he was a good bureaucrat who wanted harmony in the ranks. He retained the examination system, elaborating it in Mandarin detail while softening its rigors, but he kept the examination results the property of the bureaucracy.

Despite occasional rhetoric about independence of mind, King and Crawford made it clear in their reports that the school system was to inculcate certified thoughts and proper deportment. "Habits of obedience, attention, promptness in recitation, neatness of copy-books, and a carefully prepared program of the daily work, are some of the characteristics and attractions of most of the schools," said King in 1875. He believed that "children should be taught to obey the commands of their teachers at once, and a slight tap of the pencil [should] be intelligible to any class." As children passed from class to class, they displayed "a military air and discipline that is truly commendable and pleasant." Even compositions should display martial virtues as pupils "draw up their words in orderly array and march through many sentences preserving order in the ranks and an unbroken line." Eliot believed that in their handwriting students "should strictly conform to given positions and rules, however awkward and constrained they may seem at first; for in penmanship, as in everything else of man's development, true liberty is obedience to law." And the law, there was no doubt, was the curriculum prescribed by the bureaucracy.

The uniform curriculum of the common school—an unbroken "chain" King called it—included the three R's, grammar, and a smattering of natural and social science. From test questions it is possible to discover what children learned to remember long enough to repeat on the examinations. The curriculum was neatly parceled into semester segments, the teachers were closely supervised and had to drill students on the material covered in the tests, and a premium was placed on uniformity of output. King's report for 1877 listed the questions asked at the end of the eighth grade and the examinations in the various high school subjects. With few exceptions the questions required definitions, facts, memorization of textbook explanations. These are some examples (the last three are aimed at eighth graders, the others at high school students):

> *A man pays 6 dollars yearly for tobacco, from the age of 16 till he is 60, when he dies, leaving to his heirs $500; what might he have left them if he had dispensed with this useless habit and loaned the money at the end of the year at 6 per cent compound interest?*
>
> *Define Imaginary Quantity, Surd and Pure Quadratic Equation.*
>
> *What system did Kepler adopt? Give his three laws. Tell how he discovered each.*
>
> *Define Diction. What is necessary to give one a command of words? What kind of New Words should be avoided? If any, specify the objections to the use of each of the following words: Exit, talkist, alibi, conversationalist, boyist, skedaddle, donate.*
>
> *How do the two kinds of engines differ? How is the power of steam engines estimated?*
>
> *What was the Kansas-Nebraska Bill?*
>
> *What causes earthquakes? Describe the Desert of Sahara. Give the area of the Atlantic ocean.*
>
> *Write and punctuate the Lord's Prayer.*
>
> *Give the principal parts of the verbs lay, lie, go, cut, shoe. Give the second person singular of elect in all its moods and tenses.*
>
> *Give the five provisions of the Compromise of 1850.*
>
> *Spell: Burlesque, Ichneumon, Heliotrope, Analytically, Diaphragm, Panegyric.*

The fact that about 93 percent of the high school students answered questions like these correctly that year testifies to the marvelous capacity of the human race to suffer trivia patiently. Year after year, until the bombshell of the Cubberley report in 1913, the curriculum changed but little; it was mostly taken for granted.

An essential phase of the bureaucratization of the schools was the establishment of definite qualifications, salaries, and duties for teachers. In 1881 Crawford complained about untrained and inexperienced teachers and decried the pressure on the school board to hire incompetent teachers with influential friends. He urged that professional competence be the only criterion for employment. He also suggested a normal "training class" for high school students intending to teach. In 1881 the school board adopted a uniform pay schedule for teachers based on years of experience and level of instruction. Two years later the board set standards of eligibility and performance for each position and published twenty-two rules regulating teachers' examinations and certificates. Although technically there was no segregation into positions by sex, in effect a class system soon developed in which men became predominantly the supervisors and women the supervised; only in the high school was it respectable for men to teach. This feminization of elementary school teaching had gone so far by 1905 that all teachers of the grades were women. Twenty-three out of twenty-seven elementary school principals that year were men—almost, but not quite, a caste system, for some upward mobility was possible for women. This sex differential, coupled with the low pay, low prestige, and inadequate education of the elementary school teachers, helped to reinforce the autocratic structure of the bureaucracy.

Although certification is regarded today as a form of professional licensure, in its early stages in cities like Portland certification was a branch of civil service reform: a means of ensuring that public servants possessed at least minimal competence for their tasks and a way of preventing an educational spoils system. These objective standards of competence and rewards were common characteristics of bureaucracies in all fields, though in public agencies during the gilded age corruption and special favors were notorious problems. In Portland, however, civil service reform came early, and with the exception of alleged improper influence of the "book trust" of the American Book Company, in the 1890s, Portland was relatively free from scandal.

In 1883 the school board issued a booklet of *Rules and Regulations* which codified the practices standardized during the previous decade. There was bureaucracy, in black and white: the classification of schools; the uniform curriculum; the hierarchy of offices and delineation of duties; the time schedules; the elaborate plan of examinations and promotions. As chief policeman the superintendent was required to "see that the grade work is strictly followed, that the rules and regulations are observed and enforced, and [to] report any and all delinquencies to the Board." Principals were the intermediate inspectors and disciplinarians, instructed by the board, among other duties, "to prohibit the playing of marbles on or about the school premises." Nothing was left to chance in the duties of the teachers: they were told to open the windows at recess;

to suspend a thermometer from the ceilings and to keep their rooms between 67 and 71 degrees; to assemble for at least two hours at their monthly institute (they were fined two dollars for failing to attend and one dollar for being tardy); "to subscribe for, take and read, at least one periodical devoted to educational work"; and to "*cheerfully* cooperate with the City Superintendent in executing the prescribed work of the grades." Uneven in education and skill, teachers were to be governed by rules, not professional norms. Once a month the teachers read to the students the "Duties of Pupils" commanding obedience, punctuality, industry, and respect for school property. Thirty-seven rules dealt with absence, tardiness, excuses, and suspensions; eight outlined examinations and promotions. Obscurity was not one of the faults of the Portland Public Schools; complacency was.

The bureaucratization of the schools had not gone unchallenged in Portland or elsewhere. In 1880 the crusty and conservative editor of the *Oregonian*, Harvey Scott, launched an attack on the "cumbrous, complex and costly system" of the public schools. "In nearly every city there has been growing up during the last ten years an elaborate public school machinery," he wrote, "largely managed and directed by those whom it supports. Nominally it is controlled by the taxpayers of the districts, but in reality by associations of persons who live as professionals upon the public school system." What was needed, he said, was a return to "the simple yet effective system of the old common schools." Scott was sure that citizens were "decidedly in favor of reducing the 'establishment,'—as the system has been called since it grew to its present proportions." Methods of instruction have grown "to a complexity which puzzles the learner and which works the teacher harder out of school hours in making up trivial reports, calculated on percentages of proficiency, behavior, etc., than in the . . . schoolroom." (Perhaps teachers not inclined to "cheerfully cooperate with the City Superintendent" had been talking out of turn.)

Scott sent reporters out to gather the opinions of the businessmen of Portland about the "new-fangled, finical stuff" going on in the schools; the complex machinery, the new subjects introduced into the grades and the high school (which Scott thought quite unnecessary for the common child). Most of the businessmen interviewed thought common schools necessary, but many questioned the need for expensive "flummery." "A child who has a good English education, if he has any snap about him," said one, "will succeed better than the average graduate of the high school who knows a little of every thing." Another said flatly, "The prominent and useful men of this city are not men of high education." Some glorified the simple, cheap, old-time district school: just the three R's, under the eye and thumb of the community. And one believed that the Portland schools were "being controlled by a school ring and not by taxpayers or directors." Just inculcate the right values cheaply, said the self-made men.

Even George Atkinson had misgivings about the dominant role the school was beginning to play in the life of the child. During pioneer days children had learned the discipline of manual labor at home, he wrote in 1879, but as the school took over more and more of the student's life there was a danger that it might "graduate whole regiments of sickly sentimentalists: young gentlemen unused and unfit to work, and young ladies decked in the latest fashion. . . ." Parents should be forced to certify that their children were doing some manual labor for at least six months of the year, thereby correcting "a good part of the evils which are likely to grow out of improved public instruction."

Atkinson's comment that "evils . . . are likely to grow out of improved public instruction" suggests the complexity of the issues raised in the revolt of 1880 against the school bureaucracy. Many motives impelled Scott and his fellow critics. Scott thought the schools were producing "shyster lawyers, quack doctors, razor-strop and patent-soap peddlers, book canvassers, and bookkeepers"—not willing workers. Many opposed higher taxes, especially for secondary education. Some believed that education beyond the common school should be the province of private schools (and they were encouraged in this belief by many private schoolmen who luxuriated in laissez-faire rhetoric). Some wanted the simple days of the old district school when parents saw the school as a community center in which families were more citizens than subjects. Others resented the fact that the schools were taking over functions previously performed by family, church, and economic units. And above all, the schools seemed to be out of touch, insulated, irresponsible and irresponsive to the public, remote, and haughty.

Scott had said that no one could expect self-criticism from the professional establishment; the letters to the press of administrators like Crawford and the state superintendent of public instruction displayed a shocked and self-righteous attitude. The depth of feeling against the bu-

159

reaucrats was illustrated in a letter from "C" which appeared in the *Oregonian* on February 26, 1880: "We, the defenders of the common school system, are between the upper and nether millstones, the impracticables and the destructives. . . . It can only be perpetuated by relieving it of the complex character it has assumed by reason of the inflated, pedantic and self-aggrandizing character of the faculty, who from one entrenched foothold of aggression against popular rights have advanced to another, until we see the result in the superficial, overloaded and overtaxing system now prevailing."

Such attacks hurt and bewildered Crawford. He had earnestly gone about his business of liquidating tardiness and ignorance, organizing the schools according to the best Eastern models, cultivating his own bureaucratic garden. The impersonal rules, the uniform curriculum, the school hierarchy—did these not serve as a buffer between the teacher and the community, affording protection against the tyranny of parents, the spoils system of urban politicians, the insecurity of ambiguity? Crawford did admit that school patrons "have an undoubted right to sit in judgment on the general and even particular conduct of teachers who are public servants. What a teacher does out of the school room as well as in it comes within the purview of the public." Then as now, the superintendency was an anxious profession and the school a vulnerable institution. Bureaucracy became the schoolman's moat and castle, and bureaucrats tended to regard an attack on their particular system as an attack on the principle of public education. That label which would be heard again and again in the years to come—"enemies of the public school"—they tried to pin on their opponents.

In 1880 the main task of defending the schools fell to the Reverend George Atkinson, then general missionary for the American Home Mission Society. Atkinson knew how to smother brush fires by committee. Thus at a heated meeting of taxpayers on March 1, 1880, Atkinson as private citizen diplomatically proposed an impartial investigation of the charges which had been leveled against the system and a report on the condition of the schools. He summarized the complaints: that the machinery of the schools was too costly and cumbersome; that the studies were too difficult and numerous; and that the high school was not properly a part of the common school system (certain college preparatory subjects had been singled out for attack). Atkinson was chosen chairman of the investigating committee. This was rather like asking the Pope to study irregularities in the Vatican, for Atkinson was the most eloquent advocate of the bureaucracy (though not technically a member of the "school ring").

As author of the report Atkinson said that the "machinery" of education, far from being too cumbersome and costly, "seems hardly to keep pace with the growth of the city." He maintained that "large classes permit the best division of labor" and that the systems of grading and examinations "encourage every class in habits of promptness, order and diligence." Over a third of the grammar school graduates of the past five years were continuing their education, over one-half were working at home or in trades; and only 1 percent were "of questionable character." But Atkinson reiterated that parents should "train their children, in manual labor" and teachers should give "lessons about the real work of life." The best proof of the quality of the schools was "that few idlers or hoodlums have ever been connected with the public schools of Portland." The high school he saw as an "extension of the grades and classes," well justified as a means of spreading "the purest morals and the best possible culture among great masses of people, who make and execute their own laws."

In this report Atkinson reminded the people of Portland of the rationale for uniform and efficient public education: "The self-government of the people is still on trial, and every hour great currents sweep from other lands against its foundations and test the pillars of its strength. How shall the incoming tens and hundreds of thousands be moulded into our body politic and made homogeneous with ourselves except by the public school—training every child in our own tongue and habits of thought, and principles of government and aims of life?" The perils of diversity dictated uniformity in the schools. Thomas Eliot concurred:

The justification of our public school system really lies where people seldom look for it, viz.: In the necessity of a republic's preserving a homogeneous people; the necessity of having one institution which effectively mingles and assimilates all classes and castes. It is the "imperium in imperio," the democracy within the democracy of our national existence. The nation can afford to trust education of every kind to the parental instinct; but, it cannot afford to trust to chance the

unifying processes; the sentiment which welds the people; and the com-
mon school as bringing all classes together at an impressionable age is
the forge it sets up and maintains as its most powerful instrumentality
against aristocracy and mobocracy (communism) and every other
"ocracy."

Still grumbling about the establishment, Portland accepted Atkinson's report and its rationale. Not until Cubberley and his team of experts descended in 1913 would there be another full-scale investigation of the bureaucracy.

When Crawford resigned from the superintendency in 1888 the basic character of the school system was well established. For the next three years a talented woman, Ella Sabin, was superintendent. During her brief tenure she attempted to recast the curriculum and teaching methods in accord with "the enlivening influence of the 'new educa- tion' " (the movement which later became "progressive education"), but the patterns of behavior already established in the bureaucracy per- sisted and were reinforced by the regimentation required by her succes- sors; she left her mark chiefly by a residue of progressive rhetoric, here and there, in the teachers' guide. Irving Pratt, who took her place in 1891, became best remembered for declaring that "19 of his teachers [were] excellent. . . . All the rest were a poor lot."

Frank Rigler spent his seventeen years as superintendent (1896–1913) largely in perfecting the machine he had inherited. In his first report he assured the taxpayer that *he* was no devotee of the "new education": "The friends of our schools who are apprehensive that the schools have become too modern are needlessly alarmed. I am not aware that our schools have any (approved) features that were not to be found a genera- tion ago. . . ." Like a good general, he supported his troops: "every teacher now in our schools is making an effort, each according to her ability, to do the kind and extent of work that has been done by the best teachers for many years." The *Oregon Journal* reported the claim of one of Cubberley's colleagues that there had been no changes for the better during Rigler's long regime, an accusation which infuriated the super- intendent. In Rigler's final report, written just before his resignation, he listed the improvements made during his tenure—manual training schools, a program for deaf and defective children, medical examinations of pupils and so on—but his sense of priorities was evident in the first three items on his list of achievements:

1st   *The construction of the buildings has changed from wood to steel and concrete.*

2nd   *A system of ventilation and heating has been introduced which expresses the latest views of competent ventilating engineers.*

3rd   *The toilet facilities of the schools have been made equal to those of the best dwellings and hotels.*

Indeed, a committee of leading educators admitted in 1890 that community pressures on imaginative administrators were such that "it is not surprising that so many really capable superintendents settle down to the running of the school machine as it is . . . the strongest and wisest of educators may be pardoned if he degenerates into a not ignoble specimen of arrested development."

Rigler, however, never was tempted to be anything but a guardian of tradition. His maxim "was to play the game straight according to the prescribed rules." Criticized he was, for conservatism and autocracy; never for being too liberal. Stern, efficient, logical, a master of detail, he ran the bureaucracy like an army. At teachers' meetings he went through the textbooks page by page, telling his staff what questions to ask and what answers to accept. It was common knowledge in Portland that Rigler "could sit in his office and know on what page in each book work was being done at the time in every school in the city." He revived Crawford's plan of internships in teaching for high school graduates and personally indoctrinated the young girls in his rigid course of study (the bureaucracy in Bel Kaufman's *Up The Down Staircase* seems permissive by comparison). The basic curriculum remained what it had been in the 1870s: the three R's, grammar, history, civics, geography, drawing, and various subjects in natural science. But Rigler took great pride in splitting the former thirty-six divisions of the curriculum into fifty-four "cycles" (each spelled out by pages in the textbooks) and in turn subdivided them into fast and slow sections.

In Rigler's monotonous reports one looks in vain for reflections on the philosophical or sociological rationale of his administration. A fellow superintendent, Aaron Gove of Denver, was not so reticent; in an

NEA address he bluntly expressed the premises which underlay the Portland bureaucracy as well as his own. Gove opposed " 'soft pedagogy' and 'mellow education' " and believed that the grammar school years were "the time for drill, memory training, severe application to tasks with an accounting for their accomplishment." Similarly he had no taste for democratic school administration. The limits of the superintendent's authority should be clearly stated, he said, "in the formal rules and regulations of the board of education." Within these bounds the superintendent's authority was unlimited, though he would be well advised to exercise it politely: "The autocracy of the office of the superintendent of a public-school system is necessary for the accomplishment of his purposes, but that despotism can be wielded with a gloved hand." Teachers can no more constitute a democracy than can policemen. Teachers may from time to time give *advice*, but "dictation must come from the other end." The teacher has only "independence like that of a man in a shoe factory who is told tomorrow morning to make a pair of No. 6 boots"—that is, he "can work rapidly or slowly," but he must make the boots. Gove saw in the "War Department of the nation" the best analogy for proper school organization. The general—the superintendent—must control all his troops, but must leave first-hand inspection up to his inspector-general's department. "The executive department of a school system of thirty thousand pupils would be ideal with one superintendent and four school inspectors who shall spend their entire time, as does the inspecting officer of the army, in reviewing and examining in detail every part of the enterprise and reporting promptly and often, in a very careful way, what he finds. . . ."

So far had bureaucracy gone down the down staircase that the nature of education had been subordinated to the demands of the organization. To the survey team in 1913 schooling seemed a vast percolation of words for the student, teachers robots, administrators themselves captives of the rules and the system. This was the trained incapacity, the blindness to alternatives, which bureaucracy often (though not necessarily) produced. Cubberley and his colleagues were determined to jar Portland out of its rut.

To Cubberley's group Portland symbolized much that was wrong with "traditional education." They deplored the abstract, uniform curriculum and gagged on grammar tests that asked students to define attribute complements and independent elements. They attacked the military model of teaching by routine and drill. They satirized the autocratic and rule-constipated structure of the schools. They believed that the new science of education, new conceptions of learning, new tasks for the school, and new views of the teacher's role had rendered obsolete most of the bureaucratic system which Portland had labored for fifty years to build.

Cubberley was convinced that education should be functionally differentiated according to the needs of students and society. Furthermore, he was committed to professional expertise for both teachers and administrators. These are elements of what has come to be called educational progressivism. The old-fashioned military model of bureaucracy in which hierarchy depended more on power than on function made sense only so long as the goals of education were stated in very generalized terms, such as producing homogeneous good citizens. By 1913 many school administrators believed that educational progress depended on Spencer's "differentiation of structure and . . . specialization of function," and their model of such functional specialization was contemporary industrial organization. In Cubberley's view,

> Our schools are, in a sense, factories in which the raw materials [children] are to be shaped and fashioned into products to meet the various demands of life. The specifications for manufacturing come from the demands of the twentieth century civilization, and it is the business of the school to build its pupils to the specifications laid down. This demands good tools, specialized machinery, continuous measurement of production to see if it is according to specification, the elimination of waste in manufacture, and a large variety in output.

Cubberley believed in "large variety in output," for one of the key faults of traditional education was its lack of specialization. Portland's schools were "much in the condition of a manufacturing establishment which is running on a low grade of efficiency," said Cubberley, for it was based on an antiquated bureaucratic model. "The waste of material is great and the output is costly—in part because the workmen in the establishment are not supplied with enough of the right kind of tools; in part because the supervision of the establishment is inadequate and emphasizes wrong points in manufacture; but largely because the establishment is not equipped with enough large pieces of specialized machinery, located in special shops or units of the manufacturing plant, to enable it to meet modern manufacturing conditions." Cubberley believed that urban schools should "give up the exceedingly democratic idea that all are equal, and that our society is devoid of classes," and should adapt to existing social classes. Portlanders "should apply to the management of their educational business principles of efficiency similar to those which control in other forms of manufacturing." He believed that the school system should train students for specialized roles in the economy while still striving to produce *morally* homogeneous citizens.

The school should have a highly trained staff headed by a captain of education similar in stature to a captain of industry. A bureaucracy it should be, but a specialized one controlled by professionals, not drill sergeants. The caliber of a school, said Cubberley, "depends much more on the quality of the leadership at the top and the freedom given the leader or leaders to work things out in their own way, than upon any scheme of organization which can be devised." The Portland School Board was still trying to oversee minute administrative details and relied on rules rather than men, not realizing that "what a school system is, it is largely because of the insight, personality, and force of the Superintendent of Schools." Likewise, this leader should be given responsibility to select administrators and teachers who could exercise professional discretion within their specialized spheres. Cubberley believed that a staff which had grown from 294 in 1900 to 928 in 1913 needed effective supervision; but he also was convinced that no one man could decide what was best for the 43,000 children in the district. To professionally trained teachers fell "the responsibility, under wise guidance and leadership, of adapting the educational process, both in content and method, to individual needs." In short, the bureaucracy was to be looser structurally, the superintendent and his administrative staff adapting the schools as a whole to the needs of society, and the teachers adapting lessons to the needs of the child. A new tension was thus introduced which had hardly existed in Rigler's despotic system: the uneasy and sometimes conflicting demands of consistent and orderly administration on the one hand and professional autonomy and freedom to experiment on the other.

Cubberley had really stated a dilemma rather than solved a problem, a dilemma faced by urban schoolmen everywhere. As Cubberley knew, bureaucracy in some form was here to stay in large American school systems, however it might be modified by new conceptions of education, and inherent in bureaucracy was the impulse toward regularity. In a small rural school, or in a Freud-inspired private school, an individual teacher might single-handedly put the tenets of progressive education into practice. Progressives might protest against the regimentation common in urban school systems at the turn of the century, but the effects of rigid bureaucratization could not easily be erased by reading *Democracy and Education*, by introducing new subjects into the curriculum, by workshops on new methods, by developing new ways to classify pupils, by new theories of administration, by new patterns of professional training. It was difficult indeed to capture the spirit of progressive education in a crowded slum school, to transform a class of forty polyglot children into the sort of family at cooperative work which Dewey described as the ideal school. As a result, many "progressives" like Cubberley sought essentially to substitute a new version of bureaucracy for the old. But at the turn of the century perceptive schoolmen recognized that the quest for standardized schooling—that once had been a reform—had become a kind of despotism. It would require all their ingenuity to control their creation and to subordinate the schools to education.

ORIGINS OF THE CATHOLIC PAROCHIAL SCHOOL
Robert D. Cross

The way to secure a proper religious and moral education has always posed problems for religious minorities. During the common school revival of 1830 to 1850, the public schools moved in the direction of a nonsectarian Protestantism. This usually consisted of such practices as reciting the Lord's Prayer, the singing of a hymn, and a daily reading from the Bible. Supposedly this approach was religiously neutral. In fact, it reflected the views of and was acceptable to virtually all of the Protestant denominations, but was noxious to those of other faiths. In addition, many non-Protestants objected to the cleansing of public school subjects of a specific religious content. They maintained that all branches of learning, being parts of a unified system of doctrine, had to make manifest their philosophical and theological foundations. No mode of adjustment to nonsectarian Protestant influence on the public schools was more significant than the Catholic parochial school movement. Professor Cross, a specialist in American religious and immigration history, links the establishment of parochial schools with the cultural as well as religious needs of Catholic immigrants from Europe.

For the strength of Protestant interest in establishing and influencing the public schools, see Timothy L. Smith, "Protestant Schooling and American Nationality, 1800–1850," *Journal of American History*, 53 (1967), pp. 679–695, and David Tyack, "The Kingdom of God and the

Common School: Protestant Missionaries and the Educational Awakening in the West," *Harvard Educational Review*, 36 (1966), pp. 447–469. An interesting collection of Catholic statements on education is in Neil G. McCluskey, ed., *Catholic Education in America: A Documentary History* (New York: Teachers College Press, 1964).

Two convictions of the nineteenth century made the education or socialization of the young a pressing concern for every public man and every public institution. The first was that education was too important to be entrusted to informal processes—too important for society to indulge the belief that family solicitude, neighborhood interest, the proximity of the church, or the tutelage of farm or factory work would add up to education. Formal schools were needed, not just for the very special purposes for which they had for so long been cherished, but for all kinds of education.

The second conviction of the era was that all youth required formal education. A growing democratization of opportunity, the extension of the suffrage, a more complex urban life, an apparent increase in the amount of available and usable knowledge combined to make plausible the demand. Eventually faith in universal education outran faith in the universal desire for education, and governments began to enact compulsory school laws.

This commitment of nineteenth-century culture posed a serious problem for the churches, especially in America, where the "separation of church and state" and a growing sense of "denominationalism" had already raised baffling questions about the proper sphere of churchly enterprise. Should the churches abandon active responsibility for the formal schooling of the young, as they had renounced direct participation in political life and economic life? Or must each church conclude that the education of its children was so tied up with both the interests and the unique beliefs of the church that it could neither expect nor desire any government instrumentality to undertake the task?

By the middle of the nineteenth century, the Protestant churches had generally opted for only a limited commitment to provide formal education. They did not abandon, but even expanded, their support for institutions of higher education, many of which doubled as seminaries. They developed Sunday schools to make more formal and more organized the training in religion and theology that previous generations had assumed would be received in regular church services and in family devotions. But by and large they relegated to the state the task of providing formal daily education for youth. They did not imagine that they were condoning a secularized education, any more than they supposed that because they abstained from forming a separate political party they were abandoning politics to irreligion. They regarded with great contentment the wide use of the McGuffey readers, and the common custom of beginning the school day with prayer and a selection from the Bible. They rightly assumed that if a teacher proved wayward or a textbook impious, the local school board would be properly deferential to the complaints of an indignant religious citizenry.

The Protestant churches could thus justify acquiescing in "public education" as simply a division of function with a cooperative state, leaving the churches as free to devote their energies to such exclusively religious tasks as erecting more churches, or sending more missionaries to the heathen at home and abroad. For the Catholic Church in America no such easy solution to the problems of education was available. By the middle decades of the nineteenth century, its leaders were so alienated from much of American life that they regarded public education with deep suspicion and began to cast around for alternatives. It is the purpose of this paper to trace the way in which, through the rest of the century, Catholics narrowed their sense of alternatives, and particularly to give the reasons why the parochial school came by 1900 to be regarded as virtually the only genuine Catholic answer to the "school problem."

GROWING RESPONSE TO FORMAL EDUCATION

Up to about 1830 or 1840, the absence of any clear determination in American society to make formal education universally available had permitted Catholics to avoid any forced choices. Bishops and priests, avowing their responsibility for "Catholic education," could confine formal schooling to the area of higher education. For John Carroll the highest priority in education was to establish Georgetown, and Bishop Benedict Fenwick of Boston could declare that "the thing I want most (and until I attain it I am persuaded that nothing permanent can or will ever be effected in this quarter) is a Seminary and College." The hierar-

170

chy assumed that the education of most Catholics would be accomplished under "the parents' roof." There were, it is true, a handful of academies founded for young Catholics whose parents had both educational interests and financial means, while a few parishes, usually in the larger cities, had established local schools. But these parochial schools generally had neither the strong support from the priesthood nor the permanent teaching staff to differentiate them clearly from other semipublic schools. It is a striking fact that the first American Catholic almanac, appearing in 1833, made no mention of the few parochial schools that existed; obviously they did not yet constitute an important aspect of American Catholic public life. Society's commitment to formal education was not yet strong enough to force clear Catholic responses.

In the next thirty years or so—to the close of the Civil War—America did turn decisively towards public education. It was no easier a hundred years ago than today to define policies which would maintain the schools suitably "under God," without offending the predilections of some parents; still, the determination of men like Horace Mann that the public schools should be purged of mere sectarianism, along with the political needs of men like Seward, produced a strong disposition in many states to accommodate Catholic preferences. Know-Nothingism, seen in perspective, did not really alter the long-term trend to try to make the public schools open to all. Then, as now, local schools were given much leeway. They used it variously. In about the same years that a teacher in the Eliot School in Boston escaped real censure from his school board, even though he had very severely beaten an Irish Catholic student who wished to use a Douai rather than a King James Bible, Lowell, Massachusetts, was maintaining "Irish" public schools, to which only Catholic children came, in which only Catholics were employed as teachers, and where Catholic priests were allowed to conduct religious services.

Few immigrants brought to America a clear commitment to formal schooling, but in the strange land their children required some substitute for the tutelage of the extended family and the neighborhood they would have received in the old country. An Irish-American described his fear that immigrant children would not develop "obedience for holy things—for what is great and good and noble." Schools *might* help de-

171

velop such attitudes, and might, in addition, provide the special skills needed for successful adjustment to a new world. Immigrants themselves did not always conclude that schools were necessary, but there was an obvious congruence of interest.

NEED OF CATHOLIC SCHOOLS IS RECOGNIZED

On the other hand, the immigrants were usually suspicious of the institutions of their new country; and their church was able to show them why they were right to be. The Roman Catholic bishops at the Fourth Provincial Council, meeting in 1840, sensed a parallel between the "National Education" scheme England was creating in Ireland and the widespread use in American schools of Protestant hymns, prayers, and version of the Bible; "the nature of public education in many of these provinces," they concluded somberly, "is so developed that it serves heresy." A dozen years later, John Hughes, Bishop of New York, declared that education, as perpetrated in America, was "Socialism, Red Republicanism, Universalism, Deism, Atheism, and Pantheism— anything, everything, but religionism and patriotism." Such a fantastic image of public education in the era of Horace Mann and William McGuffey reflected how deeply this prominent Irish-American was alienated from American institutions.

The violence of Hughes's rhetoric was also a reflection of the growing determination to create Catholic parochial schools that would relieve parents of the difficult choice between public schools, private academies, and no school at all. Church councils urged this responsibility on priests and laymen in ever more commanding tones. Acknowledging the ability of public schools to impart some useful information and skills, church spokesmen recurred with increasing emphasis to the traditional theological distinction between "mere instruction," and "true education"; the latter developed the child morally and spiritually as well as intellectually. They elucidated this distinction in characteristically nineteenth-century ways, assuming that virtually all training of importance took place in schools, and contending that if this schooling did not constitute true education, it could at best be mere instruction, but was more likely to be a counterfeit kind of education. Only *schools* and schools that were formally Catholic, the argument concluded, could provide Catholic children with Catholic education.

172

Probably the growth of parochial schools, however, owed less to these syllogisms or to ecclesiastical fiat than to the success of the bishops in recruiting religious orders to run the schools. The teachers in the first parochial schools resembled their counterparts in the nineteenth century public school in thinking of their jobs as short-term commitments. The Sisters and Brothers won some of the prestige readily given professionals because of their lifetime dedication. Set apart, furthermore, by their costume and way of life, they were free to create a discipline and an order unknown in most nineteenth-century schools. They were reassuring to immigrant parents—not like many public school teachers, a challenge and a reproach; they did not speak for, or symbolize, the all too present and too coercive American world, but a lofty indifference to it. They did not allow the schools to degenerate into a center of carefree experience which might contrast invidiously with life with father. They taught the true religion, which the public schools sometimes ignored, sometimes openly reviled. Finally, their willingness to work for subsistence wages helped ease the burden of "double taxation" which seemed to bear most heavily on those least able to pay.

The recruitment of Sisters and Brothers was *necessary* to the development of a parochial school system, but it was not *sufficient*. Indeed, the critical period of the parochial schools lay ahead, in the last thirty-five years of the nineteenth century—years when the public schools would expand rapidly in numbers and radically in quality, and when compulsory school laws in most states would force Catholic parents to choose one kind of school or another. In this later period, it was not only the public educational situation that had changed. The Catholic population was much more diverse than in the years before the Civil War. As earlier, a large proportion of Catholics were recent immigrants, but there were two salient differences: an overwhelming percentage of the immigrant Catholics were not Irish; and a large percentage of the Irish-American Catholics were not immigrants. Each difference had important consequences for the Catholic response to the public schools.

GERMAN CATHOLIC LEADERSHIP

From the early 1850s to almost 1890, Germans made up the largest group of immigrants to America, and though only about one-third of them were Catholic, those that were brought with them a loyalty to the

Church that had been tempered by years of struggle with non-Catholic governments.

Even before education became compulsory in America, German Catholics had distinguished themselves by their willingness to create schools that would help save the children from the evils of the surrounding culture. "Without a school," a German Catholic editor declared, "children become totally ignorant, or what is worse, unbelievers, godless, and immoral." German Catholic areas of settlement led other Catholic areas in school development. "Our excellent German congregations," a Provincial Council of Cincinnati declared, "leave us nothing to desire on this subject." By the late decades of the century, a German Catholic priest could with probably only slight exaggeration inform Roman authorities that "you will hardly ever find a German church without a parochial school annexed, to which nearly all, if not all, parents send their children." The German Roman Catholic Central Verein established as a prerequisite for membership in its constituent societies the attendance of one's children at a parochial school. The German Catholics were emulated in their zeal, if not their immediate achievement, by the growing increments of Polish and French-Canadian Catholic immigrants who, like the Germans, developed in America a desperate eagerness to preserve their language and culture against the forces of assimilation. The Germans, however, took the lead in defending the foreign-language parochial school against criticism both from within and without the Church.

English-speaking Catholics sometimes alleged that the Germans were more interested in preserving the language than the faith, and it was certainly true that the German schools used a far higher percentage of lay teachers. Advocates of the public schools argued that the German schools, by scanting the teaching of English and civics, did not prepare their students for life in America; they also noted that the Germans were far less interested in providing schools for the older children. The German spokesmen of course denied both sets of allegations. But they did not wish to placate their critics by compromising. To submit to any demands from American or Americanizing agencies would mean, they felt sure, the end of Catholicism of the German immigrants. The prominent Chicago layman A. C. Hesing put the case for autonomy in a blunt address to Archbishop Feehan:

174

Our German language . . . is the tie that holds us together, and it presents our duties to our country, and even to our God and Church, more forcibly to our souls than any other language. . . . For it and for the preservation of our German parishes and parish schools we stake our best powers. Upon these two rest our steadfastness in the faith and our loyalty to religion and the Church.

IRISH IMMIGRANTS AND THE PAROCHIAL SCHOOL

The Irish immigrants of the era of John Hughes, though no admirers of the public schools, had not committed themselves so heavily to the parochial schools as had the Germans. This was the result partly of the greater poverty of the Irish immigrants, partly because schools were not needed to preserve the ethnic language, perhaps partly because there was no such clearly defined Irish "culture" as the *Deutschtum* their fellow Catholics wanted taught. At any rate, equivocal feelings toward parochial schools did not disappear with the years. The tone of Irish-American life in the last decades of the century was increasingly set by the second generation, many of whom had moved away, both in spirit and in fact, from the ghetto. These men were less inclined than their Irish-American forebears or their German contemporaries to regard American institutions like the public school as irredeemably anti-Catholic. They were willing to reconsider how separatist they had to remain in order to be good Catholics in America.

To an increasing number of Irish-Americans, the parochial school could not win acceptance simply as a fortress against Americanization. More and more parents began to find faults with the parochial schools as they knew them. The most common gravamen was the expense. "We can bear the burden no longer," a group of laymen told Archbishop John Ireland of Saint Paul. "My God! what can we do?" No doubt the cost of competing with the growing public schools was increasing, but so was the income of American Catholics. Considering the great generosity with which laymen in these years contributed to many Church causes, it is possible to interpret protests against the costs of parochial schools as in part simply doubts about their intrinsic desirability. Some Catholic parents openly wondered whether their children should be asked to go to school without regard for the social standing of their classmates. "Catholics of better condition," Archbishop Ireland

175

reported, want "higher associations for their children than they can make in the parochial school"—where very often children of recent immigrants and of unskilled laborers predominated. By contrast, some public schools included "children of the influential classes of the community, of those persons who control the social, financial, commercial, and political interests." Perhaps parents ought not to be influenced by such considerations, Ireland conceded, but he would not blink the "very obstinate" fact that many Catholics wanted their children to make friends in school with those who in the future would be "found in the banking and commercial houses of the city, and not on the streets or in the workshops."

Some laymen began to demand less emphasis on Europe and more on America. It was no longer a source of prestige that so many of the Sisters teaching in the parochial schools came straight from Europe; "the pious peasant girl just arrived in America" had less appeal to those who were outgrowing the immigrant state of mind. The parochial school continued to be valued for its tuition in Catholicism, but there were occasional mutterings about the failure to present the faith in persuasive ways. Archbishop Ireland reported that, fine as the Sisters were for the youngest children, there was "a very general complaint among parents" that the older ones were "sent forth by the Sisters from their schools less fitted for the battle of life" than those who had attended public schools. Laymen were "prone to believe," a priest added, "that when called upon to teach the sciences and literature, our Catholic teachers are not up to the mark."

SOCIAL POSITION AND THE PAROCHIAL SCHOOLS

Whether an Irish-American felt justified in looking askance at parochial schools frequently depended on his social position, which in turn was generally correlated with his escape from the ghetto. One Vicar-General reported that "when a pastor undertakes to erect a parochial school he meets with three classes of persons in his parish: the upper class which he cannot force, the middle class which he is able to force, and the poor people who are in favor of it." Yet even the middle class was occasionally stubborn in feeling that the public school was not without positive merit. Not only had many public school systems eliminated the grosser anti-Catholic discriminations from textbooks and the daily conduct of the schools, but many systems also gladly employed

176

Catholic teachers. (With parochial schools employing mostly Sisters, Catholics seeking to escape from immigrant occupations were strongly attached to public school teaching.) Where school boards contained Catholic members—on some occasions, Catholic priests—it was easy for Catholic parents to conclude that there could be nothing intrinsically non-Catholic about the public schools. Of course in some school systems Catholics were harried as students, proscribed as teachers, and inconceivable as members of the school board; but the number of such systems was declining.

The parish clergy on whom rested the duty of raising the money for a parochial school and then of supervising its work were, in most Eastern dioceses at least, divided into "schoolmen" and "anti-schoolmen." Father Thomas Scully of Cambridgeport, Massachusetts, for example, no doubt believed that a strenuous building campaign was an ideal way of developing loyalty to the parish. With a fine school built, he denounced by name from his pulpit those parents who still sent their children to the public school; he even denied them absolution, communion, and the Last Rites. His neighbor, Father John O'Brien of East Cambridge, Massachusetts, in contrast, once announced, "I hope the time will never come when I shall be obliged to build a Catholic school." His disinclination stemmed from his sense of the poverty of his parishioners, his respect for the achievements of the public schools and for the intentions of the Cambridge School Committee (of which he was a member), and his fear that an extensive parochial school system would engender new outbursts of anti-Catholicism. Other priests, like Edward McGlynn of New York City, believed that the problems of social welfare were so overwhelming that neither priest nor people had time or money to spare to devote to education. Many priests were simply "irresolute," sometimes maintaining a school, sometimes not, but always hoping for some accommodation with the state that would relieve their people and themselves from carrying, unaided, the burden of formal education.

The regular clergy and the bishops were less affected by these practical considerations and more by their estimate of the general health of the Church. Given the unprecedented conditions of late nineteenth-century America, it is little wonder that there was a sharp difference of opinion. The Church was obviously growing at a remarkable rate, but should it not be growing faster? If, as many suspected, the Church was suffering great "losses," what was the probable cause? And what modes

177

of counterattack were possible in a culture which gave no church the privileges of establishment?

Most of the German spokesmen and Irish-Americans like Bishop Bernard McQuaid of Rochester and Archbishop Michael Corrigan of New York viewed the American scene with foreboding. The public schools appeared to them as simply an aggression of the world against the faith; that these schools were steadily growing less Protestant they took as a sign of a trend toward "godlessness." McQuaid was sure that the public schools were the major reason for Catholic losses. A German priest concluded that a parish without a parochial school would have to depend on receiving members brought up in other parishes; its own children would be swept away into infidelity by the public schools. A German Redemptorist, Father Michael Mueller, was outraged at the notion that a few Catholic teachers or a Catholic priest on the school board would make the public school any less dangerous; "I assert," he wrote, "that a Catholic boy of tender years, and perhaps careless training, can be preserved from moral contamination, in public and mixed schools, by nothing less than a miracle. I will not chop logic with any one about it. It is a matter of fact." The peculiarity of Mueller's reasoning, like the intemperance of the abuse visited by these men upon the public schools, were the measures of the bewilderment they felt. Like their non-Catholic contemporaries, they jumped from the plausible assumption that formal schooling would likely have *some* effect upon the young to the conclusion that it was absolutely decisive. They concluded that the Church, in self-defense, must secure "the constant charge of her own children. She wants to control their studies, form their minds, direct their hearts, teach them, guard them . . . have them at her side and so fulfill in every detail the duty imposed on her by her Lord of feeding his flock and gathering the lambs into her bosom." In that perspective, building a parochial school and requiring all parents to send their children became almost a dogma of the faith, no less persuasive because it was based on an unsubstantiated fear, and no less revered because it was premised on a gospel of educationalism that the Church might have been expected to reject.

In striking contrast to this point of view was that held by a minority in the Church who had come to believe that American culture was enor-

178

mously hospitable to Catholicism; all that was needed for greater triumphs was Catholic readiness to respond intelligently to the promise of American life. Education these men viewed not as a shield for Catholics against America, but as an emancipation from narrow views. John Lancaster Spalding's many books and sermons typified this commitment to education, as well as a willingness to recognize that there were various ways in which children might become truly educated. These "liberals" could not, of course, approve of the absence of religious training in the public schools, but they liked to contrast the respect generally shown for religion there with the skeptical tone of public schools in putatively Catholic lands. They were optimistic that eventually the state would find ways of fostering a wholly satisfactory education that was both public and religious. Continuing to urge their priests to build parochial schools, they never ceased to explore the possibility of an entente between state and church to provide such satisfactory education.

ALTERNATE MODES OF EDUCATION

I do not have time, nor is there really any need, to rehearse here the story told ably by Father Reilly and others of the several demarches made in the 1880s and the 1890s by Archbishop Ireland, Father Thomas Bouquillon, and their liberal allies to develop an alternative, on the one hand to the public school as advocated by the National Education Association, and on the other to the parochial school as defended by men like Mueller and McQuaid. The theme of their efforts was set by Ireland in a letter to Cardinal Gibbons declaring that "the necessity for parish schools is hypothetical, . . . a Provision in certain cases for the protection of the faith." In many countries, he noted, Catholics got along very well without them. "The Church is not established to teach writing and ciphering," he continued, "but to teach morals and faith, and she teaches writing and ciphering only when otherwise morals and faith could not be taught." Regarding the parochial school not as the norm but as the last resort, Ireland explored, sometimes openly, sometimes deviously, the possibility of alternative modes of education.

Ireland received considerable support for this position in the 1890s, both in the United States and at Rome. But by 1900 or 1910 it was obvious that the American Church had publicly committed itself to the parochial school as the only Catholic solution to the educational problem. Indeed, for the next forty or fifty years debate was largely limited to the best means of completing a system of schools equal to but separate from the public schools. Diocesan organization, the training of teachers, curricular reform—these preoccupied Catholic educational thought. An occasional request for government aid was almost always accompanied with a militant assertion of the absolute autonomy of the parochial school.

Why had the possibility of alternate arrangements disappeared so rapidly and so completely? One reason was certainly the inertia of a large organization. By the 1890s three out of five parishes had created parochial schools of some sort, and though many were sustained only with great difficulty, it would have required remarkable self-abnegation for laymen to urge, or clergy to seek, or bishops to sanction, a policy which either abandoned the parochial schools or jeopardized exclusively Catholic control over them. Furthermore, building and supporting a parochial school had become a familiar and practical way of expressing one's religious commitment in a society which offered few modes so simple or so satisfying. Finally, even though the papal delegate to America, Archbishop Satolli, had specified that "absolutely and universally speaking" Rome did not require the parochial school, fifty years of episcopal strictures, exhortations, and demands had worked their cumulative effect; only men of force and orginality like Archbishop Ireland, and then only in a period of heady optimism about the Americanizing of Catholics and the Catholicizing of America, could manage to transcend this tradition. Unquestionably, too, American Catholics gathered from the papal utterances *Testem Benevolentiae*, in 1899, and *Pascendi gregis*, in 1907, that they should approach any cooperation with the non-Catholic world with great caution.

A second reason was the continuing inflow of foreign-language Catholics, and the increasing reliance on national parishes to accommodate them. The large number of Polish, South Slav, and Italian Catholics, arriving between 1900 and 1914, were mostly potential recruits for the "German" position on parochial schooling. Confronted with mandatory school laws, most of the first generation clearly preferred for their children a school which respected the old culture, both linguistically and religiously. Where public schools made a deliberate effort to safeguard the immigrant language, and parochial schools were unwilling or unable to—a case in point would be the greater responsiveness of the public schools in Milwaukee than of the largely German parochial schools there to the influx of Polish Catholics—the newcomers gave slight support to the parochial schools; but such a situation was far less common than one in which the Church proved willing to deviate from its policy of defining parishes geographically in order to cater to the ethnic interests of the new immigrants.

But probably the major reason for the failure of Ireland's détente was the unwillingness of most public school authorities to make special arrangements for any minority groups. The moral they drew from the long battle with private schools and academies was that compromises were neither necessary nor desirable. The school board must remain, one state superintendent characteristically argued, "absolutely free in the exercise of its authority for the organization and conduct of a good public school." To defer to immigrant interests would be to jeopardize the ability of the schools to Americanize. It seemed supremely important not to enter into any special arrangements with religious groups. The public school should conscientiously eliminate any religious practice which offended anyone; it should not experiment with modes of positive accommodation.

This attitude derived from more than educational principle. School boards, concerned with the efficient administration of a school system, attached great importance in this era to a rationalized districting of the city; imposed from the top, such a districting reflected bureaucratic need more than local interests. The public school which stood in the middle of such a district might be called a "neighborhood school," but school authorities would insist that the school should set the tone for the neighborhood, rather than that the neighborhood or district should determine the nature of the school. Such a system clearly left little room for nice adjustments to Catholic interests. The inevitable recourse was the parochial school.

I have argued in this paper that the decisive period in the development of the parochial schools in America was the late nineteenth century. It is, of course, possible to contend that the schools date from the acknowledgment by John Carroll of the Church's desire for the Catholic education of its children; from the determination of the Fourth Provincial Council of Baltimore in 1840 that the nature of public education was such as to serve heresy; from the First Plenary Council of

1852 which ordered priests to build schools wherever possible; from the Instruction from Propaganda in 1875; from the Third Plenary Council in 1884. Or one may contend that the decisive period did not come until recent decades, when enough Catholics were prosperous to make possible a dramatic extension of the parochial school system and when, in many parts of the country, the public school had lost the prestige it had enjoyed generally in the time of Archbishop Ireland.

My argument has been, however, that in the late nineteenth century both Catholics and non-Catholics entertained peculiar notions about the importance of formal schooling. In those years, most non-Catholics believed that the public school was a unique and irreplaceable engine of democracy and progress; and most, though not all, Catholics accepted the gross exaggeration of Bishop Hughes that if the Church was to survive, schools were more important than places of worship. The irreconcilability of these conclusions made the parochial school necessary. It exists today even though the premises about the importance of formal schooling for the preservation of the faith have been sharply challenged.

★ 12 ★

EDUCATION FOR BLACKS: BOOKER T. WASHINGTON AND W. E. B. DUBOIS
Merle Curti

With the conclusion of the Civil War, the issue of education for blacks became a national question. Since the former slaves were now citizens, and many of them, of all ages, thirsted for instruction, it was natural to shape and implement educational enterprises in their behalf. Both governmental and private agencies involved themselves. The Freedmen's Bureau of the War Department put up school buildings in Southern states immediately after the war. Church and secular charitable societies, mainly organized and funded in the North, enlisted teachers and supplied them to Southern schools. During the Radical Reconstruction period of the late 1860s, some Southern states opened their public schools to black youngsters, and Congress in later years seriously considered, although never launched, a federally financed national campaign to abolish illiteracy, which existed mainly among black and immigrant children.

Although some of these undertakings were either temporary or stillborn, permanent results were achieved. Notable was the establishment of several institutions of higher learning for black youth. Some of these, such as Fisk University in Nashville and Howard University in Washington, D.C., were modeled on the antebellum American college. Hampton Institute in Virginia, and Tuskegee Institute in Alabama, however, broke new ground by initiating programs that combined traditional collegiate instruction with vocational training. The leading spokesman for this approach was Booker T. Washington, head of Tuskegee, and soon to become a national figure. By the opening of the twentieth century, Washington's ideas, although still popular with many of those whites who were interested in supporting black education, had provoked serious challenge from within black ranks. The lead in this was taken by Dr. W. E. B. DuBois, a highly educated black scholar and publicist, who argued the case for traditional liberal arts instruction.

Students should consult Washington's classic autobiography, *Up From Slavery* (many editions), and DuBois's collection of essays, *The Souls of Black Folk* (Chicago: A. C. McClurg & Co., 1903). Other aspects of the history of black education are covered in Horace Mann Bond, *Negro Education in Alabama: A Study in Cotton and Steel* (Washington, D.C.: Associated Publishers, 1939); Louis R. Harlan, *Separate and Unequal* (Chapel Hill, N.C.: University of North Carolina Press, 1958); and Henry L. Swint, *The Northern Teacher in the South, 1862–1870* (Nashville: Vanderbilt University Press, 1941). See also C. Vann Woodward, *The Origins of the New South, 1877–1913* (Baton Rouge: Louisiana State University Press, 1951), pp. 350–368.

Just so soon as the white merchant finds that education is giving the Negro not only more wants, but more money with which to satisfy these wants, thus making him a better customer; when the white people generally discover that Negro education lessens crime and disease and makes the Negro in every way a better citizen, then the white taxpayer will not look upon the money spent for Negro education as a mere sop to the Negro race, or perhaps as money entirely thrown away.

—Booker T. Washington,
My Larger Education.

I

In 1872 a young Negro boy with fifty cents in his pocket knocked at the door of Hampton Institute. Born a slave, he had, as a toiler in the salt

184

and coal mines in West Virginia, known nothing but degradation and poverty in the turbulent years that followed emancipation. His mother was not one of the five or ten percent of her race who could read, and it was only by heroic efforts that he had succeeded in learning his letters. The elementary schools for freemen established in some places in the South by the missionary societies of Northern churches and by the Freedman's Aid Bureau had apparently not penetrated the mining region where he lived. It was consequently not his fortune to learn his three R's from any of the courageous Yankee schoolma'ams who had gone South to educate the Negro. Had he come under the influence of one of these teachers, who were regarded by Southern whites as obnoxious and who sometimes saw their schoolhouses burned by the Ku-Klux, his later social philosophy might have been very different. If it was true, as Southerners insisted, that these Yankee teachers were inculcating in the blacks pernicious ideas of racial equality and hatred toward their former masters, Booker T. Washington might have developed a militancy which would have altered his outlook on life. But he learned another lesson from his first great hero, the founder and head of the Hampton Institute.

General Samuel Chapman Armstrong had founded Hampton with the conviction that the only hope for the future of the South lay "in a vigorous attempt to lift the colored race by a practical education that shall fit them for life." He had learned from the experiences of the American missionaries in Hawaii, from whom he had sprung, the value of an education for less advanced peoples which, by training the hand for efficient industry, at the same time disciplined the mind and formed character. He taught his pupils that labor was a spiritual force, that physical work not only increased wage-earning capacity but promoted fidelity, accuracy, honesty, persistence, and intelligence. At a time when most Negroes who dreamed of education at all aspired to a knowledge, no matter how smattering, of Latin and Greek, and looked upon education as a substitute for the grinding toil of slavery, Armstrong at Hampton was teaching that the capacity to "make a living becomes enlarged into the capacity to make a life." At great personal sacrifice and with true missionary zeal he and his teachers, when Washington entered the school, were training selected colored youths to go out and lead their people by showing them how to acquire land and homes, vocations and skills; by teaching them to respect labor, especially skilled labor, and to appreciate the value that such work had for the making of character.

In the spirit of Dewey, the founder of Hampton had thus created a school which was a little world where education was to be identical with actual living and which was intended to become a potent and directing force in solving a great social problem. A new type of education was to prevent economic and political catastrophe for blacks and whites alike. "Education, to be effective for life," Armstrong declared, "must be, like the conduct of life itself, both alert and patient, beginning where people are, and creating character rather than comfort, goodness rather than goods. It must be won rather than given, and based on faith in labor as a moral force; it must inspire the will to serve rather than the will to get; it must be a struggle, not for life alone, but for the lives of others."

General Armstrong's appreciation of Booker Washington's admirable qualities—his perseverance, diligence, optimism, and submission to authority—did not assure to that boy an easy road. Hard and exemplary janitor service, a part of the self-help that prevailed at Hampton, enabled him to earn his way. He had never before known what it was to sleep in a bed, to eat regular meals with a knife and a fork, and to take the most elementary care of his body. These things he learned and, realizing their importance to the progress of his race, idealized.

Hampton taught other lessons. Booker T. Washington learned the full meaning of duty. Above all, General Armstrong imbued him with his own burning love of service to others, especially service to the black race. His doctrine that skill in labor was indispensable to the Negro was confirmed in Washington's mind when his awkwardness in waiting on table at a summer hotel brought him a cruel rebuff. Each obstacle that he overcame, however, strengthened in his mind the Hampton doctrine that personal success depended on one's ability to do some useful service that the world wanted. If this applied to the individual, it must also apply to his race.

In his first teaching experience in a small school in West Virginia Washington learned to apply the pedagogical principles which in a general way prevailed at Hampton and, in doing so, anticipated one of the most characteristic features of progressive education. Noting the listlessness of his pupils one hot June day, he prolonged their recess and by a happy accident discovered that in surveying the islands in a neighboring marsh the children learned their geography with a zeal entirely lacking when they pondered their maps and books. "For the first time the real difference between studying about things through the medium of books, and studying things themselves without the medium of books, was revealed to me." Washington ever afterward impressed on his associates the great importance of training pupils to study and analyze actual things, and to use what they had learned in the schoolroom in observing, thinking about, and dealing with the objects and situations of everyday life.

When, in 1881, Washington was called to found a normal institution at Tuskegee, he found no plant, no apparatus, and almost no money. Moreover, he found hostility on the part of the white community. Save at Hampton, Negro education had largely been a bookish training which fitted the students for teaching and preaching; and it was widely feared that this would result in making blacks dissatisfied with manual work. To provide the means for building and maintaining the school, and to break down this prejudice, Washington was virtually compelled to fuse practical and intellectual training, thus anticipating the project method which Dewey popularized many years later. If there were to be buildings, students must construct them. If there was to be food, they must produce it, for few could pay for its purchase. If it was to be prepared, they must cook it. So students were taught arithmetic by figuring the cost of constructing and painting a building, by measuring an acre of land, by estimating the cost of producing and preparing a pound of pork. When the school, to meet its own and the community's needs, developed the industry of brick-making, an opportunity was provided for studying the history of the practical arts; and all these matters formed the basis of instruction in English composition.

When students cooperated in doing all the necessary work at Tuskegee and in providing the community with many of the products it needed, and especially when the surrounding area was included in this education through extension work, education was in fact closely tied up with life. Experience and necessity taught Washington that in education it is best "to stick close to the common and familiar things—things that concern the greater part of the people the great part of the time." Education became, in short, problem-solving; and the problems were created, not by artificial devices, but by the compelling necessities of existence. Thus in the struggle to find an education which would best

187

meet the needs of his people, Washington gave the world a practical example of "a broader and more generous conception of what education is and should be than it had had before."

In spite of the Hampton precedent, it was not an easy matter to popularize practical education. Armstrong's doctrine of the moral value of industrial training was of course reiterated, but to the ambitious young Negroes who desired to raise their status by acquiring the culture of upper-class whites it was not altogether convincing. When classroom work was dropped for several days in order to prepare special exhibits and to put Tuskegee in apple-pie order for President McKinley's visit, there was much grumbling on the part of students. Dewey had not yet popularized his doctrine of the educational value of learning by doing useful and cooperative tasks, but Washington appeased his pupils by talking to them at length in very much the way that Dewey might have done. It was not, however, until 1911, when the founder of Tuskegee visited the folk schools of Denmark, that he came fully to appreciate the broader cultural value of utilitarian education. Meantime it was in his mind justified chiefly on the ground that it was necessary, not simply for the existence of Tuskegee, but for the solution of the race problem itself. It is his emphasis on the social significance of a purposeful education which lies at the heart of Washington's social philosophy and which makes him a great American educator.

Washington's emphasis on a practical education for the Negro is explained by his belief that, in order to break down racial prejudice and to achieve real progress for the black, the Southern white must be convinced that the education of the former slaves was in the true interest of the South—in the interest, in short, of the Southern white himself. Far from appealing to disinterested motives, this black leader believed in the efficacy of appealing to the self-interest of the dominant whites. In their hands lay the granting or withholding of funds for Negro schools. In their hands, moreover, lay the administration of court justice and the alternative device of the rope and faggot—the year after Washington arrived at Tuskegee 49 black men were lynched, and in 1892, ten years later, the number was 155. In the hands of the ruling race, too, lay a thousand other matters which vitally affected the blacks. It was clear to Washington that the alliance with Northern whites during Reconstruction had failed to effect any permanent guarantees to his race; and it was equally clear that the more militant and aggressive behavior of the postwar days had provoked reaction and the violence of the Ku Klux Klan. Where aggressiveness and militancy had failed, an appeal to the self-interest of the dominant whites might succeed. The founder of Tuskegee faced the facts and acted according to his light.

In his effort to enlist the sympathy and cooperation of the white community in Tuskegee, Washington was surprisingly successful. His warning that white men, by holding blacks in the gutter, would have to stay there with them, was a compelling argument when it became clear that the whole community actually did profit by what was being done for the Negro. By providing skilled services and produce that Tuskegee needed, he broke down a great deal of the existing prejudice against Negro education. By encouraging the blacks to respect the law and to cooperate with white authorities in detecting crime and punishing it, he still further won the goodwill of the old master class. When he insisted that the great majority of his race did not expect or desire social equality, he still further disarmed the whites.

The astute Negro leader also did much to dispel the bugbear of black political domination. At first he said very little about the constitutional right of the Negro to vote. Only very cautiously and gradually did he come to advocate the desirability of permitting educated and property-owning blacks to exercise the right of suffrage. He declared that the Negroes should give up their political affiliations with the Republican party, which had befriended them in Reconstruction and which they regarded as their emancipator. The Negro in the solid South should vote Democratic because that party was regarded as the true friend of the economic interests of the South, and by so voting he would still further ingratiate himself with the white people in their community. The principal of Tuskegee himself, having made it clear that he would vote only for Democratic candidates, had no trouble in casting his ballot.

To his own people Washington preached the necessity of making themselves useful to the whites and thus securing their goodwill and the favors they alone could bestow. If the Negro learned how to cultivate the land so efficiently as to produce a larger acreage of cotton, the white farmer would not only respect him but chat with him on the methods he had so successfully used. If the black mastered a skilled trade, the white employer would value his greater usefulness and recognize the potential ability of the race economically to rehabilitate the South. If he accumulated property and paid taxes, if he was able to succeed in business and trade and even to lend money to the dominant race, no barrier of skin could keep the white from associating with him. If he gave up his desire to imitate the upper-class whites by taking on a veneer of superficial polish and made himself valuable in terms of dollars and cents, he would in the long run win their respect and confidence and even break down their antipathy.

In season and out of season, therefore, Washington warned his people against the deadly sins of idleness, gambling, and drinking, and held up to them the ideals of industry, thrift, chastity, honesty, and earnestness. The Negro, he pleaded, could better afford to be wronged that the white man could afford to wrong him. Unlike the Russian who hurled dynamite to right his wrongs, or the Frenchman who applied the torch of revolution, or the Indian who flew to his tomahawk, the "Negro must lie by, must be patient, must forgive his enemies, and depend for the righting of his wrong upon his midnight moans, upon his songs, upon his four-day prayers, and upon an inherent faith in the justice of his case."

In short, the black man was to cease depending upon the humanitarian friendship of Northerners and, by making himself indispensable to the ruling class at home, to work out his own salvation. He must never forget that for the race as for the individual the more discriminations and difficulties, the more steam was required to overcome them, and the greater the victory. If this optimistic philosophy was in part compensatory for the actual handicaps of the race, it nevertheless proved to be a dynamic force, giving courage and incentive to many who came under its spell.

Washington spared nothing to get a hearing for his social philosophy among Southern whites. Aware that his public words in the North would find their way South, he took care never to say anything in that section which he would not say at home. Southerners who attended the sessions of the National Education Association in Madison in 1884 reported with approval the generous tribute he paid to the white people in Tuskegee for the sympathy they had shown toward his work. When at last an invitation came to give a five-minute talk before a Southern audience, he thought it worthwhile to make a three-thousand-mile journey in order to win the ear of those who directed matters south of the Mason and Dixon line. It is said that he even paid $1,000 to get a speech into *The Atlanta Constitution.* His great victory came in 1896

[1895-Ed.] when, notwithstanding grave doubts as to the propriety of the invitation, he was asked to give an address at the opening of the Cotton States Exposition in Atlanta.

In the famous speech which Washington delivered on that occasion he translated his social philosophy into epigrammatic terms. The opportunity to earn a dollar, he declared, was more important to the Negro than the chance to spend it in the opera house. Pleading with the Negro to make himself useful to the South and with the white to cultivate a spirit of friendliness and fairness to the black in return for this economic contribution, Washington won great applause from the governing class for concluding that "in all things that are purely social we can be as separate as the fingers, yet one as the hand in all things essential to mutual progress." Clark Howell of *The Atlanta Constitution* wired New York that the speech was one of the most notable that had ever been given to a Southern audience; it was "a revelation, a platform upon which blacks and whites can stand with full justice to each other." For the first time the white South listened seriously to a Negro, and the speech won new allies in the North as well.

Subsequent lectures, articles, and books consolidated the position thus won. In view of the bids that the South was making for Northern capital, it was not without significance that the Negro educator declared in the Atlanta speech, as he had done before and continued to do, that his people had never engaged in strikes or given any labor trouble. He announced that the hope of the Negro rested largely on such Southern leaders in finance and business as John M. Parker, a New Orleans cotton merchant who was quoted as saying that it was "important to the commercial progress of the country that the Negro should be treated with justice in the courts, in business, and in all the affairs of life." So exemplary was Washington's behavior that J. L. M. Curry could observe that in fourteen years of intimate association with him he had never once known the Negro educator to say or to do an unwise thing.

Regardless of the extent to which Washington succeeded in convincing Northern financial groups that industrial education of the Negro promised a skilled, docile, and cheap labor supply, and that racial friction would diminish, he certainly found it, after his reassuring speeches, less of a struggle to obtain endowment for his institution. Both the Peabody and Slater funds increased their subsidies; and the great railroad magnate Collis Huntington and such industrialists as

Andrew Carnegie, H. H. Rogers of the Standard Oil Company, William H. Baldwin, and Robert Ogden discovered the value of the work which was being done at Tuskegee, and contributed to its exchequer.

In 1905 Ogden wrote that, in view of the ill effects of excitement on the race question, *"peaceful patience* should control the utterances from Hampton" and doubtless the same advice was given to Tuskegee. On one of the rare occasions when Washington referred to the race question, which he thought must be *"lived* down, not *talked* down," he took particular pleasure in Curry's praise of his remarks. William Henry Baldwin, manager and vice-president of the Southern Railway, was, in Washington's words, "always particularly interested and even anxious that in all my public utterances I should say the right thing and, above all, that I should say the helpful thing."

Convinced that the Negro was at his best in the country and that he showed up worst in the city, Washington made every effort to persuade his people to acquire the farms on which they lived. Yet, as the years passed, he came more and more to sympathize with the Negro businessman and to reverence the business ideal of life. In part this change was due to new associations. He learned to admire such men as H. H. Rogers, William Baldwin, Robert Ogden, and the Negro business leader Charles Banks. In part, however, his increased interest in business was merely a recognition that American life was becoming urbanized and that business success offered the great road to advancement. He took it for granted that a people able to organize and conduct large business corporations, banks, insurance companies, and other forms of corporate enterprises was destined to survive and prosper.

If the Negro businessman was successful, Washington felt that then prejudice and color could not long shut the race out from a share in any of the responsibilities of the community in which they lived, or in any opportunity or position that a self-respecting people would desire to possess. "Our people," he declared, "must learn not merely the lessons of industry and thrift; they must also learn to employ corporate action for the achievement of their ends as individuals and a race, in the same way that the white man has learned to employ it." He sponsored the National Negro Business League and in refutation of the charge that the race was lacking in thrift, executive talent, and organizing ability, cited with pride the success of colored men in business.

The black leader was merely accepting the dominant business philosophy of his day. Like most Americans, he did not ask how fortunes were made, nor question the ethics of the captains of industry and finance. Accepting the tenet that whenever the Negro failed to find steady employment, it was due to his shiftlessness, his unreliability, and his easygoing ways, he begged his people, in heart-to-heart talks, to cultivate the business virtues.

In plain words Washington reminded his race that one of their sins was their inability to handle other people's property honestly. He held up for praise the successful boy who did a dollar's worth of work for fifty cents, was at hand before starting time, and stayed after the closing hour to ask the employer if there were not something more to be done before he went home. The Negro was urged to anticipate the wants of his employer and to remember that it did not pay to do anything less than his very best. Above all, he was advised to accumulate a bank account. Frugality, industry, foresight, financial responsibility, and independence—these were prominent among the virtues that Washington begged his people to cultivate as the surest means of getting ahead.

Believing that if the blacks knew something of the burdens borne by the masses of Europe they would realize that their own position was by no means unique or hopeless, as many had supposed, Booker T. Washington went to Europe in 1910 to study the "man farthest down." He came back with an optimistic message for his people. If they could have heard one race in Austria-Hungary denouncing another in the most virulent terms, they would realize that race prejudice was not a matter of color. Could they have visited with him the desolate slums of the great European cities, seen the degradation, the beggary, the unemployment, they would have seen sights, he declared, far worse than anything which existed in the Negro quarters of Southern cities or in the most wretched cabins in the countryside.

In Europe Washington found conditions bad indeed. There the overcrowded land was owned by a few great landlords; in the South, there was plenty for everyone to own an ample farm. In Cracow, women toiled in the granite quarries. In Sicily existed moral degeneracy that made the Negro seem in comparison a model of virtue. In Bohemia, the Czechs, in addition to the discriminations inflicted on them by the ruling Germans, spoke a different language and adhered to a different faith: the Negro spoke the tongue and attended the church of the Southern white. However meager the educational opportunities of American

193

Negroes, boys and girls shared them alike. In Europe, on the other hand, the women farthest down were burdened with additional discriminations because of their sex. In short, while the Negro had suffered as a slave and was still discriminated against, his position was by no means exceptional. Indeed, in some respects he fared better than the man farthest down in the Old World. In finding people lower still than they, Washington seemed to lift his own race to a higher level.

Although Washington found much evidence that the masses in Europe were getting ahead, he doubted whether trade unions, strikes, Socialism, and revolution could improve their lot. Wherever the governing classes had made concessions, wherever remedial measures and reforms had been granted, the spirit of revolution had subsided. While he admitted that he did not very clearly understand Socialism, he expressed doubt whether, human nature being what it was, the Socialist program could be realized in the way its adherents believed. It was the American individualist of the middle class, not the Negro, who spoke when he declared that as human capacities differed, so opportunities and rewards must also differ. As a Southerner he paid tribute to the *laissez-faire* theory that the best government was that which governed least; and as an American, he repudiated reform by revolution and by political machinery which directed and controlled the individual from the outside. Neither his own race nor the substantial friends of Tuskegee could doubt where he stood. Possibly, however, there was something of an ironical warning in his statement that the dominant class in Europe had patriotically striven to strengthen the existing order by freeing it from the defects that endangered its existence.

In a truly American middle-class spirit this educator looked to philanthropy, collaboration between classes and races, and, above all, to education, to effect a great, silent, peaceful revolution in the lot of the European masses. "The effect of this movement, or revolution as I have called it, is not to 'tear down and level up,' in order to bring about an artificial equality, but to give every individual a chance to 'make good,' to determine for himself his place and position in the community by the character and quality of the service he is able to perform." The industrial training which European governments provided for the masses confirmed him in his belief that he had done well to emphasize that type of education for his race.

Washington's social philosophy was, in fine, more typical of middle-class white Americans, whom he wanted his people to be like, than it was of the Negro as such. It is true that in appealing to former slaves and their offspring to eschew militancy and conflict with the whites in the effort to improve the status of the race, he capitalized the black man's way of getting along by laughing, dancing, and singing. But little was said about the qualities of gaiety, humor, and wistful whimsicality, virtues and gifts which some thought might enrich and soften the driving, efficient, and machinelike ways of the American whites. On the contrary, Washington made simplicity, earnestness, frugality, and industry the great desiderata. One searches his writings in vain for any appreciation of the aesthetic and cultural values of the African background, of the "spirituals," or of the generally pleasant, easygoing ways of the black man. Although very occasionally he made a bow to the need of cultivating the beautiful, he resembled Franklin in paying much greater deference to whatever was useful and practical.

In other ways Washington was like the average American. His insistence on looking at the bright side of things, his devotion to getting ahead by self-help, his conviction that every one had his future in his own hands, that success came to him who was worthy of it, and that the greater the obstacles, the greater the victory over them—all this characterized the thought and feeling of most Americans. Equally typical of the dominant psychology of the middle and upper classes was his denial of any conflict or cleavage of interest between worker and employer, white and black. His was the gospel of class cooperation. His boast that his race had never been guilty of declaring strikes was pleasant to Americans who loved to think that there could be no justification in such disturbances to decency and public order. His patriotic belief that, however bad conditions were for his race at home, the masses of Europe were even worse off, was likewise good American doctrine.

II

Characteristically middle-class though his social thinking was, it met with criticism. After the Atlanta speech, when Washington was accorded recognition as the leader of his race, Negroes took him to task for truckling to the dominant whites in the South. Some felt he should speak out more openly in regard to the violation of the civic rights of Negroes. Others lamented that his philosophy lacked the spirit of the Declaration of Independence. His complacency and his desire to give

195

no offense seemed to many a betrayal of the best aspirations and hopes of the race.

Outstanding among his critics was Dr. W. E. Burghart DuBois. A graduate of Fisk and of Harvard, DuBois had studied at the University of Berlin and won distinction as a scholar and as a writer. What he especially resented was the overshadowing emphasis which Washington placed on industrial education. It seemed to obscure the legitimate desires of many Negroes for professional, literary, and artistic distinction. College education, which promised to teach the Negro the values and meaning of life, seemed relegated to a back place by all the insistence on training to get ahead in the trades, in farming, and in business. If the race was to have leadership, if Negroes were not to be simply more efficient hewers of wood and drawers of water, then, it was held, something more than industrial training was imperative. If the Negro were to win equality with the white, he must equal the white in culture, in creative scholarship, and in the arts. He must prize the best in his racial heritage; he must hold his head high, and stop turning the other cheek; he must, in short, cast off the psychology of the slave. Between these two ideals of education a bitter fight was waged. In spite of the passionate and tenacious sincerity that characterized both sides, each made concessions. But on the whole, at least among the leaders of the race who succeeded Washington, the point of view for which Dr. DuBois stood gained an increasingly important place.

Yet, as Dr. DuBois himself later admitted, much could be said in defense of the position that Washington took. When he insisted that no end of talk would refute the evidence that the blacks did not equal in condition and capacity the majority of the whites with whom they came in contact, he added the significant remark that to insist that such was not the case was merely to admit that slavery had not been a handicap to the race. While professional men were indeed necessary, and while culture must be kept in mind, the race for the time needed above all else the knowledge and skill which would ensure the material necessities of life.

Washington's position is better understood when it is remembered that he began his work when race hatred was at its height and when emotions were strained and tense. The temper of the times was against the black man. Washington felt that much could be gained if attention were diverted from the fear of whites for the integrity and supremacy of their race, a fear deeply ingrained by hundreds of years of experience as a master class. That fear might be diverted if the ignorant black could be made to seem a more serious danger than the educated Negro. The satisfaction of the stronger race that came from insults could perhaps best be undermined by the black if he capitalized his defensive sense of humor. If defiant passion were met with resistant passion, conflict rather than conviction promised to result. A wise strategy would shift the proof of the capacity of the black race from the subjective to the objective plane. The emotional resistance of the whites to such objective proof must be swept aside, not by a frontal attack, but by a diversion— by allaying the fear of the dominant group that its self-interest and integrity were threatened by the lower.

Education of the hands helped, in fact, to bridge the gap between slavery and freedom; it taught thousands of Southern whites to accept Negro education, not merely as a necessary evil, but as a possible social benefit. The goodwill that Washington won was at least partly responsible for increasing public support to Negro colleges and schools. But this support has remained to our own day both inadequate and unequal to that given the schools for white children. While in 1931 an average of $45.63 was spent by Southern states for the education of the white child, only $14.95 was spent for that of the black. Of the total school expenditure in the South, only 10.7 percent went to the Negro race.

The industrial school was, nevertheless, realistic and not without victories in its practical object of aiding the black man to find a place in American life in which he could make a decent living as the foundation of culture. In the words of its early critic Dr. DuBois, "it tempered and rationalized the inner emancipation of American Negroes. It made the Negro patient when impatience would have killed him. If it has not made working with the hands popular, it has at least removed much of the stigma of social degradation. It has made many Negroes seek the friendship of their white fellow citizens, even at the cost of insult and caste. And thus through a wide strip of our country it has brought peace and not a sword."

Yet, as Dr. DuBois has pointed out, industrial training did not keep the Negro farm population from decreasing; it did not enable the Negro artisan to gain proportionately in industry; it did not establish Negro business on a sound footing. Leaders of the movement ignored the fact that at the very time when the crusade for industrial training was being launched, the technological basis of industry was rapidly shifting from that of the skilled artisan to machine production. They failed to see that the machine, by invading the farm, was already beginning to push even the established farmer to the wall. They did not come to grips with the stubborn and fettering problem of tenantry. They were blind to the fact that in business a new technique of worldwide combination, the use of credit on a vast scale and the rise of the mail order house and chain store, was stacking the cards against the success of the Negro businessman. Above all, they failed to see the weaknesses in the dominant industrial and financial system into which industrial education was trying to fit the Negro. They made the grave mistake of assuming that it was both sound and unchanging. In short, Washington failed to see the problem of democracy in industry; he failed to seek an alliance with the labor movement, or with any group that sought to remake the existing order along more equitable and more stable lines.

In view of the hostility of organized labor to the black and the general ineffectiveness of Socialism on the one hand and the friendliness of men of great wealth on the other, it was, of course, entirely natural for Washington to take the stand he did. Moreover, there was much justification for his emphasis on the immediate amelioration of his race within the system that actually existed. Until collaboration with the dominant class among the whites had been proved to be ineffective as an instrument for elevating the race, it was natural to pin great faith to it. Even the majority of white educational leaders, far better equipped than a former slave to penetrate and to interpret events, did not see any fundamental inadequacies in the existing order.

With much mellowness and philosophical insight Dr. DuBois has criticized also the cultural type of Negro education which supinely imitated the white college and university. If it provided much intelligent leadership, it too had failed to comprehend the age for which it was presumably fitting its students. Like other colleges, it had often turned attention away from a disposition to study and solve fundamental economic and cultural problems.

If the Negro were to fit into the existing system—and what could seem more natural and desirable to a former slave?—Washington offered a realistic approach to the problem. His ideas and his leadership were widely appreciated. Probably the most representative and influential educational leader of the period, William T. Harris, declared that

Washington's solution for the Negro problem was of "so universal a character that it applies to the down-trodden of all races, without reference to color." If in spite of his positive contributions in helping Negroes adjust themselves to a system, Booker T. Washington failed to criticize fundamental weaknesses within that system, his failure was hardly a personal one. He was merely accepting the prevalent American doctrine of self-help and the belief that the best man gets ahead, and, considering his background, it is not strange that he failed to see that this holds even less true for the humble Negro than for the average white man. The limitations of his social thinking were not, primarily, those of a Negro—they were those of the class which, on the whole, determined American values and governed American life.

★ 13 ★

JOHN DEWEY'S CONTRIBUTION TO EDUCATION
Oscar Handlin

John Dewey, the American philosopher, educational theorist, and liberal intellectual, was undoubtedly the most important American thinker of the early twentieth century and—for good or ill—its most influential educator. Evaluating his role in the changes wrought in American education from the late nineteenth century to the present remains one of the largest problems in writing American educational history.

In *The School and Society,* published at the turn of the century, Dewey referred to the school as a "legatee institution," one inheriting functions other institutions, such as the family, workshop, or local community, could no longer perform. Perhaps this central insight suggests better than anything else why modern schools have been the objects of such severe criticism. They were where the buck stopped: they inherited the problems that could not be passed on to any other institutions (except perhaps the police). Oscar Handlin in the selection below shows the basis of Dewey's indictment of the schools. School conditions at that time suggest the magnitude of the job that progressives were tackling. Perhaps Dewey's error was to arouse unrealistic expectations for achieving giant social purposes merely through reform of the schools.

The principal study of Dewey's influence is Lawrence A. Cremin, *The Transformation of the School* (New York: Alfred A. Knopf, 1961), which can be read in conjunction

200

with John Dewey, *Democracy and Education* (New York: The Macmillan Company, 1916). See also Richard Hofstadter, *Anti-Intellectualism in American Life* (New York: Alfred A. Knopf, 1963), pp. 299–390.

THE IMPORTANCE OF THE CONTEXT

The simplicity of historical chronology is often deceptive. It is tempting but dangerous to hang the interpretation of a long-term development upon a succession of striking events. We know, for example, that John Dewey opened his experimental school at the University of Chicago in 1896. In 1904 he went to Columbia University. His *Democracy and Education* was published in 1916; and three years later the Progressive Education Association was established. The direct line from date to date lends plausibility to the assertion that the progressive movement in education began in 1896 and grew steadily thereafter. Thence it is but a short step to holding Dewey responsible for everything that has happened to American education since 1896.

This trap has claimed some of Dewey's defenders and many of his critics. Recent comments all too often leave the impression that the schools since the 1890s have been entirely dominated by "progressive" ideas or by "Deweyism." Actually, it has been shown that while Dewey and others were thinking along lines that might be called progressive in the 1890s, their theories were not widely spread until after the First World War; and their genuine importance came much later still. It is fallacious to ascribe either the evils or the virtues of American education before 1917 to progressive education or to John Dewey.

This clarification is not merely a matter of setting the historical record straight. It is also essential in comprehending the significance of Dewey's ideas. The movement in which he played a part has often been described as a revolt. But to understand its character it is necessary to begin by recognizing the established patterns against which the revolt was directed. Yet the central features of the *ancien régime* in American education are but vaguely remembered; otherwise we would not now hear so much talk of the return to a "good old system" that was neither good nor old—nor indeed, much of a system. This paper will outline the social and cultural context of American education in the period between 1870 and 1910, in order to make clear the shortcomings against which Dewey and his collaborators directed their criticism. Only in the light of that context does the significance of progressive education become meaningful.

The forty years after 1870 were a period of critical change, both in the nation and in its schools. Unfortunately, although, for reasons which are themselves important, there was a vast discrepancy between what happened to the schools and what happened to the nation. The development of education, shaped by the ideals of an earlier America, opened a widening gap between the school and the society evolving around it and created burdensome problems for both. It was against the unwillingness to face those problems, many of which plague us still, that Dewey revolted. We shall not understand either his revolt or the problems themselves without understanding first the context within which both developed.

CHANGES IN SCHOOLS AND NATION

These four decades witnessed a radical transformation in American education. The number of students rose steadily, driven upward by the growth of population through natural increment and through immigration. The concentration of an ever larger percentage of the population in urban places and the extension of the duration of schooling also contributed to the increase. The result was a marked, if chaotic, attempt to clarify the functions of the schools at every level. Rapid changes in the curriculum and continuous, agitated questioning about the character of education reflected a pervasive uncertainty concerning the proper purpose and even the proper form of these institutions. "A thorough, orderly, and scientific organization of education is at length needed," complained W. W. Folwell in 1875. By the end of the century such an orderly structure was defined, in a pattern still recognizable today. The schools were public, secular, compulsory, and free; and they fell into the threefold division of elementary, secondary, and higher.

In the same forty years, however, the United States also changed. Its empty continental spaces rapidly filled up as railroads bound the nation together. Its population more than doubled, with an ever larger percentage of its residents concentrated in great metropolitan centers rather than spread across the rural countryside. Its wealth more often was drawn from factories, manned by a depressed labor force, than from the farms of independent husbandmen. Its economic, cultural, and political interests stretched far beyond the limits of the two oceans. The life of

202

the men who were shortly to confront a world war was thus radically different from that of their forebears who had emerged from the Civil War.

The human beings who suffered the shock of these cataclysmic changes could not immediately adjust their habits of thought and action to the new circumstances. To many contemporaries the nation seemed to be "whirling down the descending grade to destruction." The signs of its peril were unwieldy populations crowded into great cities and factories, the loss of the sense of individual responsibility in the face of the complex issues of modern life, materialism and excessive ambition, and the immense social gulf between "the apes of fashion and the reckless horde." The result was that liberty was mistaken for license, the anarchist and capitalist alike defied the government, and mobs hissed the American flag.

At the heart of these complaints was a sense of communal disintegration. The shock of the Civil War produced social effects felt for decades thereafter. Industrialization, the development of massive metropolitan centers, the creation of gigantic fortunes in the hands of new men, the peculiar conditions of life on the prairie farms, the undermining of family relations over a whole continent, and the attenuation of supernatural beliefs in religion—all these were factors in the cataclysmic collapse of communal institutions. And that collapse accounted for the sense of drift and lack of guidance or standards so characteristic of these years.

Under these circumstances, the common assumption was that it was the duty of the school to intervene, to supply the guides to action that the individual could no longer acquire through the slow accretion of experiences, to impart the instruction that the family and the church had offered in more stable societies and that now were simply lacking.

President Charles W. Eliot of Harvard University summarized the need most cogently: "In spite of every effort to enlighten the whole body of the people, all sorts of quacks and imposters thrive. . . . The astrologer in the Middle Ages was a rare personage . . . but now he advertises in the public newspapers and flourishes as never before. Men and women of all classes . . . seek advice . . . from clairvoyants, seers, Christian Scientists, mind-cure practitioners . . . and fortune tellers. The ship of state barely escapes from one cyclone of popular folly, like the fiat-money delusion or the granger legislation of the seventies, when another blast of ill-informed opinion comes down on it, like the actual legislation which compels the buying and storing of silver by Government." It was the same "in this matter of aesthetics." Popular tastes were hopeless; a fresh start with the children was essential.

The very statement of the problem hinted at the answer. Experience could not be counted on to endow a man with the cultural equipment for life's decisions. The school would have to do so.

THE SCHOOL AS PREPARATION FOR LIFE

The task of the schools was commonly described as that of preparing its students for life, an admirable general proposition with which few could disagree. Yet the meaning of the phrase became alarmingly elusive when efforts were made to reduce it to concrete terms. It could variously be applied to readiness for further education, to the acquisition of a trade, to training for citizenship, and to equipment with a general culture. The ambiguity is significant and deserves extended examination.

The analysis which follows could apply to every aspect of American education in this period. But it will focus primarily upon the high school, to which, in these years, all other levels of teaching accommodated themselves.

As the registration figures of the high schools soared after 1870, the academies of an earlier period declined precipitously in number and in influence. Few survived unless they were able to transform themselves into select college preparatory schools, specializing in the training of the sons of elite men of wealth. As a result the colleges were deprived of students prepared to carry on the existing courses of study; and they ultimately adjusted their instruction to the level of preparation provided by the high school. A system of accrediting standardized a uniform pattern of preparation. No longer did a boy enter by examination whenever he was ready; he now did so when he left high school. In the same way the high school shaped the character of the elementary instruction by regularizing the eight-year primary course that supplied it with students.

Yet the high school was not simply an institution that completed the studies of the elementary school, nor yet simply one that initiated the studies of college. It did both, and more besides. The commonly expressed views as to its complex functions reveal some of the American expectations of education at the close of the nineteenth century.

The high school tried to prepare some of its students for college. Yet the preponderant number of graduates did not go on, and the percentage who did so remained relatively unchanged in this period. Such considerations led the National Education Association's Committee of Ten on Secondary School Studies to conclude that the program of these institutions ought to be designed "for those children whose education is not to be pursued beyond the secondary school. The preparation of a few pupils for college or scientific school should . . . be the incidental, and not the principal object." That judgment reflected the existing situation; high school instruction was not primarily shaped to fit some students for college.

In the beginning, indeed, this had been regarded as a terminal institution to equip young men with trades; and its objective continued to be, in part at least, vocational training. Rapid economic change stimulated a demand for the "opportunity of learning how to do more and better work"; and courses in the manual and mercantile arts had demonstrable utility. Low wages, it was argued, were not due to the capitalist or to society but to faulty education. Particularly since the old system of apprenticeship was declining, it was "the duty of the state, as a business manager," to establish secondary technical schools in order to assure the nation's industrial supremacy. A careful development of "country schools preparatory to agriculture" and city schools preparatory "to the mechanic and manufacturing arts" would assure the efficient application of science to the productive system.

However, there was a seemingly irresistible trend toward the perversion of vocational into general courses. No sooner was a trade inserted into the curriculum than its sponsors began to urge it as a study upon all children. It was a truism that every boy ought to be taught to work— even, some said, before he was taught to read. Such training bridged over social cleavages, inculcated a love of labor, prevented idleness, and might be useful in later life. About the story of a clerk who took the place of a striking blacksmith and saved the day for the construction company, the editor moralized, "By his manual training that lad had become an American of the old school."

Some educational theorists had always given high value to the cultural implications of manual training. But the insistence that such courses were general deprived them of their vocational character, in a process similar to that which was also turning the land-grant colleges away from their original purpose. The labor unions were therefore frequently hostile; and artisans and craftsmen continued to learn their trades at the bench rather than in the classroom. Significantly, the popular conception of success rarely ascribed a man's rise in the world to the quality of his education.

Vocational education was pushed toward the general because it was oriented toward the past rather than toward the present. There were frequent verbal acknowledgments that the struggle for existence was becoming fiercer in consequence of the denser population and the disappearance of the empty lands of the frontier and that therefore "our artisans and mechanics must be trained to compete with those from the technical and industrial schools of European countries." But in practice the schools did not conceive it their function to prepare students for the jobs the economy actually offered. They hoped rather to preserve the archaic handicraft skills of a productive system that was already disappearing. This function, then, was detached from the actualities of life outside the school.

EDUCATING CITIZENS

Preparation for life had a wider meaning also. The schools, as "an element of national strength," had an obligation to train good citizens. The only justification for taking "the people's money for public instruction," it was often said in these years, was that the common school was "the corner-stone of our national order of Republican society."

There had been a time, of course, when education had not been deemed essential to good citizenship. Back in 1798, William Manning had argued that learning was actually a threat to democracy. Every yeoman knew his own interests, and schooling was not likely to further his capacity to act intelligently in politics. As late as 1871 Governor Brown of Missouri still denied there was a connection between education and citizenship and pointed out "your prime rascals are educated rascals."

Well before the Civil War, this assurance had begun to fade. Instead, the spread of public education was justified by the contention that the good citizen needed some minimal schooling to understand his own and his country's interests. Only thus could he act intelligently on the manifold issues of public policy decided by his vote. In the closing decades of the century the change went much further. It was no longer enough to give each citizen the ability to read, and to count on him then "to cast the ballot intelligently and wisely." The function of the schools was to indoctrinate their students with a positive pattern of beliefs, "political and moral axioms and principles" that would guide their acts as citizens. There were even proposals that only those so educated should be allowed to vote.

This conception received formal expression at the hands of the Herbartians. If one could teach morals through literature and history, then it followed that those subjects should so be taught as to imbue the young with the moral values upon which the society agreed. It was a short step from that point to J. B. McMaster's conclusion that history was to teach Americans the lofty ideals by which the United States had always been animated. Furthermore, almost every subject could be related to the same end. Even physical education was justified on the ground that it developed a sense of discipline and respect for law; and there were discussions as to which of the sports was most "fully in accord with the Zeitgeist." Thus education for citizenship became identified with patriotism. It was the task of the schools, through moral and intellectual training, to impart to the child that love of country which was the only reliable basis of correct political action.

The conflation of these values and emotions was evident in the Columbian Public Schools Celebration of 1892. Initiated by the magazine *Youth's Companion*, the idea for a mammoth commemoration of the four-hundredth anniversary of the discovery of America was taken up by the National Convention of Superintendents of Education and sanctioned by an act of Congress. During the course of the celebration there was a significant association of Columbus, the flag, and the public schools. The public schools, symbolized by the "little red schoolhouse" in the parades, were "the noblest expression of the principle of enlightenment which Columbus grasped by faith, . . . the master force which, under God, has been informing each of our generations with the peculiar truths of Americanism." The mere flying of the flag "over the schoolhouses, also, impressed powerfully upon the youth that we are a nation," and developed "brave manly boys and womanly girls."

The flag had itself by now become an object of ritual veneration. Careful consideration was given to ceremonies that would stimulate the respect of the young. The fervent quality of this iconoduly may be gauged from the horrified comments of an editor who observed a group of New England boys throwing snowballs at some girls in sight of the flag. "The American flag means fair play, equal chance, protection of the weak, . . . honor to women." In hoisting the flag, "the pupils of the school make a profession of the American religion, a leading principle of which is respect and consideration" for women.

Yet even that editor was, on occasion, forced to acknowledge that raising the flag was not enough. "Genuine love of country" called not only for the "recitation of deeds of heroism and past public service," through literature and history. It called also for "a special tie to the soil—a feeling which allies itself to the trees, the flowers, the birds, the prairies . . . the hills, the wild creatures of the woods and fields, and everything that is distinctively American."

The concealed premise of this statement—that it was possible to define a homogeneous pattern of American emotions and attitudes—ran counter to all the changes that made American life more heterogeneous through these decades. Sectional, ethnic, and urban-rural divisions were becoming more rather than less pronounced. Yet the schools continued to cling to uniformity as an ideal toward which their students were to be trained.

That insistence was most clearly revealed in attitudes toward the immigrants. There were, of course, exceptional teachers who appreciated the distinctive qualities of their foreign-born pupils and who rose to the challenge of working with them. But the predominant view was that under the impact of a "flood of imported barbarism" the "whole upper strata of society" were "becoming debauched." Fear of the consequences led sober, law-abiding men to go so far as to justify the lynching of Italians in New Orleans.

Although their children were but a small proportion of the school population, the newcomers were often described as a "distinct national menace." No one could live exposed to them without infection. They were making "a sorry mess" of the nation's language, for instance. "Their speech," to which they stubbornly clung, was "but a mangled product" of "fragments from many tongues." To permit them thus to corrupt English was disloyal and unpatriotic.

The foreigners not only perverted American tastes; they also brought with them an "antagonism to fixed institutions and ideas," and they actually led the native-born into idleness and crime. "All the trade unions of the country are controlled by foreigners," *The Century* explained. "While they refuse admission to the trained American boy, they admit all foreign applicants with little or no regard to their training or skill."

Hence the susceptibility of American young men to idleness, crime, and error.

Thus in discussions of the function of the schools, civic education was as little related to the needs of the present as vocational training. In reference to both, the assumption prevailed that it was desirable to cut the school apart from the main currents of the life about it. That assumption did not arise merely out of respect for an archaic past. It was rather the product of a newly developed view of culture and of its place in the curriculum.

CULTURE AND THE CURRICULUM

It was all very well to assert that the truly good citizen was "a man of large sympathies," educated to have a wide familiarity in the sciences and arts. Such general statements met with universal assent, for culture was conceded to be a universal good. Almost as a matter of course the schools, and particularly the high schools, accepted the task of educating young people in that sense. The importance of that function will become clear from a concrete examination of precisely what culture the schools transmitted to students through the evolving curriculum of these years.

The course of study was at no time the logically structured entity it has sometimes appeared to be in retrospect. The actual curriculum of the high school, for instance, was a conglomeration of traditional and new materials inserted or retained in the adjustment to a variety of pressures. In discerning the relationship of education to culture, however, these pressures are less significant than the means by which they were rationalized. There was an intense rivalry among all teachers to further their own subjects. But there was a striking uniformity to the justifications they gave for them. All argued that their subjects were part of the American's general equipment in dealing with his life's problems. No subject was to be taught merely, or primarily, because of the inherent importance of its content, but rather because of its contribution to an arsenal of weapons with which to deal with those problems. That was why the Committee of Ten recommended that "the best course of study" even for "the future common laborer" was a "portion of the longer course of study designed to educate the professional man."

That was also why President Eliot had criticized the older curricula.

"No amount of such studies will protect one from believing in astrology, or theosophy, or free silver, or strikes or boycotts, or in the persecution of Jews or of Mormons or in the violent exclusion of non-union men from employment." He himself thought, and many agreed with him, that only the sciences which gave men "practice in classification and induction" could impart the methods of right reasoning.

Science was not, however, to be narrowly limited to the physical or natural sciences. "All sciences," it was agreed, "involve the same methods and employ the same faculties." Mathematics was obviously useful for its training in logic. History, too, had become a science with a laboratory method of its own; a well-known textbook aimed to train the pupil to think for himself "by giving him as material for his work, *Historical Sources*." And claims of equal validity were made for "the most difficult science of government and lawmaking" and for economics and social science. As a matter of fact, the identical case was made for domestic science and a multitude of other subjects.

Often, however, simple instruction in the correct procedures seemed inadequate. It was not enough to teach children who lived in slums that "a healthful, beautiful location, good construction, perfect drainage, perfect plumbing, and perfect sanitary conditions generally, are indispensable to the house beautiful"; or to illustrate the proper mode of dining with quotations from Homer, Plutarch, and Boswell. It was essential, in addition, that the students' tastes be bent toward desirable, and therefore previously defined, goals.

Thus the function of the school was also to soften and ennoble its charges. "Beware of the boy who was never in love with his schoolmistress; he will become a man who will bear vigorous watching, even in the pulpit." That end could be attained through the development of an appreciation of the higher aspects of culture. Domestic science, for instance, led to an awareness of the artistic elements in decoration and to an understanding of the beauties of English, French, German, and Italian furniture. Students were thus to be exposed to the noble, gentle styles of life so different from their own.

The development of high school education in music was particularly enlightening from this point of view. The underlying emphasis at the start, and for a long time thereafter, was upon singing for an uplifting purpose. "We need more songs of home, of country, of simple praise to God and love to man." Singing was important because of its subject

210

matter. It dealt with "such subjects as Love of Country, Home-loving, the Golden Rule, etc." These, the teachers knew, "will surely develop like sentiments in the children who sing them." Since music regulated the emotions, "the habitual use of vocal music by a family" was "an almost unfailing sign of good morals and refined tastes."

Furthermore, music also had value "as a disciplinary study" with power "to develop the mind and will of the child." It taught patriotism, morality, temperance, and obedience to the law. Singing was even "to some degree a safeguard against those diseases which affect the breathing organs." The need for proper attention to music was particularly great in the United States. "The social results of a developed rhythmical sense in considerable masses of people . . . are far-reaching. It cultivates a feeling for order and regularity. . . . It gives . . . a measure of values. . . . With our heterogeneous population, our widespread opposition of social classes, and the dreadful monotony of living among the lower classes . . . it surely is worth our while to cultivate in all classes and in every kind of social group the feeling for order and symmetry." A "refined sense of harmony" was also essential. "The street noises that assault our ears and exhaust our nerves; the hideous architecture of our great cities, and the deadly architectural monotony of our factory towns; the excesses of public advertising; and our widespread disregard for the natural beauties of land, river and sea,—what are these but the inevitable outspeakings of a people to whom life has not yet became harmonious?"

In the logical progression of this argument, music had become not that which people enjoyed, but that which was good for them. A little story made this unmistakably clear. The young girl, sent by the town's subscriptions to study at the Conservatory in Boston, returns to Auroraville. Asked to play "Home, Sweet Home" or "Rocked in the Cradle of the Deep," she refuses: "You see, I have really learned what is good music." The townspeople are antagonized when she plays instead Moszkowski's Sonata, an "unmelodious, incomprehensible clatter." They withdraw their support. But she persists; and in time they acknowledge that they were wrong and she was right. "The people of no town were ever prouder of a native who had won distinction than the Auroraville people now are of that brilliant performer on the piano, Miss Hettie Ketchum."

The result, in the schools, was a steady shift in emphasis to courses that would identify good music and bring "added culture and refinement" into children's nature. It followed also that musicians had to avoid the opprobrium "of being deficient in general culture."

So too, the teaching of art was desirable because it encouraged accuracy of observation and contributed to success in later life. But the objects had to be carefully chosen; in a defective painting, the effect was "exactly like that of powder and rouge on a woman's face." "The purification and elevation" of "a vitiated and crude public taste" was "manifestly to be achieved by the systematic education of the youth" in the appreciation of great art, "however difficult that might be."

But above all else, a knowledge of great literature was important. "Literature," said Professor Woodrow Wilson, "will keep us pure and keep us strong." "Literature is a power," said the financier to the aspiring young hero in a novel. It could rescue the language from the deterioration with which it was threatened. Journalistic style, "short, direct talk," and passages "characterized by terse sentences" were corrupting the written language as books became sensational and magazines were marred with pictures and headlines. The spoken language was even worse. The old-time preaching and oratory were out of fashion and slang intruded into conversation. Yet "vocal form," Henry James pointed out, was "the touchstone of manners" and the symbol of civilization. Under these circumstances the teaching of good literature, of good speech, even of how to read a good newspaper were inescapable duties of the school.

There was a common assumption concealed in all these obligations loaded upon the school. When the teacher asserted that cleanliness, order, and honesty were basic to art, or when she was instructed, "In discussing beautiful objects as distinguished from those which are simply gaudy, it will be better to borrow objects from the stores, as we do not wish to criticize objects which the children bring from their own homes," it was an affirmation that the culture communicated through the school was unrelated to the life of its students. The teacher might hope that the good influences he generated would spread to the homes and elevate the parents. But figuratively and actually, he envisioned the school as cut off from, and battling against, the dominant currents of the civilization within which it existed.

212

The culture communicated by the schools had thus become entirely detached from experience. The disjunction was not the product of forces peculiar to education. It sprang rather from the rapid changes of the period in the whole social context of the nation.

The term "culture," as commonly used in the schools and outside them, comprehended the possession of knowledge through science as a guide to right action in every sphere of personal and social life. But it also included the possession of certain symbols of gentility and quality, primarily in the arts. Medicine or economics or natural science supplied the right answers to questions of health or business or the character of the natural universe; and music or painting or literature supplied the right modes of emotional expression.

To discriminate right from wrong in science or art, however, was by no means easy. Social science and Christian Science, phrenology and zoology and astrology all justified their claims with their own credentials. Why should one believe in a Neolithic Age but not in a lost continent of Atlantis? A scientific magazine discussed the birds of the grasslands and a new star in the Milky Way, the conservation of the mackerel supply and the cabalistic shapes numbers naturally assumed. All were science. And, alas, the confusion of claims in the arts was more confounded still. Some standard of judgment was desperately required.

The urgency was most acute among men and women of wealth, whether inherited or newly acquired. Such people were most sensitive to the need for dependable criteria of thought and action. They lived always under the pressure of insecurity about their possessions and of uncertainty about how to play their own roles. Their frenetic eagerness to develop a "Society" was an effort to bring into being the norms that would determine who belonged and who did not and that would establish the appropriate modes of thought and behavior. Reluctant to base status solely upon riches, which were easily gained and lost, those who aspired to leadership wished to make the possession of culture one of the major tests for admission to, or exclusion from, Society. "Changes in manners and customs," Edith Wharton had said, "originate with the wealthy or aristocratic minority, and are thence transmitted to the other classes." It was thus the responsibility of Society to provide cultural guidance to the nation.

The years after 1870 saw the development and elaboration of an apparatus for defining the official culture of this Society. It included institutions like museums, symphony orchestras, opera companies, and learned societies; and an array of journals and publications that passed judgment on taste and ideas. This apparatus was in the hands of a few key figures, the critics and influential scholars who were the ultimate arbiters. The critic in this role was the source of discipline, the man who "screws down the brakes," rather than "the sentimentalist irresponsibly swept into folly by the fury of the crowd, or the demagogue whooping its shibboleth." At the core of this apparatus was the university, in which science and art were joined. In its development, Society shared the control and supplied the funds; and in return it sought and generally, although not always, secured a certified set of standards it could accept. The union of the college and the university in a manner unique to the United States significantly reflected the function they were to serve. The university defined taste and knowledge while the college imparted them to the children of the elite, who were thereby set off as a group.

The struggle to effect such a definition and to certify what was officially correct in this sense was fought in every field of American culture. It may most clearly be perceived in the fate of medical practice. By the end of the nineteenth century the dozens of medical sects that had formerly had respectable followings had been extinguished by state action and but "one mode of healing" had been given "exclusive control." That mode was one certified by approved medical schools and societies—that is, by those linked to the universities, by those whose practitioners had heeded the advice given to the Philadelphia medical students, that "of all men, the medical practitioner should be, above all things, a perfect gentleman," and should "move only in the best, unquestioned society." These institutions developed the practitioners influential in Society; and that influence brought them the victory of official and exclusive recognition.

What happened in medicine happened also in the other professions. All came to recruit their practitioners from among the graduates of schools linked to the universities. Most of them achieved some degree of social and legal recognition through a formal process of certification; and in most of those callings the old pattern of relatively free access disappeared.

More important, an analogous process, although without legal sanctions, operated in all phases of American culture. No degree or certificate or qualifying examination, but a validating process no less formal and stringent marked out the music or painting or book that received an approved place in the culture.

It was more difficult to secure the acceptance of these standards by the population at large. The problem and its resolution were illustrated in a boys' story. Snobbish Schuyler Rivington of New York is appallingly unlovely in his contacts with the residents of a small western town. But he is redeemed in the eyes of the likable old lady who comes to the city to be cured of a brain illness. New York was "not all fashion and frivolity"; it was, after all, justified by "the science and knowledge stored in the great city." Science, like the culture Hettie brought back from the conservatory in Boston, was perhaps hard to take. But it was good for you.

THE SCHOOLS AND THE DIFFUSION OF CULTURE

And here we return to the schools and particularly to the high school. Their function was to diffuse the values of the officially defined culture. They did so not only by preparing some pupils for college but, more important, by securing the universal acceptance of the defined culture through their courses in science, history, politics, economics, art, music, and literature.

That acquiescence was secured because the school was also a significant channel of upward social mobility; American boys and girls were "all climbers upon a ladder." Cautious protests that the school ought "not to push the pupil beyond his environment" had no effect. Its very structure and organization encouraged mobility. For students, the reward for accepting its values, that is, for doing well, was access to the colleges, to the professions, and even to the opportunities business afforded. The reality of these rewards was an incentive of enormous attractiveness toward acceptance of the established cultural norms. The school thus permitted the wide diffusion of the officially defined culture with relatively little strain or tension.

The more serious damage was to culture itself. Detached from their lives, it did not meet the needs of many Americans. While accepting the privileged status of that which was defined as culture, they turned for their own satisfaction and enjoyment to forms which developed outside the range of established controls and, to that extent, were popular.

Only a "few people of refinement and culture" appreciated the best drama for "art's sake" and for its function "in educating the noblest faculties of the mind," a critic observed sadly. The masses went to the theater for entertainment, to gratify "exotic tendencies" and "to ease the stress of sensuous toil" when weary of "the hard, hopeless grind of business and household cares." Such people were not heedful of the critics. The theater they patronized developed spontaneously and independently.

In the same way the popular medicine of unorthodox healers and patent medicines served more people than that of the M.D.; the popular sciences of the Sunday supplements convinced more readers than the official science of the learned journals; men sang and danced to popular music, however much they were taught to appreciate the official music of the schools. The dime novels and the magazines made popular a literature and art of which the critics took no cognizance at all. A perceptive observer, criticizing the methods of "Art Study" in 1906, pointed out, "The children are living with the houses and the furniture and the wallpaper—God help them!—and the Buster Browns and Nervy Nats of to-day, and the ever present influence of these will not be overcome by ignoring them and summoning Giotto and Velásquez for ten minutes from the past."

This was evidence of a disjunction between popular and official culture. That separateness was new to American life. In its development American education had had an important part, although one but slightly perceived and but little understood by those who participated in it.

Conversely the gap between popular and official culture also affected education. Hostile critics complained of the tendency toward making "a sort of college" of the free public school by offering instruction in science, literature, music, and art and by tolerating fraternities and organized athletics. The urban high school, in their view, offered "a four years' course in an institution modelled on the plan of the university-fitting school of a generation ago;—four years of cramming in Latin and mathematics, with a little dabbling in science and a mild flirtation with English literature." Such cultural fripperies had no place in free education. "We have no right to appropriate a dollar of the people's money" to make "scholars, in the university sense." From this point of

216

view, the "rage for intellectual culture" was "the Moloch in the American school-room," sought only by parents infuriated with ambition for their children.

DEWEY AND THE PROBLEMS OF EDUCATION

It was the achievement of John Dewey to have couched his criticism of the divorce between experience and education in more meaningful terms. His practical contact with the problems of the schools of the 1880s and 1890s stimulated his philosophical inquiries into the nature of knowledge; and his understanding of the learning process supplied a theoretical basis to his views on proper pedagogy. The development of his ideas was thus meaningfully related to the context of the times in which he lived.

When Dewey came as instructor to the University of Michigan in 1884, he brought with him intellectual attitudes shaped by two forces. His early upbringing in Vermont had been permissive to the point of chaos; the most valuable lessons he had learned had been outside the classroom and independently carried forth. His own training had thus been almost casual and had certainly been free of the rigidity to be imposed on American schools after 1870. Recollections of his experience as a student no doubt influenced his later critical view of what education was becoming in the last quarter of the nineteenth century.

His philosophical background also raised questions with regard to current assumptions. From his graduate work under George S. Morris at Johns Hopkins he carried away a commitment of Hegelian idealism, which nurtured his hostility to dualisms of every sort and left him dubious as to the validity of all such dichotomies as those between education or culture and society or life.

But at Michigan, Dewey's formal philosophical views and his personal memories were challenged by the necessities of instruction and by his immersion in the life of a community. To make his ideas comprehensible to the young men and women in his classrooms was but a fraction of his task. In addition, he had to be aware of the relationship of his work to the world about him; and as a member of the faculty of a state university, he also had to concern himself with the problems of the public school system related to it. President Angell always regarded it as one of the chief duties of the university "to keep in close touch with the state system of public education." That preoccupation was reflected in Dewey's proposal to publish a general "Thought News"; and it emerged also in his earliest books, the core of which was analysis of the ways of knowing. The title of the volume in which he collaborated in 1889 was significant: *Applied Psychology: An Introduction to the Principles and Practices of Education*.

His marriage in 1886 and the move to Chicago in 1894 added to the weight of the practical considerations in the development of his thought. The intellectual associations at the exciting new university were undoubtedly stimulating; but the exposure to the immediate problems of teaching in a great and expanding metropolis were fully as much so. Experiments in new education were already in progress in Chicago; and the Deweys at the Experimental School undoubtedly profited from them. But it is, in any case, clear that the main outlines of their work were set up on a pragmatic rather than a theoretical basis. That is, Dewey began to treat the problems of education not from an abstract, previously defined position of what ought ideally to be, but rather from a concrete estimate of deficiencies that actually existed.

The systematic exploration of these problems did not follow until later. The first extensive exposition of Dewey's position came in the lectures collected as *The School and Society* (1899), a work which was still largely critical and negative. A fuller analysis appeared seventeen years later in *Democracy and Education*. But the general propositions enunciated in that work rested upon a very careful case-by-case study of particular experiments in the new education. Dewey's general conclusions were thus the products of more than twenty years of experience. His ideas were not formulated in the abstract but through the encounter with the conditions of learning in the United States in the closing decades of the nineteenth century.

The necessity for grappling with a development that had divorced the school and its culture from society and its life was an irritant that compelled Dewey to define his ideas on education. Those ideas were integrally related to his comprehensive conceptions of the character of knowledge, the mind, human nature, the experimental process, and the values of democracy. As he clarified his thoughts on education he also refined his views on these more general philosophical issues.

But his conceptions also had a pragmatic attractiveness that converted many Americans who did not accept or were unfamiliar with the wider implications of his philosophy. His ideas were persuasive because they revealed the evident weaknesses of the schools as they were.

WHAT WAS WRONG WITH AMERICAN EDUCATION

The realm of the classroom in the 1890s was totally set off from the experience of the child who inhabited it. The teachers' lessons encrusted by habit, the seats arranged in formal rows, and the rigid etiquette of behavior all emphasized the difference between school and life. Hence learning consisted of the tedious memorization of data without a meaning immediately clear to the pupil.

Dewey, whose own education as a boy was free of all such rigidity, objected strenuously that these conditions stifled the learning process, for they prevented the student from relating his formal studies to his own development as a whole person.

The educator therefore had to narrow the distance between the classroom and the world outside it. Society was changing rapidly under the impact of urbanization and industrialization, and not always for the better. But the teacher ought not therefore pretend that his pupils still walked along the lanes of an eighteenth-century village back to a rustic farmhouse. He had to take account of the city streets and of the American home as it actually was.

The educator could end the school's isolation by pulling it into a closer relationship with the family and the community. Awareness of the homes, the neighborhood environment, and the business and professional life about it would enable the school to function more effectively and also to widen its influence. By recognizing the unity of the child's experience, it could communicate more directly with him and at the same time break down the pernicious "division into cultured people and workers." It would then cease to be alien and hostile in the eyes of its students and become instead a natural part of their habitat within which they sought satisfaction of their own needs.

In such schools, the "subject matter in history and science and art" could be so presented that it would have "a positive value and a real significance in the child's own life." What was taught would justify itself because it answered questions the student himself asked. He would not be forced to study the map to learn what the world was like, but, exploring the world about him, would come to wonder how it looked on the map. History and literature would cease to be the elegant furnishings of an abstract culture; the pupil would be drawn to them out of his own desire to know himself and his origins. Mathematics would no longer be a burdensome exercise in mental discipline but would be sought as a practical way of managing quantities.

Instruction, under such conditions, could be carried forward as a succession of direct experiences on the child's part. From Rousseau, Dewey had learned that education was not something to be forced upon youth. It involved rather a process of growth antedating the pupil's admission to the school and extending beyond his departure from it. In teaching, it was essential always to take account of the conditions of learning, to impart the ability to read, to write, and to use figures intelligently in terms that were themselves meaningful and real. That meant at the lower grades an emphasis on activities over abstractions, not as ends in themselves but as means of evoking stimulating questions.

Learning would then become incidental to the process of dealing with authentic situations. Children who played at making things readily learned to weave, but in doing so began to wonder how cotton and wool came to be formed into their own garments. Those who had practice in electing a class president found it natural to inquire how the city elected a mayor.

The school was thus not simply to pander to a child's liking for interesting activities. It was to select those which led him on to a widening of significant achievements. Knowledge of geography, government, history, and arithmetic was acquired through the continual reconstruction of the student's own experiences. As he absorbed the significance of what he did, he was able to direct his attention to ever broader and more meaningful subjects. Furthermore, interest in the achievement of a practical end could steadily be transformed into interest in the process, that is into "thinking things out" intellectually or theoretically. The whole of education could thus be conceived as the process of learning to think through the solution of real problems.

A school firmly oriented in the world of its pupils could dispense with discipline through the external force of keeping order. Children whose interest was actively engaged in their studies did not need policing. They could be permitted more than the usual amount of freedom, not for the purpose of relaxing real discipline, but to make possible the assumption of larger and less artificial responsibilities, the performance of which would evoke order from within.

The establishment of voluntary patterns of obedience not only facilitated the teacher's task; it also emphasized that which was most important in education—its moral purpose. "All the aims and manners which are desirable in education are themselves moral. Discipline, natural development, culture, social efficiency, are moral traits—marks of a person who is a worthy member of that society which it is the business of education to further." Education was not simply a preparation for what would later be useful. It was more, "getting from the present the degree and kind of growth there is in it." From the very start, therefore, the child would become acquainted with, and through his life learn ever better, the relationship of knowledge to conduct. That was the most worthy function of his schooling.

THE RELEVANCE OF DEWEY'S CRITIQUE

Dewey's central conceptions of education are thus directly related to criticisms of the system that had developed in the United States between the time when he had ended his own schooling in Vermont and the time when he moved to Chicago. The conditions that evoked his revolt have changed radically since 1894; yet his comments have by no means lost their timeliness.

In some sixty years since the experimental school in Chicago opened its doors, John Dewey's ideas have had a profound effect upon American education. Despite the occasional errors in their application to practice and despite the distortions by uncritical enthusiasts, the schools have profited immensely from his influence.

There have been failings, but due largely through a disregard of the spirit of Dewey's intentions. In the hands of mediocre or incompetent teachers, new techniques have sometimes become ends in themselves. Dewey valued the experiment and the laboratory as means through which the pupil could learn by discovery. But when instruction is so routinized that the student knows from the manual what he will find before he puts his eye to the lens, the microscope has added nothing to his education. There is no point to substituting modern for ancient languages if dull teachers make one as dead as the other.

The danger of the abuse of techniques as ends in themselves has certainly been heightened by the tendency in many states to emphasize method over content in the preparation of the teacher. Yet Dewey always insisted that method could not be divorced from content. The subject matter and the means of communicating it were inextricably bound together; and a successful performance depended on the mastery of both. It is ironic now to find Dewey often blamed in retrospect for the proliferation of empty courses in "education" and for the "certification racket" that makes completion of a formal quota of methods courses the prerequisite to teacher licensing. "Consider the training schools of teachers," he wrote in 1899. "These occupy at present a somewhat anomalous position for thus they are isolated from the higher subject matter of scholarship, since, upon the whole, their object has been to train persons *how* to teach, rather than *what* to teach."

Much of Dewey's writing was addressed to the problems of the elementary school, which in his day were most pressing. But neither at that nor at any other level did he regard familiarity with techniques as an alternative to command of the substance of subject matter. The two were inseparable at any level, for each acquired meaning from its relationship to the other.

Insofar as they are focused upon these abuses the complaints of the critics of Deweyism have a measure of validity. But the accusation that progressive education has kept Johnny from learning how to read or how to use a slide rule is unfounded and dangerous. It tends also to obscure the genuine improvements that have emanated from his influence.

In 1928, in an article on Soviet education, John Dewey pointed to the significance of the Russian achievement—far earlier than his detractors of thirty years later. But he did not then take, nor would he now have taken, technological proficiency or advances in rocketry as a test of the excellence of an educational system. He was certainly not impressed in the 1930s by the accomplishments of the Nazis in the same fields. Nor would he have overlooked in any comparison the counter-balancing achievements of our own educational system in medicine, in the peaceful branches of science, and in the humanities.

The crucial test, rather, was the extent to which education served as a vital instrument teaching the individual to behave in the world about him. In his own society, Dewey warned that "academic and scholastic, instead of being titles of honor are becoming terms of reproach." He took that as a measure of the isolation of the schools and the negligence of the culture; and he feared that without an immediate reform schools would become empty and ineffective and the culture would be weakened from within. That accounted for the urgency with which he wrote.

Dewey did not intend that his criticisms should become the creed of a sect or party; and he was uncomfortable when the label "Progressive" was attached to his ideas. He directed his revolt not against tradition but against a rather recent development—the gap created by the inability of Americans to adjust their conceptions of education and culture to the terms of the changing world about them. Unwilling to limit the scope of either education or culture by the lines of an artificial definition, he insisted upon broadening both by reestablishing their relationship to life.

Late in life, reflecting upon the developments of a half century, he made this clear, when he defined the new education as hostility to "imposition from above," to "learning from texts and teacher," to "acquisition of isolated skills and techniques by drill" to "preparation for a more or less remote future" and to "static aims and materials." Against those aspects of the school of the late nineteenth century he had called for the "expression and cultivation of individuality," for "learning through experience," and for "acquaintance with an ever-changing world."

That much can be ascribed to the reaction against the trends of the 1880s and 1890s. But Dewey had no intention of proceeding entirely upon a basis of rejection. "When external authority is rejected," he pointed out in another connection, "it does not follow that all authority should be rejected, but rather that there is need to search for a more effective source of authority." In his times, the disjunction between the school and society had enshrined external and arbitrary authority in American education. His revolt, which is comprehensible in terms of his times, aimed to end that disjunction and sweep away that authority as a step in the reconstruction of education on a sounder basis.

★ 14 ★

THE OBJECTIVES AND IMPACT OF SCIENTIFIC TESTING
Clarence J. Karier

The emergence of large corporations supplying national and international markets had parallels in the realm of education. Industries were vitally interested in rationalizing production through lowering costs, matching supply with demand, managing the work force, and introducing a more centralized supervision of investment and production in the whole economy. Similarly in education, efficiency, cost accounting, rationality, and central direction acquired a new significance. Science was one of the most important channels for unifying educational goals and criteria. While science had acquired many meanings by the twentieth century, the most important for educational purposes was the belief that inborn intelligence could be abstracted and quantified to provide a rational basis for the curriculum and educational planning. Central influence was pursued through standardization of teacher training and certification, the establishment of national organizations for teachers and school administrators, and the projects of philanthropic foundations. Although immediate control of schools and their funding remained in local hands, many other parts of the educational enterprise began to respond to nationalizing tendencies.

In this essay Clarence J. Karier explores the interrelations between the emergence of new forms of economic organization and the spirit of science, specialization, and control in education. Other relevant writings include Robert H. Bremner, *American Philanthropy* (Chicago: University of Chicago Press, 1960); Raymond Callahan, *Education and the Cult of Efficiency* (Chicago: University of Chicago Press, 1962); and Geraldine Joncich, *The Sane Positivist: a Biography of Edward L. Thorndike* (Middletown, Conn.: Wesleyan University Press, 1968).

America's entry into the war brought to a head certain trends which were evolving within the progressive era. . . . The larger corporations found profitable ways to work with government and a large cadre of social science experts tried out their new-found techniques for the management of the new corporate state. John Dewey, for example, saw in the war the great possibility for "intelligent administration" based eventually on a solid social science. The corporate liberal state emerged from the war stronger than ever. Progressive liberal reform did not come to an end with the war but rather became institutionalized. Henceforth, most social change would be institutionally controlled and the interest of government, corporate wealth, and labor more securely managed. The state which thus emerged included a mass system of public schools which served the manpower needs of that state. One of the more important ways that system served the needs of the state was through the process of rationalizing and standardizing manpower for both production and consumption of goods and services.

For many "professional educators," the school as a trainer of producers and consumers necessarily led to a view of the school as a business model or factory. Ellwood P. Cubberley spoke for many professional educators in the twentieth century when he said:

> *Every manufacturing establishment that turns out a standard product or a series of products of any kind maintains a force of efficiency experts to study methods of procedure and to measure and test the output of its works. Such men ultimately bring the manufacturing establishment large returns, by introducing improvements in processes and procedure, and in training the workmen to produce larger and better output. Our schools are, in a sense, factories in which the raw products (children) are to be shaped and fashioned into products to meet the various demands of life. The specifications for manufacturing*

*come from the demands of twentieth-century civilization, and it is the
business of the school to build its pupils according to the specifications
laid down. This demands good tools, specialized machinery, continuous measurement of production to see if it is according to specifications, the elimination of waste in manufacture, and a large variety in
the output.*

The testing movement, financed by corporate foundations, helped meet
the need for "continuous measurement" and "accountability." It also
served as a vital part of the hand which helped fashion the peculiar
meritocracy within that state.

Although the testing movement is often viewed as getting under way
with the mass testing of 1.7 million men for classification in the armed
forces in World War I, the roots of the American testing movement lie
deeply imbedded in the American progressive temper, which combined
its belief in progress, its racial attitudes, and its faith in the scientific expert working through the state authority to ameliorate and control the
evolutionary progress of the race. While America has had a long history
of eugenics advocates, some of the key leaders of the testing movement
were the strongest advocates for eugenics control. In the twentieth century the two movements often came together in the same people under
the name of "scientific" testing and for one cause or the other received
foundation support.

One such leader of the Eugenics Movement in America was Charles
Benedict Davenport, who, having seriously studied Galton and Pear-
son, sought to persuade the new Carnegie Institution of Washington to
support a biological experiment station with himself as director. In 1904
he became director of such a station at Cold Spring Harbor on Long
Island. As his interest in experiments in animal breeding began to
wane, he used his influence as secretary of "the Committee on
Eugenics of the American Breeders Association" to interest others in the
study of human heredity. Supported by the donations of Mrs. E. H.
Harriman, Davenport founded the Eugenics Record Office in 1910,
and by 1918 the Carnegie Institution of Washington assumed control.
The work of the Record Office was facilitated by the work of committees
on: "Inheritance of Mental Traits," which included Robert M. Yerkes
and Edward L. Thorndike; "Committee on Heredity of Deafmutism,"
with Alexander Graham Bell; "Committee on Sterilization," with

H. H. Laughlin; and "Committee on the Heredity of the Feeble Minded," which included, among others, H. H. Goddard.

These committees took the lead in identifying those who carried defective germ-plasm and disseminating the propaganda which became necessary to pass sterilization laws. For example, it was Laughlin's "Committee to Study and Report on the Best Practical Means of Cutting off the Defective Germ Plasm in the American Population," which reported that "society must look upon germ-plasm as belonging to society and not solely to the individual who carries it." Laughlin found that approximately 10 percent of the American population carried bad seed and called for sterilization as a solution. More precisely, he defined these people as "feeble-minded, insane, criminalistic (including the delinquent and wayward), epileptic, inebriate, diseased, blind, deaf, deformed and dependent (including orphans, ne'er-do-wells, the homeless, tramps and paupers)." Social character, from murder to prostitution, was associated with intelligence and the nature of one's germ-plasm. The first sterilization law was passed in Indiana in 1907, followed in quick succession by fifteen other states. In Wisconsin such progressives as Edward A. Ross and Charles R. Van Hise, president of the University of Wisconsin, took strong public stands supporting the passage of sterilization laws. America pioneered in the sterilization of mental and social defectives twenty years ahead of other nations.

Between 1907 and 1928, twenty-one states practiced eugenical sterilization involving over 8,500 people. California, under the influence of the Human Betterment Foundation, which counted Lewis B. Terman and David Star Jordan as its leading members, accounted for 6,200 sterilizations. California's sterilization law was based on race purity as well as criminology. Those who were "morally and sexually depraved" could be sterilized. Throughout the sterilization movement in America ran a *Zeitgeist* reflecting the temper of pious reformers calling for clean living, temperance, and fresh air-schools as well as sterilization. The use of sterilization for punishment reached the point where laws were introduced which called for sterilization for chicken stealing and car theft, as well as prostitution.

H. H. Goddard, fresh from G. Stanley Hall's seminars at Clark University, translated the Binet-Simon scale (1908) using the test to identify feebleminded at the training school at Vineland, New Jersey. Various scales and tests which were freely used and patterned after the original scale were later proven to lack reliability to the extent that, according to some testers, upward of half the population was feebleminded. From the Binet scale, Goddard went on to publish *The Kallikak Family*, which showed the family history of Martin Kallikak as having sired both a good and bad side to his family tree. The bad side, which began with his involvement with a feebleminded girl, contributed such "social pests" as "paupers, criminals, prostitutes and drunkards." Goddard's next book, *Feeble-mindedness: Its Causes and Consequences*, gave further "scientific" justification to the notion of the relationship between feeblemindedness and moral character.

Interestingly enough, the liberal tradition in America from Jefferson on usually assumed a positive relationship between "talent and virtue." It was then not surprising to find people assuming that anyone with less talent will have less virtue. This relationship was assumed in the passage of most sterilization laws. Society would rid itself of not only the genetic defective but, more importantly, the socially undesirable. Laughlin, Goddard, Terman, and Thorndike all made similar assumptions. Terman argued that the feebleminded were incapable of moral judgments and, therefore, could only be viewed as potential criminals. He said:

> . . . *all feeble-minded are at least potential criminals. That every feeble-minded woman is a potential prostitute would hardly be disputed by anyone. Moral judgment, like business judgment, social judgment or any other kind of higher thought process, is a function of intelligence.*

The same thinking which guided Terman to find a lower morality among those of lesser intelligence had its mirror image in the work of Edward L. Thorndike, who found a higher morality among those with greater intelligence. Thorndike was convinced that "to him that hath a superior intellect is given also on the average a superior character." The sterilization solution to moral behavior problems and the improvement of intelligence continued to be advocated by Thorndike, as well as by his pupils. By 1940, in his last major work, he concluded that:

> *By selective breeding supported by a suitable environment we can have a world in which all men will equal the top ten per cent of present men. One sure service of the able and good is to beget and rear off-*

spring. One sure service (about the only one) which the inferior and vicious can perform is to prevent their genes from survival.

The association of inferior with vicious and intelligence with goodness continued to appear in the psychology textbooks. Henry E. Garrett, a former student and fellow colleague with whom Thorndike was associated, who won a "reputation for eminence," continued to project the story of Martin Kallikak in terms of goods and bads in his textbook on *General Psychology* as late as 1955. Just in case someone might miss the point, the children of the feebleminded tavern girl were pictured as having horns, while the "highest types of human beings," were portrayed as solid Puritan types.

This view of the Kallikaks was no accident. As chairman of Columbia's department of psychology for sixteen years and as past president of the American Psychological Association, as well as a member of the National Research Council, Garrett was in sympathy with Thorndike's views on the place of the "inferior and vicious" in American life. By 1966, as a Professor Emeritus from Columbia, in the midst of the civil rights movement, he produced a series of pamphlets which drew out what he believed to be the implications of sixty years of testing in America. Sponsored by the Patrick Henry Press, over 500,000 copies of his pamphlets were distributed free of charge to American teachers. In *How Classroom Desegregation Will Work, Children Black and White,* and especially in *Breeding Down,* Garrett justified American racism on "scientific" grounds. Going back to Davenport and the Eugenics Record Office as well as Terman's work and others, Garrett argued:

> *You can no more mix the two races and maintain the standards of White civilization than you can add 80 (the average I.Q. of Negroes) and 100 (average I.Q. of Whites), divide by two and get 100. What you would get would be a race of 90s, and it is that 10 per cent differential that spells the difference between a spire and a mud hut; 10 per cent—or less—is the margin of civilization's "profit"; it is the difference between a cultured society and savagery.*
>
> *Therefore, it follows, if miscegenation would be bad for White people, it would be bad for Negroes as well. For, if leadership is destroyed, all is destroyed.*

He went on to point out that the Black man is at least 200,000 years behind the Whites and that intermarriage, as well as desegregation, would destroy what genetic lead the White man had achieved through "hard won struggle" and "fortitudinous evolution." The state, he argued, ". . . can and should prohibit miscegenation, just as they ban marriage of the feeble-minded, the insane and various undesirables. Just as they outlaw incest."

The style and content of Garrett's arguments were but echoes of similar arguments developed earlier by Davenport, Laughlin, Terman, Brigham, Yerkes, and Thorndike. For example, C. C. Brigham spoke of the superior Nordic draftees of World War I and seriously worried about inferior germ-plasm of the Alpine, Mediterranean, and Negro races in *A Study of American Intelligence*. What disturbed Brigham as well as the U.S. Congress was, of course, the fact that 70 percent of the total immigration in the early 1920s was coming from Alpine and Mediterranean racial stock. H. H. Laughlin of the Carnegie Foundation of Washington provided the scientific evidence to the Congress in his report "An Analysis of America's Melting Pot." Using information from the Army tests and from his Eugenics Record Office dealing with the insane and feebleminded, Laughlin built a case that the new immigrant from Southern Europe was of inferior racial stock by virtue of the numbers that appeared as wards of the state.

Supported by the Commonwealth Fund, Lewis M. Terman reported similar evidence from his study. Addressing the National Education Association at Oakland, California, on July 2, 1923, he expressed concern about the fecundity of the superior races. As he put it:

> *The racial stocks most prolific of gifted children are those from northern and western Europe, and the Jewish. The least prolific are the Mediterranean races, the Mexicans and the Negroes. The fecundity of the family stocks from which our gifted children come appears to be definitely on the wane. . . . It has been figured that if the present differential birth rate continues, 1,000 Harvard graduates will at the end of 200 years have but 50 descendants, while in the same period 1,000 South Italians will have multiplied to 100,000.*

It was this kind of "scientific" data derived from the testing and Eugenics Movement which entered into the dialogue which led to the restrictive immigration quota of 1924, that clearly discriminated against southern Europeans.

After World War I, America had moved toward a more restrictive immigration policy. While small manufacturers, represented by the National Association of Manufacturers and Chambers of Commerce, tended to favor a sliding-door policy which would open according to the labor needs of the small manufacturers, most larger manufacturers and labor unions, represented by the National Civic Federation, favored restricting immigration. Perhaps the motivation was best stated by Edward A. Filene of Boston, a pioneer in employee management, when he said:

> *Employers do not need an increased labor supply, since increased use of labor-saving machinery and elimination of waste in production and distribution will for many years reduce costs more rapidly than wages increase, and so prevent undue domination of labor.*

The Carnegie money that Laughlin used in his campaign for greater restrictions was ultimately money well spent in the interest of the larger manufacturer. Nevertheless, the rhetoric of the times and of the testers was, perhaps, best put when President Coolidge proclaimed, "America must be kept American."

The nativism, racism, elitism, and social class bias which were so much a part of the testing and Eugenics Movement in America were, in a broader sense, part of that *Zeitgeist* which was America. This was the land of the Ku Klux Klan, the red scare, the Sacco-Vanzetti and Scopes trials as well as the land of real opportunity for millions of immigrants. It was this kind of contradictory base in which the corporate liberal state took firm root, building a kind of meritocracy that even Plato could not have envisioned. Just as Plato ascribed certain virtues to certain occupational classes, so, too, Lewis Terman assigned numbers which stood for virtue to certain occupational classes. It was clear to Terman that America was the land of opportunity, where the best excelled, and the inferior found themselves on the lower rungs of the occupational order. Designing the Stanford-Binet intelligence test, Terman developed questions which were based on presumed progressive difficulty in performing tasks which he believed were necessary for achievement in ascending the hierarchial occupational structure. He then proceeded to find that, according to the results of his tests, the intelligence of different occupational classes fit his ascending hierarchy. It was little wonder that I.Q. reflected social class bias. It was, in fact, based on the social class order. Terman believed that, for the most part, people were at that level because of heredity and not social environment. He said:

> Preliminary investigations indicate that an I.Q. below 70 rarely permits anything better than unskilled labor; that the range from 70 to 80 is preeminently that of semi-skilled labor, from 80 to 100 that of the skilled or ordinary clerical labor, from 100 to 110 or 115 that of the semi-professional pursuits; and that above all these are the grades of intelligence which permit one to enter the professions or the larger fields of business. Intelligence tests can tell us whether a child's native brightness corresponds more nearly to the median of (1) the professional classes, (2) those in the semi-professional pursuits, (3) ordinary skilled workers, (4) semi-skilled workers, or (5) unskilled laborers. This information will be of great value in planning the education of a particular child and also in planning the differentiated curriculum here recommended.

Plato had three classes and Terman had five; both maintained the "myth of the metals" and both advocated a differentiated curriculum to meet the needs of the individuals involved. Terman so completely accepted the assumption of the social class meritocracy and the tests which were based on that meritocracy that he never seemed to even wonder why, in his own study of the gifted, "the professional and semi-professional classes together account for more than 80 per cent. The unskilled labor classes furnish but a paltry 1 per cent or 2 per cent."

Social class was not the only problem with the tests. Whether one reads Terman's Stanford-Binet or his Group Test of Mental Ability or the Stanford Achievement Tests, the Army tests, or the National Intelligence Tests, certain characteristics emerge. They all reflect the euphemisms, the homilies and the morals which were, indeed, the stock and trade of *Poor Richard's Almanac*, Noah Webster's Blue-back *Speller*, as well as *McGuffey's Readers*. The child who grew up in a home and attended a school where these things were in common usage stood in distinct advantage to the newly arrived immigrant child. At a time when over half the children in American schools were either immigrants or children of immigrants, this movement represented discrimination in a massive way.

By 1922 Walter Lippmann, in a series of six articles for *The New Republic*, questioned whether intelligence is fixed by heredity and whether the tests actually measure intelligence. While Lippmann challenged the validity of the test, he did not attack the presumption of meritocracy itself. Although Lippmann seemed to get the best of the argument, Terman fell back to the high ground of the condescending professional expert who saw little need to debate proven "scientific" principles.

Conscious of the social implications of their work, Goddard, Terman, and Thorndike viewed themselves as great benefactors of society. The concern for social order and rule by the intelligent elite was everpresent in their writings. Goddard put it bluntly when he argued that "the disturbing fear is that the masses—the seventy or even eighty-six million—will take matters into their own hands." The "four million" of "superior intelligence" must direct the masses. Throughout the literature of this period the fear of the masses appears as a constant theme. Under such circumstances one could hardly turn to the masses for an enlightened solution. The assumed role of the "professional" scientific expert was to lead the masses out of the irrational morass of ignorance. The definition of democracy had changed. It no longer meant rule by the people, but rather rule by the intelligent. As Thorndike put it, "The argument for democracy is not that it gives power to men without distinction, but that it gives greater freedom for ability and character to attain power."

Luckily, mankind's wealth-power-ability and character were positively correlated. This, indeed, was not only Plato's ideal, but the testers' view of the meritocracy which they in fact were fashioning. Late in life, Thorndike reflected on these concerns and said:

> It is the great good fortune of mankind that there is a substantial positive correlation between intelligence and morality, including good will toward one's fellows. Consequently our superiors in ability are on the average our benefactors, and it is often safer to trust our interests to them than to ourselves. No group of men can be expected to act one hundred per cent in the interest of mankind, but this group of the ablest men will come nearest to the ideal.

To be sure, there have been and still are inequities between men of intelligence and of wealth, Thorndike argued, but through the "beneficence of such men as Carnegie and Rockefeller," this discrepancy had been somewhat overcome.

Although Thorndike was directly involved in the army classification testing during World War I and the creation of the National Intelligence Test after the war, all of which skyrocketed the testing movement in American schools, perhaps his most profound influence on American schools came through his work in organizing the classroom curriculum. His name appears on approximately 50 books and 450 monographs and articles, including the much-used Thorndike *Dictionary*. He wrote many of the textbooks, tests, achievement scales, and teachers' manuals. In short, he told the schoolteachers what to teach and how to teach it and, in turn, how to evaluate it. Much of his work was, indeed, made possible through the beneficence of Carnegie. The Carnegie Foundation from 1922 to 1938 had made grants supporting his work totaling approximately $325,000. It was men like Thorndike, Terman, and Goddard, supported by corporate wealth, who successfully persuaded teachers, administrators, and lay school boards to classify and standardize the school's curriculum with a differentiated track system based on ability and values of the corporate liberal society. The structure of that society was based, then, on an assumed meritocracy, a meritocracy of White middle-class, management-oriented professionals.

The test discriminated against members of the lower class—southern Europeans and Blacks—indirectly by what they seemed to leave out, but more directly by what they included; for example: on a Stanford-Binet (1960 revision), a six-year-old child is asked the question "Which is prettier?" and must select the Nordic Anglo-Saxon type to be correct. If, however, the child is perhaps a Mexican-American or of southern European descent, has looked at himself in a mirror, and has a reasonably healthy respect for himself, he will pick the wrong answer. Worse yet is the child who recognizes what a "repressive society" calls the "right" answer and has been socialized enough to sacrifice himself for a higher score. The same is true in the case of the Black six-year-old. Neither Blacks nor southern Europeans were beautiful according to the authors of the Stanford-Binet, but then, there was no beauty in these people when Goddard, Laughlin, Terman, Thorndike, and Garrett called for the sterilization of the "socially inadequate," the discriminatory

234

closing of immigration, and the tracking organization of the American school, or for that matter, defined their place in the meritocracy.

The test, then, discriminated in content against particular groups in the very questions that were used as well as the questions that were not used with respect to particular minority experiences. While some educational psychologists sought to eliminate bias from the content of the test, as well as introduce a broader cultural basis for the test, others sought the impossible: a culturally free I.Q. test. Still other educational psychologists, hard-pressed to define intelligence, fell back to the assertion that it was simply that which the tests measured. Although many gave up their concern about intelligence, others argued that the various intelligence tests were achievement tests which could also be good predictors of success within both the corporate society and the bureaucratic school system which served that society. At this point, the testers had come full circle, ending up where Terman started.

Terman's tests were based on an occupational hierarchy which was, in fact, the social class system of the corporate liberal state which was then emerging. The many varied tests, all the way from I.Q. to personality and scholastic achievement, periodically brought up to date, would serve a vital part in rationalizing the social class system. The tests also created the illusion of objectivity, which on the one side served the needs of the "professional" educators to be "scientific," and on the other side served the need of the system for a myth which could convince the lower classes that their station in life was part of the natural order of things. For many the myth had apparently worked. In 1965 the Russell Sage Foundation issued a report entitled, *Experiences and Attitudes of American Adults Concerning Standardized Intelligence Tests.* Some of the major findings of that report indicated that the effects of the tests on social classes were "strong and consistent" and that while "the upper class respondent is more likely to favor the use of tests than the lower class respondent," the "lower class respondent is more likely to see intelligence tests measuring inborn intelligence."

The lower-class American adult was, indeed, a product of fifty years of testing. He had been channeled through an intricate bureaucratic educational system, which, in the name of meeting his individual needs, classified and tracked him into an occupation appropriate to his socioeconomic class status. The tragic character of this phenomenon was

235

that the lower class not only learned to believe in the system, but worse, through internalizing that set of beliefs, made it work. It worked because the lowered self-image which the school and society reinforced on the lower-class child did result in lower achievement. A normal child objectified as subnormal and treated by the teacher and the school as subnormal will almost surely behave as a subnormal child. Likewise, the lower-class child who is taught in many ways to doubt his own intelligence can be expected to exhibit a lower achievement level than those children who are repeatedly reminded that they are made of superior clay and therefore are of superior worth.

Intelligence and achievement tests used throughout American society are a vital part of the infrastructure which serves to stabilize and order the values of that society. Arthur R. Jensen put it well when he said, "Had the first I.Q. tests been devised in a hunting culture, 'general intelligence' might well have turned out to involve visual acuity and running speed, rather than vocabulary and symbol manipulation." Jensen, as Terman and others, argued that:

> . . . what we now "mean" by intelligence is something like the probability of acceptable performance (given the opportunity) in occupations varying in social status.
>
> So we see that the prestige hierarchy of occupations is a reliable objective reality in our society. To this should be added the fact that there is undoubtedly some relationship between the levels of the hierarchy and the occupations' intrinsic desirability, or gratification to the individual engaged in them. Even if all occupations paid alike and received equal respect and acclaim, some occupations would still be viewed as more desirable than others, which would make for competition, selection, and again, a kind of prestige hierarchy.

The hierarchy, Jensen argued, was inevitable because "most persons would agree that painting pictures is more satisfying than painting barns, and conducting a symphony orchestra is more exciting than directing traffic." While the hierarchy was culturally determined, it is clear that certain values which Jensen preferred appeared to him more intrinsic than others. Nevertheless, he admitted that "we have to face it: the assortment of persons into occupational roles simply is not 'fair' in any absolute sense. The best we can hope for is that true merit, given equality of opportunity, act as the basis for the natural assorting pro-

236

cess." Herein lies the crucial weakness of the argument. Given the current racist, economic, and socially elitist society where wealth, power, and educational privilege are so unevenly distributed, what does it mean, then, to assume "equality of opportunity" and "hope" that "true merit" will somehow result from a "natural assorting process"?

Jensen, like Thorndike and Terman before him, assumed an ideal liberal community where "equality of opportunity" balanced with lively competition produced a social system where "true" merit was rewarded. Although the "Jefferson-Conant" ideal of the good community is in itself questionable, the problem was compounded when the ideal society was confused with the real society. In spite of Terman, Thorndike, and Jensen's idealized assumptions about "equal opportunity" and "natural assorting process," all based their objective data on the real world of economic and social privilege. With highly questionable sociological data they proceeded to even more questionable biological conclusions. The leap from sociology to genetics was an act of faith.

Most testers refused to admit the possibility that they were, perhaps, servants of privilege, power, and status, and preferred instead to believe and "hope" that what they were measuring was, in fact, true "merit." This was also an act of faith, a faith based on the belief that somehow the "prestige hierarchy of occupations" and the people in it who provided the objective standard upon which the tests were based were there not because of privilege, wealth, power status, and violence, but because of superior talent and virtue. This was a fundamental axiom in the liberal's faith in the meritocracy which emerged in twentieth-century American education.

Throughout this century, within this liberal faith, there emerged a series of doctrinal disputes engaging the attention of millions of people. The nature-nurture argument was one such continuous dispute from Galton to Jensen. The course of this dispute reflected little more than increasing refinement of statistical techniques and accumulation of data on both sides of the issue. Given the extent of unprovable propositions on both sides of the issue, one finds the choice between heredity or environment more a matter of faith than hard evidence. In many respects, the nature-nurture argument is a misleading issue. One can accept a strong hereditarian position and still advocate political, economic, and social equality, just as one might accept a strong environmentalist position and still argue for political, economic, and social inequality. There

237

is in fact no inherent logic either in the mind of man or in the universe which predetermines that differences in intellectual ability necessarily should mean differences in social power. Why, for example, should one be more favorably rewarded because, through no effort of his own, he happened to inherit a superior intelligence or because he happened to be born into a superior social environment? Repeatedly, from Terman to Hermstein, psychologists have attempted to link ability to the meritocracy without questioning the values inherent in the meritocratic principle itself.

Most psychologists did not take their position to its logical conclusion, for to do so would be to question not only the ideal assumption upon which the meritocracy rests (such as equal opportunity and the inherent value of competition) but to further question the hierarchy of values which undergird the work of the professional knowledgeable expert in the liberal society. The professional expert, with his esoteric knowledge, is a vital element in both the creation and maintenance of the corporate meritocracy. His economic and political self-interest as well as his very survival is at stake. Thus it is understandable that so few in the professional middle class are disturbed by the presumed meritocracy, or are seriously inclined to question it. Those who have done well by the system can hardly be expected to be its best critics. To be sure, some are willing to suggest that we ought to look at the social system from the bottom up, and out of humanitarian motives, or perhaps survival motives, allow more opportunity for those who have been cut out of the system, but few are willing to doubt critically the validity, if not the equity of the system itself.

It is also understandable that those who have been severely cut out of the system should provide the most vehement source of criticism. The unusual thing, however, is that in the past half century there have been so few real challenges. The meritocracy issue was bound to surface as the U.S. Supreme Court attacked segregation of children in the public schools in the 1954 Brown decision. The same effect of segregation on the basis of race could be achieved in most communities through segregation on the basis of "tested" ability. If, in fact, the tests were based on socioeconomic class, then the net result of segregation was possible.

In *Bolling* v. *Sharpe* (1954) the court ordered the desegregation of the District of Columbia schools, and in 1956 the Board of Education adopted a tracking system for the Washington public schools based on so-called "ability grouping." In *Hobson* v. *Hansen* (District Court case, 1967) Skelly Wright, a U.S. circuit judge, wrote the opinion which not only challenged the use of ability tracking in the Washington public schools to circumvent desegregation, but went further by questioning the basis of tracking in the first place. While the school board insisted that the tracking system was based on meeting the needs of individuals through curricular adjustment according to their ability, they also denied racial bias but admitted that enrollment in the tracks was related to socioeconomic status of the students.

. . . .

The tests, whether measuring intelligence or achievement, as well as the meritocracy itself, served to so mask power as to effectively immobilize any real revolutionary opposition. If a man truly believes that he has a marginal standard of living because he is inferior, he is less likely to take violent measures against that social system than if he believes his condition a product of social privilege. In the nineteenth century, Daniel Webster said that "public education is a wise and liberal system of police, by which property, and life, and the peace of society are secured." In the twentieth century, a similar condition prevails. In this sense, the foundations' deep involvement in educational policy, whether it was the Ford Foundation in educational television or the Carnegie Foundation in testing or the Rockefeller Foundation in Black education, all had an interest in an effective, efficiently managed system. The foundations' management of educational policy in the twentieth century has been clearly at the cutting edge of every educational reform from the "Carnegie Unit" to the "open classroom."

Even the rhetoric which engages the professional educators seems fairly well managed. Throughout the last four decades, the pendulum of educational rhetoric has swung from the child-centered discussion of the thirties to the society-determined needs of the fifties, then, again, to the child-centered needs of the seventies. In the thirties the Carnegie Foundation supported the Progressive Education Association with over four million dollars, while in the fifties James Conant's study of American schools was supported by Carnegie, as was the project which culminated in Charles Silberman's *Crisis in the Classroom* in the 1970s. It is interesting to note that during periods of labor surplus our educational rhetoric tends to be child-centered, while in periods of shortage the rhetoric shifts to society-oriented needs. This may be the propelling factor. It is interesting, however, that when the rhetoric becomes so heated that people can be heard suggesting that we do away with the system or radically change it, Carnegie Foundation supported James Conant, who, in effect, said the system was basically sound but then co-opted the rhetoric of the attackers to recommend limited change. It was, after all, the survival of the system which Conant had in mind when he spoke of social dynamite in the ghettoes. By the 1970s, when most manpower projections clearly indicated surplus of labor for the next decade, the educational reform rhetoric shifted from training scientists and engineers to open classrooms. Again critics could be heard suggesting that the system be radically altered if not abolished, and once again the Carnegie Foundation supported a study by Silberman which, in effect, said that the system was basically sound but needed some reforming. Once again, the rhetoric of the attackers was co-opted for limited change. While the Carnegie Foundation obviously does not control the pendulum, they have played a major role in managing the rhetoric at critical points when the system is in acute danger. It is this function as governor of the educational machinery which prevents destructive unmanaged revolution that foundations have performed so well. One, then, is left to ponder the question of whether Charles W. Eliot was right when testifying before Congress (1913) that he had "never known a charitable or educational corporation to do anything which threatened the welfare or the liberties of the American people." Or was the majority of that committee which heard his testimony perhaps more correct when they concluded that the policies of the foundations would inevitably be those of the corporations which sponsored them, and that "the domination of men in whose hands the final control of a large part of American industry rests is not limited to their employees, but is being extended to control the education and social services of the nation."

PEOPLE OF PLENTY
David Potter

"What then is the American, this new man?" asked Michel-Guillaume de Crevecoeur during the American Revolution. From that beginning, observers have recognized an American character that was in some sense new to the world and have sought to define and explain it. Some have pointed to political institutions, others to the experience of settling an unpeopled frontier, or to the mixture of immigrant groups, as the definition and manifestation of a distinctive American character. David Potter sought in the 1950s for a causal explanation that would cover all of American life. He found it in the fact of economic abundance throughout the nation's history. American politics, social structure, and even the development of personality were at every point, he argued, profoundly affected by almost unlimited resources. In the section printed below, Potter explores the effect of economic plenty on the life of a six-month-old child. Much of society's expectations for that child ultimately rest on the wealth available to his family; the observation illuminates the great problem of educating the disadvantaged in a nation whose very existence implies an affluent society.

A sense of material progress in America can be obtained from Robert S. and Helen M. Lynd, *Middletown* (New York: Harcourt, Brace & Co., 1929).

In . . . view of the factors currently being examined by students of personality, it is now evident that social psychology is steadily reaching out more widely to bring the major tendencies of the political, economic, and social spheres within the range of its analysis. Topics such as "advertising," or "the frontier," or "the democratic ideal" no longer seem so remote from the study of personality as they once appeared.

Also, these topics are not so far removed from "the most intimate features of man's self" as a literal approach to them might indicate. It is true that historical discussion of such topics is usually couched in general or collective terms, so that one thinks of democracy in connection with public decisions; of advertising in connection with the mass media; or of the frontier in connection with the temporary absence of public institutions and services such as law, organized religion, and organized medicine. But all these clearly have their bearings upon the individual in his personal capacity. American ideas of equality, for instance, apply not only politically between fellow citizens but also within the family, where relations between husband and wife or even between parent and child do not reflect the principle of authority nearly so much as in most countries which share the Western tradition. The frontier exercised many imperatives upon the individual, for it determined rigorously the role which he had to fill: he had to be capable of performing a very wide variety of functions without relying upon anyone else, and he had to exercise his own judgment in deciding when to perform them. From his early youth this was what society required of him. Also, it expected him to show a considerable measure of hardihood, and to do this from childhood, especially if he were a boy. To take the example of advertising, this also trains the individual for a role—the role of a consumer—and it profoundly modifies his system of values, for it articulates the rationale of material values for him in the same way in which the church articulates a rationale of spiritual values.

In the same way, almost all public and general forces can be found operating in the private and individual sphere. Hence it is not at all far-fetched to argue that even a discussion of the general aspect of one of these forces is full of implicit indications which touch the personal lives and the conditioning and response of individuals. . . . But, if the utility of the historical approach in an understanding of the factors of personality formation is to be adequately proved, something more than an indirect or implicit relationship must be established. The questions recur: What, if anything, does the factor of abundance have to do with the process of personality formation (insofar as this process is understood) in the United States? How does the process differ from that in countries where the measure of abundance is not so great?

To these questions, I believe, some highly explicit answers are possible. Let us therefore be entirely concrete. Let us consider the situation of a six-month-old American infant, who is not yet aware that he is a citizen, a taxpayer, and a consumer.

This individual is, to all appearances, just a very young specimen of *Homo sapiens*, with certain needs for protection, care, shelter, and nourishment which may be regarded as the universal biological needs of human infancy rather than specific cultural needs. It would be difficult to prove that the culture has as yet differentiated him from other infants, and, though he is an American, few would argue that he has acquired an American character. Yet abundance and the circumstances arising from abundance have already dictated a whole range of basic conditions which, from his birth, are constantly at work upon this child and which will contribute in the most intimate and basic way to the formation of his character.

To begin with, abundance has already revolutionized the typical mode of his nourishment by providing for him to be fed upon cow's milk rather than upon his mother's milk, taken from the bottle rather than from the breast. Abundance contributes vitally to this transformation, because bottle-feeding requires fairly elaborate facilities of refrigeration, heating, sterilization, and temperature control, which only an advanced technology can offer and only an economy of abundance can make widely available. I will not attempt here to resolve the debated question as to the psychological effects, for both mother and child, of bottle-feeding as contrasted with breast-feeding in infant nurture. But it is clear that the changeover to bottle-feeding has encroached somewhat upon the intimacy of the bond between mother and child. The nature of this bond is, of course, one of the most crucial factors in the formation of character. Bottle-feeding also must tend to emphasize the separateness of the infant as an individual, and thus it makes, for the first time, a point which the entire culture reiterates constantly throughout the life of the average American. In addition to the psychic influences which may be involved in the manner of taking the food, it is also a matter of capital importance that the bottle-fed baby is, on the whole, better nourished than the breast-fed infant and therefore likely to grow more rapidly, to be more vigorous, and to suffer fewer ailments, with

243

whatever effects these physical conditions may have upon his personality.

It may be argued also that abundance has provided a characteristic mode of housing for the infant and that this mode further emphasizes his separateness as an individual. In societies of scarcity, dwelling units are few and hard to come by, with the result that high proportions of newly married young people make their homes in the parental ménage, thus forming part of an "extended" family, as it is called. Moreover, scarcity provides a low ratio of rooms to individuals, with the consequence that whole families may expect as a matter of course to have but one room for sleeping, where children will go to bed in intimate propinquity to their parents. But abundance prescribes a different regime. By making it economically possible for newly married couples to maintain separate households of their own, it has almost destroyed the extended family as an institution in America and has ordained that the child shall be reared in a "nuclear" family, so called, where his only intimate associates are his parents and his siblings, with even the latter far fewer now than in families of the past. The housing arrangements of this new-style family are suggested by census data for 1950. In that year there were 45,983,000 dwelling units to accommodate the 38,310,000 families in the United States, and, though the median number of persons in the dwelling unit was 3.1, the median number of rooms in the dwelling unit was 4.6. Eighty-four percent of all dwelling units reported less than one person per room. By providing the ordinary family with more than one room for sleeping, the economy thus produces a situation in which the child will sleep either in a room alone or in a room shared with his brothers or sisters. Even without allowing for the cases in which children may have separate rooms, these conditions mean that a very substantial percentage of children now sleep in a room alone, for, with the declining birth rate, we have reached a point at which an increasing proportion of families have one child or two children rather than the larger number which was at one time typical. For instance, in the most recent group of mothers who had completed their childbearing phase, according to the census, 19.5 percent had had one child and 23.4 had had two. Thus almost half of all families with offspring did not have more than two children throughout their duration. In the case of the first group, all the children were "only" children throughout their childhood, and in the second group half of the children were "only" children until the second child was born. To state this in another, and perhaps a more forcible, way, it has been shown that among American women who arrived at age thirty-four during the year 1949 and who had borne children up to that time, 26.7 percent had borne only one child, and 34.5 percent had borne only two. If these tendencies persist, it would mean that, among families where there are children, hardly one in three will have more than two children.

The census has, of course, not got around to finding out how the new-style family, in its new-style dwelling unit, adjusts the life-practice to the space situation. But it is significant that America's most widely circulated book on the care of infants advises that "it is preferable that he [the infant] not sleep in his parents' room after he is about 12 months old," offers the opinion that "it's fine for each [child] to have a room of his own, if that's possible," and makes the sweeping assertion that "it's a sensible rule not to take a child into the parents' bed for any reason." It seems clear beyond dispute that the household space provided by the economy of abundance has been used to emphasize the separateness, the apartness, if not the isolation, of the American child.

Not only the nourishment and housing, but also the clothing of the American infant are controlled by American abundance. For one of the most sweeping consequences of our abundance is that, in contrast to other peoples who keep their bodies warm primarily by wearing clothes, Americans keep their bodies warm primarily by a far more expensive and even wasteful method: namely, by heating the buildings in which they are sheltered. Every American who has been abroad knows how much lighter is the clothing—especially the underclothing—of Americans than of people in countries like England and France, where the winters are far less severe than ours, and every American who can remember the conditions of a few decades ago knows how much lighter our clothing is than that of our grandparents. These changes have occurred because clothing is no longer the principal device for securing warmth. The oil furnace has not only displaced the open fireplace; it has also displaced the woolen undergarment and the vest.

This is a matter of considerable significance for adults but of far greater importance to infants, for adults discipline themselves to wear warm garments, submitting, for instance, to woolen underwear more or less voluntarily. But the infant knows no such discipline, and his garments or bedclothes must be kept upon him by forcible means. Hence primitive people, living in outdoor conditions, swaddle the child most rigorously, virtually binding him into his clothes, and breaking him to them almost as a horse is broken to the harness. Civilized peoples mitigate the rigor but still use huge pins or clips to frustrate the baby's efforts to kick off the blankets and free his limbs. In a state of nature, cold means confinement and warmth means freedom, so far as young humans are concerned. But abundance has given the American infant physical freedom by giving him physical warmth in cold weather.

In this connection it may be surmised that abundance has also given him a permissive system of toilet training. If our forebears imposed such training upon the child and we now wait for him to take the initiative in these matters himself, it is not wholly because the former held a grim Calvinistic doctrine of child-rearing that is philosophically contrary to ours. The fact was that the circumstances gave them little choice. A mother who was taking care of several babies, keeping them clean, making their clothes, washing their diapers in her own washtub, and doing this, as often as not, while another baby was on the way, had little choice but to hasten their fitness to toilet themselves. Today, on the contrary, the disposable diaper, the diaper service, and most of all the washing machine, not to mention the fact that one baby seldom presses upon the heels of another, make it far easier for the mother to indulge the child in a regime under which he will impose his own toilet controls in his own good time.

Thus the economy of plenty has influenced the feeding of the infant, his regime, and the physical setting within which he lives. These material conditions alone might be regarded as having some bearing upon the formation of his character, but the impact of abundance by no means ends at this point. Insofar as it has an influence in determining what specific individuals shall initiate the infant into the ways of man and shall provide him with his formative impressions of the meaning of being a person, it must be regarded as even more vital. When it influences the nature of the relationships between these individuals and the infant, it must be recognized as reaching to the very essence of the process of character formation.

The central figures in the dramatis personae of the American infant's universe are still his parents, and in this respect, of course, there is nothing peculiar either to the American child or to the child of abundance. But abundance has at least provided him with parents who are in certain respects unlike the parents of children born in other countries or born fifty years ago. To begin with, it has given him young parents, for the median age of fathers at the birth of the first child in American marriages (as of 1940) was 25.3 years, and the median age of mothers was 22.6 years. This median age was substantially lower than it had been in the United States in 1890 for both fathers and mothers. Moreover, as the size of families has been reduced and the wife no longer continues to bear a succession of children throughout the period of her fertility, the median age of mothers at the birth of the last child has declined from 32 years (1890) to 27 years (1940). The age of the parents at the birth of both the first child and the last child is far lower than in the case of couples in most European countries. There can be little doubt that abundance has caused this differential, in the case of the first-born by making it economically possible for a high proportion of the population to meet the expenses of homemaking at a fairly early age. In the case of the last-born, it would also appear that one major reason for the earlier cessation of childbearing is a determination by parents to enjoy a high standard of living themselves and to limit their offspring to a number for whom they can maintain a similar standard.

By the very fact of their youth, these parents are more likely to remain alive until the child reaches maturity, thus giving him a better prospect of being reared by his own mother and father. This prospect is further reinforced by increases in the life-span, so that probably no child in history has ever enjoyed so strong a likelihood that his parents will survive to rear him. Abundance has produced this situation by providing optimum conditions for prolonging life. But, on the other hand, abundance has also contributed much to produce an economy in which the mother is no longer markedly dependent upon the father, and this change in the economic relation between the sexes has probably done much to remove obstacles to divorce. The results are all too familiar. During the decade 1940–1949 there were 25.8 divorces for every 100 marriages in the United States, which ratio, if projected over a longer period, would mean that one marriage out of four would end in divorce. But our concern here is with a six-month-old child, and the problem is to know whether this factor of divorce involves childless couples predominantly or whether it is likely to touch him. The answer is indicated by the fact that, of all divorces granted in 1948, no less than 42 percent were to couples with children under eighteen, and a very large proportion of these children were of much younger ages. Hence one might say that the economy of abundance has provided the child with younger parents who chose their role of parenthood deliberately and who are more likely than parents in the past to live until he is grown, but who are substantially less likely to preserve the unbroken family as the environment within which he shall be reared.

In addition to altering the characteristics of the child's parents, it has also altered the quantitative relationship between him and his parents. It has done this, first of all, by offering the father such lucrative opportunities through work outside the home that the old agricultural economy in which children worked alongside their fathers is now obsolete. Yet, on the other hand, the father's new employment gives so much more leisure than his former work that the child may, in fact, receive considerably more of his father's attention. But the most vital transformation is in the case of the mother. In the economy of scarcity which controlled the modes of life that were traditional for many centuries, an upperclass child was reared by a nurse, and all others were normally reared by their mothers. The scarcity economy could not support many nonproductive members, and these mothers, though not "employed," were most decidedly hard workers, busily engaged in cooking, washing, sewing, weaving, preserving, caring for the henhouse, the garden, and perhaps the cow, and in general carrying on the domestic economy of a large family. Somehow they also attended to the needs of a numerous brood of children, but the mother was in no sense a full-time attendant upon any one child. Today, however, the economy of abundance very nearly exempts a very large number of mothers from the requirement of economic productivity in order that they may give an unprecedented share of their time to the care of the one or two young children who are now the usual number in an American family. Within the home, the wide range of labor-saving devices and the assignment of many functions, such as laundering, to service industries have produced this result. Outside the home, employment of women in the labor force has steadily increased, but the incidence of employment falls upon unmarried women, wives without children, and wives with grown children. In fact, married women without children are two and one-half times as likely to be employed as those with children. Thus what amounts to a new dispensation has been established for the child. If he belongs to the upper class, his mother has replaced his nurse as his full-time attendant. The differences in character formation that might result from this change alone could easily be immense. To mention but one possibility, the presence of the nurse must inevitably have made the child somewhat aware of his class status, whereas the presence of the mother would be less likely to have this effect. If the child does not belong to the upper class, mother and child now impinge upon each other in a relationship whose intensity is of an entirely different magnitude from that which prevailed in the past. The mother has fewer physical distractions in the care of the child, but she is more likely to be restive in her maternal role because it takes her away from attractive employment with which it cannot be reconciled.

If abundance has thus altered the relationship of the child with his parent, it has even more drastically altered the rest of his social milieu, for it has changed the identity of the rest of the personnel who induct him into human society. In the extended family of the past, a great array of kinspeople filled his cosmos and guided him to maturity. By nature, he particularly needed association with children of his own age (his "peers," as they are called), and he particularly responded to the values asserted by these peers. Such peers were very often his brothers and sisters, and, since they were all members of his own family, all came under parental control. This is to say that, in a sense, the parents controlled the peer group, and the peer group controlled the child. The point is worth making because we frequently encounter the assertion that parental control of the child has been replaced by peer-group control; but it is arguable that what is really the case is that children were always deeply influenced by the peer group and that parents have now lost their former measure of control over this group, since it is no longer a familial group. Today the nursery school replaces the large family as a peer group, and social associations, even of young children, undergo the same shift from focused contact with family to diffused contact with a miscellany of people, which John Galsworthy depicted for grown people in the three novels of *The Forsyte Saga*. Again, the effects upon character may very well be extensive.

Abundance, then, has played a critcal part in revolutionizing both the physical circumstances and the human associations which surround the American infant and child. These changes alone would warrant the hypothesis that abundance has profoundly affected the formation of character for such a child. But to extend this inquiry one step further, it may be worth while to consider how these altered conditions actually impinge upon the individual. Here, of course, is an almost unlimited field for investigation, and I shall only attempt to indicate certain crucial points at which abundance projects conditions that are basic in the life of the child.

One of these points concerns the cohesive force which holds the family together. The family is the one institution which touches all members of society most intimately, and it is perhaps the only social institution which touches young children directly. The sources from which the family draws its strength are, therefore, of basic importance. In the past, these sources were, it would seem, primarily economic. For agrarian society, marriage distinctively involved a division of labor. Where economic opportunity was narrowly restricted, the necessity for considering economic ways and means in connection with marriage led to the arrangement of matches by parents and to the institution of the dowry. The emotional bonds of affection, while always important, were not deemed paramount, and the ideal of romantic love played little or no part in the lives of ordinary people. Where it existed at all, it was as an upper-class luxury. (The very term "courtship" implies this upper-class orientation.) This must inevitably have meant that the partners of the majority of marriages demanded less from one another emotionally than do the partners of romantic love and that the emotional factor was less important to the stability of the marriage. Abundance, however, has played its part in changing this picture. On the American frontier, where capital for dowries was as rare as opportunity for prosperous marriage was plentiful, the dowry became obsolete. Later still, when abundance began to diminish the economic duties imposed upon the housewife, the function of marriage as a division of labor ceased to seem paramount, and the romantic or emotional factor assumed increasing importance. Abundance brought the luxury of romantic love within the reach of all, and, as it did so, emotional harmony became the principal criterion of success in a marriage, while lack of such harmony became a major threat to the existence of the marriage. The statistics of divorce give us a measure of the loss of durability in marriage, but they give us no measure of the factors of instability in the marriages which endure and no measure of the increased focus upon emotional satisfactions in such marriages. The children of enduring marriages, as well as the children of divorce, must inevitably feel the impact of this increased

250

emphasis upon emotional factors, must inevitably sense the difference in the foundations of the institution which holds their universe in place.

In the rearing of a child, it would be difficult to imagine any factors more vital than the distinction between a permissive and an authoritarian regime or more vital than the age at which economic responsibility is imposed. In both these matters the modern American child lives under a very different dispensation from children in the past. We commonly think of these changes as results of our more enlightened or progressive or humanitarian ideas. We may even think of them as results of developments in the specific field of child psychology, as if the changes were simply a matter of our understanding these matters better than our grandparents. But the fact is that the authoritarian discipline of the child, within the authoritarian family, was but an aspect of the authoritarian social system that was linked with the economy of scarcity. Such a regime could never have been significantly relaxed within the family so long as it remained diagnostic in the society. Nor could it have remained unmodified within the family, once society began to abandon it in other spheres.

Inevitably, the qualities which the parents inculcate in a child will depend upon the roles which they occupy themselves. For the ordinary man the economy of scarcity has offered one role, as Simon N. Patten observed many years ago, and the economy of abundance has offered another. Abundance offers "work calling urgently for workmen"; scarcity found the "worker seeking humbly any kind of toil." As a suppliant to his superiors, the worker under scarcity accepted the principle of authority; he accepted his own subordination and the obligation to cultivate the qualities appropriate to his subordination, such as submissiveness, obedience, and deference. Such a man naturally transferred the principle of authority into his own family and, through this principle, instilled into his children the qualities appropriate to people of their kind—submissiveness, obedience, and deference. Many copybook maxims still exist to remind us of the firmness of childhood discipline, while the difference between European and American children—one of the most clearly recognizable of all national differences—serves to emphasize the extent to which Americans have now departed from this firmness.

This new and far more permissive attitude toward children has arisen, significantly, in an economy of abundance, where work has called urgently for the workman. In this situation, no longer a suppliant, the workman found submissiveness no longer a necessity and therefore no longer a virtue. The principle of authority lost some of its majesty, and he was less likely to regard it as the only true criterion of domestic order. In short, he ceased to impose it upon his children. Finding that the most valuable trait in himself was a capacity for independent decision and self-reliant conduct in dealing with the diverse opportunities which abundance offered him, he tended to encourage this quality in his children. The irresponsibility of childhood still called for a measure of authority on one side and obedience on the other, but this became a means to an end and not an end in itself. On the whole, permissive training, to develop independent ability, even though it involves a certain sacrifice of obedience and discipline, is the characteristic mode of child-rearing in the one country which most distinctively enjoys an economy of abundance. Here, in a concrete way, one finds something approaching proof for Gerth and Mill's suggestion that the relation of father and child may have its importance not as a primary factor but rather as a "replica of the power relations of society."

If scarcity required men to "seek humbly any kind of toil," it seldom permitted women to seek employment outside the home at all. Consequently, the woman was economically dependent upon, and, accordingly, subordinate to, her husband or her father. Her subordination reinforced the principle of authority within the home. But the same transition which altered the role of the male worker has altered her status as well, for abundance "calling urgently for workmen" makes no distinctions of gender and, by extending economic independence to women, has enabled them to assume the role of partners rather than of subordinates within the family. Once the relation of voluntarism and equality is introduced between husband and wife, it is, of course, far more readily extended to the relation between parent and child.

If abundance has fostered a more permissive regime for the child, amid circumstances of democratic equality within the family, it has no less certainly altered the entire process of imposing economic responsibility upon the child, hence the process of preparing the child for such responsibility. In the economy of scarcity, as I have remarked above, society could not afford to support any substantial quota of nonproductive members. Consequently, the child went to work when he was as yet young. He attended primary school for a much shorter school year than the child of today; only a minority attended high school; and only the favored few attended college. Even during the brief years of schooling, the child worked, in the home, on the farm, or even in the factory. But today the economy of abundance can afford to maintain a substantial proportion of the population in nonproductive status, and it assigns this role, sometimes against their will, to its younger and its elder members. It protracts the years of schooling, and it defers responsibilities for an unusually long span. It even enforces laws setting minimal ages for leaving school, for going to work, for consenting to sexual intercourse, or for marrying. It extends the jurisdiction of juvenile courts to the eighteenth or the twentieth year of age.

Such exemption from economic responsibility might seem to imply a long and blissful youth free from strain for the child. But the delays in reaching economic maturity are not matched by comparable delays in other phases of growing up. On the contrary, there are many respects in which the child matures earlier. Physically, the child at the lower social level will actually arrive at adolescence a year or so younger than his counterpart a generation ago, because of improvement in standards of health and nutrition. Culturally, the child is made aware of the allurements of sex at an earlier age, partly by his familiarity with the movies, television, and popular magazines, and partly by the practice of "dating" in the early teens. By the standards of his peer group, he is encouraged to demand expensive and mature recreations, similar to those of adults, at a fairly early age. By reason of the desire of his parents that he should excel in the mobility race and give proof during his youth of the qualities which will make him a winner in later life, he is exposed to the stimuli of competition before he leaves the nursery. Thus there is a kind of imbalance between the postponement of responsibility and the quickening of social maturity which may have contributed to make American adolescence a more difficult age than human biology alone would cause it to be. Here, again, there are broad implications for the formation of character, and here, again, abundance is at work on both sides of the equation, for it contributes as much to the hastening of social maturity as it does to the prolongation of economic immaturity.

Some of these aspects of the rearing of children in the United States are as distinctively American, when compared with other countries, as any Yankee traits that have ever been attributed to the American people. In the multiplicity which always complicates social analysis, such aspects of child-rearing might be linked with a number of factors in American life. But one of the more evident and more significant links, it would seem certain, is with the factor of abundance. Such a tie is especially pertinent in this discussion, where the intention of the whole book has been to relate the study of character, as the historian would approach it, to the same subject as it is viewed by the behavioral scientist. In this chapter, especially, the attempt has been made to throw a bridge between the general historical force of economic abundance and the specific behavioral pattern of people's lives. Historical forces are too often considered only in their public and overall effects, while private lives are interpreted without sufficient reference to the historical determinants which shape them. But no major force at work in society can possibly make itself felt at one of these levels without also having its impact at the other level. In view of this fact, the study of national character should not stand apart, as it has in the past, from the study of the process of character formation in the individual. In view of this fact, also, the effect of economic abundance is especially pertinent. For economic abundance is a factor whose presence and whose force may be clearly and precisely recognized in the most personal and intimate phases of the development of personality in the child. Yet, at the same time, the presence and the force of this factor are recognizable with equal certainty in the whole broad, general range of American experience, American ideals, and American institutions. At both levels, it has exercised a pervasive influence in the shaping of the American character.

A NOTE ON FURTHER STUDY

Those students who wish to pursue the history of American education beyond the treatment it receives in these essays and the works here cited in the headnotes should turn for bibliographic assistance to Jurgen Herbst, compiler, *The History of American Education* (Northbrook, Illinois: AHM Publishing Co., 1973). This valuable list of works, one of the series of "Goldentree Bibliographies in American History," is available in an inexpensive paperback edition.

Scholarly periodicals that regularly or occasionally publish research articles, book reviews, and bibliographical lists on this subject include *The History of Education Quarterly, Harvard Educational Review, The American Historical Review, American Quarterly, The Journal of American History, The Journal of Negro History,* and *The Journal of Negro Education.*

INDEX

Fitzhugh, George, 59, 68
Five Hundred Pointes of Good Husbandrie, 11
Filene, Edward A., 231
Finney, Charles G., 139
Fisher, Alexander Metcalf, 114–15
Fisk University, 183
Flag, the, 207–8
Fleet, John H., 97
Florence, Italy, 129
Folwell, W. W., 202
Food, infants', 243
Ford Foundation, 239
Forsyte Saga, The, 249
Forum, 146
Foundation of Christian Religion, Gathered into Sixe Principles, The, 8
Foundations, 239
Four Generations, 2
France and the French, 18, 64, 82; Revolution, 59
Franklin, Benjamin, 137
Fraser, on parents, 34
Fredericksburg, 91–92
Freedmen's Bureau, 183, 185
French, the. *See* France and the French
French-Canadian immigrants, 174
French Revolution, 59
Friends. *See* Quakers
"Fritz, Little," 36
Fuller, Margaret, 113, 120–30

Galsworthy, John, 249
Garrett, Henry E., 229–30, 234
General Psychology (Garrett), 229
Genetics. *See* Heredity
Gentleman's Calling, The, 9
Geography books, 50, 59ff.
George, W. L., 35

Georgetown, Md., 97
Georgetown University, 170
Georgia, 76, 86, 90
German Catholics, 173–75, 178, 180–81
Gibbons, Cardinal, 179
Gibbs, Sir Philip, 44
Gilbert, Charles B., 149–50
Girls. *See* Women and girls
Gladden, Washington, 143
Gobineau, Joseph, 59
Goddard, H. H., 227–28, 233, 234
Godwyn, Morgan, 17
Gookin, Daniel, 17
Gove, Aaron, 163–64
Great Awakening, 27
Greeley, Horace, 125
Greene Street School (Providence), 124
Grevan, Philip, Jr., 2
Grimké, Sarah, 91
Griswold, Rufus, 126
Group Test of Mental Ability, 232
Guilds, 11–12
Guyot (author), 60, 61

Hall, G. Stanley, 227
Hamilton, Alexander, 57
Hampton Institute, 183, 184–86
Handlin, Mary F., 18
Handlin, Oscar, 18, 200–23
Harlan, Louis R., 184
Harper's Weekly, 132
Harriman, Mrs. E. H., 226
Harris, Sarah, 96
Harris, Rev. William, 88
Harris, William T. (educational leader), 198–99
Hartford, Conn., 115
Harvard Educational Review, 169
Harvard University, 17, 230

Noyes, James, 8
Noyes Academy, 95
Nursery school, 249

O'Brien, John, 177
Occupations, 231–32. *See also* Apprenticeship
Ogden, Robert, 192
Ohio, 93, 94
Old Textbooks, 47
Oregon, 93, 145–67
Oregon City, 152
Oregon Journal, 162
Oregonian, 160
Original sin, 136, 141
Origins of the New South, The, 184
Ossoli (married Margaret Fuller), 128, 130
Outhouse, John, 152

Page, Thomas Nelson, 68
Panoplist, 104
Parents. *See* Families
Parker, John M., 191
Parker, Theodore, 121
Parry (schoolmaster), 90
Parton, James, 132
Pascendi gregis, 180
Patrick Henry Press, 229
Patriotism, 207–8. *See also* Nationality
Patten, Simon N., 251
Peabody, Elizabeth, 125
Peabody fund, 191
Peake, Mrs. (schoolmistress), 91
Pearce, Harvey, 108
Pennsylvania, 4, 49, 87, 98. *See also* Philadelphia
Perkins, William, 8
Peter, Hugh, 8

Philadelphia, 95, 214
Physical education, 207
Physiology and Calisthenics, 118
Pilgrim's Progress, The, 8
Pinchbeck, Ivy, 1
Plato, 231ff.
Plymouth, Mass., xvii, 4
Pocohontas, 62
Polish (Catholic) immigrants, 174, 180–81
Poor Law of 1601, 5
Poor Man's Family Book, The, 8, 9
Portland, Ore., 145–67
Portugal, 64
Potter, David, 241–54
Practise of Pietie, The, 8, 9
Pratt, Irving, 162
Presbyterians, Presbyterianism, 29, 101, 117, 133, 134
Primers, 7–8
Princeton University, 87
Progressive Education Association, 201, 239
Prose Writers of America, The, 126
Prostitution, Beecher on, 135
Protestantism. *See* Religion
Providence, R.I., 124
Prussia, 79
Punishment. *See* Discipline; Morals
Puritan Family, The, 2
Puritans, Puritanism, 3, 28, 41, 53, 55. *See also* Religion

Quakers (Friends), 28, 86ff., 92, 96
Quarterly Review, The, 126

Races and racism, 56–57, 193 (*see also* Blacks; Indians); and teachings in 19th-century schools, 59–68; and testing, 229ff.

Souls of Black Folk, The, 184
South, the, 69–84. *See also* specific
    places
South Carolina, 76, 86, 89, 91
South Slavs, 180
Southern Literary Messenger, 70, 78
Spain, 64
Spalding, John Lancaster, 179
Spanish America, 62
Spellers, 51–52, 66
Spencer, Herbert, 147, 165
Spender, Harold, 46
Sports, 207
Stanford Achievement Tests, 232
Stanford-Binet test, 231–32, 234
*Statement of the Theory of Education
    in the United States, A,* 148–49
Stathesk, John, 44
Statute of Artificers, 5, 11
Steevens, George, 45
Sterilization, 227
Stockbridge Reservation, 100
Stowe, Harriet Beecher, 119, 140
Stuart-Wortley, Lady Emmaline, 34
Study of American Intelligence, A, 230
Sturgis, Caroline, 127, 130
Success, Beecher's lectures on,
    131–44
Supreme Court, 238
Sunday school (Sabbath school), 91ff.,
    169–70
Swint, Henry L., 184

Tappan, Arthur, 95
Taylor, William R., 69–84
Teachers and schoolmasters, 48–49,
    80–81, 146ff., 208, 211 (*see also*
    specific places, teachers); and edu-
    cation of Negroes before Civil War,
    85–97; parochial school, 173, 176,
    177

Teen-agers. *See* Adolescents
Temple School, 124
Terman, Lewis B., 227, 228, 230,
    231–33ff.
Testem Benevolentiae, 180
Testing, scientific, 224–40
Textbooks, 7–9; 19th-century, 47–58
Thackeray, William Makepeace, 34,
    75
Theater, 216
Thomas, M. Carey, 123
Thoreau, Henry, 121
Thorndike, Edward L., 226, 228–29,
    233–34, 237
Tocqueville, Alexis de, 75, 118, 139
Toilet training, 246
Trades. *See* Apprenticeship; Boarding
    schools
Transformation of the School, The,
    200–1
Turner, Nat, 88, 91ff.
Tuskegee Institute, 183, 187–89, 192
Tusser, Thomas, 11
Tyack, David B., 145–67, 168

United Foreign Mission Society, 110
Universalists, 28
Universities vs. colleges, 214
Unmarried persons, 4–5
Up from Slavery, 184
Up the Down Staircase, 163

Vachell, Horace, 37–38
Vaile, P. A., 35
Van Hise, Charles R., 227
Van Imborch, Gysberg, 12
Veblen, Thorstein, 151
Vineland, N.J., 227
Virginia, 62, 65, 72, 73, 86, 89, 90
    (*see also* Hampton Institute); Colo-
    nial, 4ff., 15ff.; correspondents of